Edited by JOHN NICHOLS

AGAINST THE BEAST

A DOCUMENTARY HISTORY OF AMERICAN OPPOSITION TO EMPIRE

NATION BOOKS · NEW YORK

AGAINST THE BEAST
A Documentary History of American Rebellion

Published by
Nation Books
An Imprint of Avalon Publishing Group Inc.
245 West 17th St., 11th Floor
New York, NY 10011

AVALON
publishing group incorporated

Library of Congress Cataloging-in-Publication Data is available.

ISBN 1-56025-513-7

9 8 7 6 5 4 3 2 1

Book design by Pauline Neuwirth, Neuwirth & Associates, Inc.

Printed in Canada
Distributed by Publishers Group West

Empire is a most complex and persistent beast. And it has claws.

—LINDA COLLEY

I am an anti-imperialist and against having the eagle grasp some other country in its claws.

—MARK TWAIN

Contents

Author's Note

This compendium of anti-imperialism writings, assembled over many years in the manner of Jefferson's commonplace books, does not propose to serve as the comprehensive record of American anti-imperialism. Rather, it explores nine critical periods in American history when anti-imperialist sentiment flared. The general pattern is chronological, forming a loose record of the progression of the American experiment from its earliest days to the present. The book avoids examining some periods that other writers will find good reason to explore. At the same time, it explores some periods from multiple and, at times, overlapping perspectives. The voices recorded here are mostly, though not exclusively, those of prominent political and cultural figures from the periods that are examined. An emphasis was placed on seeking out voices from traditionally dispossessed groups that, often, were most damaged by the excesses of imperialism. The particular passages contained in the nine sections of the book were selected, much as the bullet points in a lawyer's brief, with the purpose of establishing the case that the impulse toward anti-imperialism is at once necessary, noble, and patriotic.

PREFACE
A Beastly Time

I traveled light, carrying only an out-of-print book by William Appleman Williams and a bootleg CD from a Phil Ochs concert.

It was October 2001, and I found myself in a frail, frightened land, where the flag was flown as a threat and the term "patriot" had been captured by the warriors against liberty. Men of great power were plotting to make a crime against humanity into an excuse for what was shaping up as an extremely profitable crusade. War was certain. The preparations, begun even before the excuse had been provided, were nearing completion. Borrowing a favorite phrase from history's darkest authoritarians, those in power began to refer to this place as "the homeland." Borders had been sealed. Refugees were being rounded up. In the airports, young men in uniform brandished automatic weapons. Disembodied voices chanted instructions for proper behavior.

This was my country. But this was not my time, nor that of my kind.

I followed a path cut through the landscape by dissenters who had been written out of history by the new rulers. When the president of this time declared that my country would return to the ways of the crusaders, pursuing an endless war against the blowbacks he had created, I rallied with those who followed the president of another time. It came as no surprise that the lies of George Bush sounded louder than the truths of James Madison. While Bush commanded his congress and his media to spread the gospel of perpetual war, Madison could muster only the weak tug of memory and conscience. And there was no comfort in the knowing that, each day, Bush provided confirmation of Madison's warning that, "No nation can preserve its freedom in the midst of continual warfare."

But we were not of a surrendering class. We chose to mount our challenge to the ethos of the day, knowing that we would be dismissed as traitors and fools—just as our forebears had been when they took up the fight against another empire of another time.

In that gray fall, I traveled across the western United States, city to city, town to town, meeting with those who remained faithful to another America. I carried messages from Madison and Frederick Douglass and Bob La Follette and Barbara Lee. In Seattle, I picked up the newspaper and read that the local congressman, Jim McDermott, had questioned the rush to war. Already, he was being vilified. Yet, his dissent was a sign of the stirring. The pressure toward silence and acquiescence was strong, but not quite strong enough to achieve complete conformity of thought or action. By the time I got to Boise, my friend Lark Corbeil had already organized teach-ins and peace rallies. In the most Republican and conservative state in the nation, Lark and her friends had chosen to stand once more against the ignorance and superstition of a dark age. They were the guardians of that fire of freedom that had been kindled centuries before. And, it was good to be among them. I did not know where we were headed, but I knew we were on a singularly American journey. When the speaking was done and the folding chairs had all been put away, I walked out into the afternoon. I had a few hours and a few questions. I would take my time and my questions to the Moses of my country's middle passage.

Dead now for six decades, William Borah is buried in a quiet cemetery near the heart of Boise. I visited his grave alone, and without interruption. Even in Idaho, which he represented for thirty-three years in the United States Senate, Borah's star has faded. Few recall that when he chaired the Senate Foreign Relations Committee in the 1920s, Borah was considered by foreign leaders to be a force more powerful than the presidents of his time. Fewer still recall that he exercised his immense power not for the purpose of personal or national aggrandizement, but in the pursuit of a moral vision that had at its core the faith that policies of entanglement, expansion, and empire would destroy not just lives and property but something even more precious: democracy itself. He denounced the "Dollar Diplomacy" that linked the interests of U.S. corporations and U.S. foreign policy, he rejected "the fetish of force" that would send

American troops to distant lands "to invade territory, to tear down governments and to set up other governments," and he promised that under his watch America's actions would be guided by the principle that the greatest threat to the United States came not from external foes but from those who would "yoke a government whose fundamental maxim is that of liberty to a government whose first law is that of force."

Borah knew that liberty in America, not to mention the rest of the world, would be assured only if the United States chose to operate on the world stage as "a great moral force, disentangled" from the tentacles of empire that choked away the freedoms of the powerful as surely as they did those of the weak. Standing at Borah's grave, seized by the certainty of his vision, I felt an optimism come over me. A country that could produce a William Borah, and give him the power to enforce a moral vision of foreign policy, could do so again. Even in the worst of times, there must remain the seed planted in better days. It was not so much a matter of discovering a new way as it was of renewing the faith that had been so assaulted by the passage of years. As Borah's champion, William Appleman Williams had said, "We can as citizens deal with the question of what to do, therefore, only after we cope with the issues raised by the meaning of the history."

The hour had grown late. The sun was setting across the western hills.

I could hear the call of another history. It was high time for a homecoming.

INTRODUCTION
Anti-Imperialist Reunion

My great-grandfather lived his entire life in Blue River, Wisconsin, a village that took its name from the Wisconsin River that flowed past the tight little assemblage of houses, churches, and taverns on the way to the Mississippi. As Blue River's elected village president in the first years of the twentieth century, he struck up a friendship with John Blaine, who then served as the mayor of the nearby city of Boscobel. Blaine would go on to serve as Wisconsin's attorney general and then as the state's governor. But he never lost touch with his roots in the farm country of southwest Wisconsin, from which a seam of Midwestern populism snaked its way west across Iowa and Minnesota, through the Dakotas and out toward Montana and Idaho.

In 1926, John Blaine decided to run for the United States Senate, and my great-grandfather campaigned for him in the farm valleys and hamlets of Grant and Vernon counties. America was not at war. Yet, Blaine and his supporters talked a great deal about foreign policy. They argued that, as successive American presidents had become more and more entangled with the affairs of European kings and kaisers, the country's revolutionary spirit was being worn away. They were horrified that soldiers of the United States now were garrisoned on islands in the Caribbean and the Pacific, enforcing occupations that were indistinguishable from the colonialism of the British monarchs they had been taught to despise in their American history classes. And, they were repelled by the way in which the armies of the United States were being used to advance the international business interests of the same American corporations that had stacked the deck against farmers and factory workers in the Midwest. Blaine said he was "against every commitment that in any way bound us in the slightest degree to the wars and quarrels of foreign governments." And, he raged against "Dollar Diplomacy," declaring that, "We have turned the Monroe Doctrine into an agency of mischief for America, not for her protection or the protection of weaker nations and peoples (but as an instrument that made American intervention), the wet nurse for alien governments, money lenders, adventurers, and concession grabbers in their career of expansion, extension, and exploitation."

In the Republican primary of that year, John Blaine defeated the incumbent senator, and when he took his seat the following winter, he began an agitation against the U.S. occupations of Haiti, Nicaragua, and other Caribbean and Latin American lands. Allied with Senate Foreign Relations Committee Chairman William Borah and other progressives, Blaine investigated the influence of corporations on U.S. foreign policy, averted a U.S. invasion in Mexico and forced the United States to begin the withdrawal of troops from Nicaragua, the Dominican Republic, and other lands. "Liberty and independence, justice and equality are the cornerstones on which America was begun," Blaine declared. "They are the only cornerstones upon which we can build for an enduring peace."

When he was done, Blaine came home to southwestern Wisconsin. He and my great-grandfather would sit on the front porch of our family home in Blue River and watch the Fourth of July parade go by. They saluted the flag that they believed should fly only on American soil. The work that consumed them, they said, was not merely politics, nor even governance, but the redemption of America.

Blaine and my great-grandfather had a name for the political principle that guided their campaigning for a righteous foreign policy. They called themselves "anti-imperialists." Their fear was entanglement with the turmoil and troubles of other lands and continents; their enemy was empire. And they believed that America could realize her promise as a free and honorable land only if she abandoned the ugly relativism of the powerful and adopted the absolute morality of the good.

Their faith was not unique to their time. Nor was their language.

Indeed, when they spoke of themselves as anti-imperialists, as the sworn enemies of empire, and the bitter foes of expansion, entanglement, and conquest, they borrowed from an American lexicon that was older than the country itself. As the *New York Evening Post* observed in the first years of the twentieth century, "Anti-imperialism is only another name for old-fashioned Americanism."

In the first years of the twenty-first century, as the United States embarked upon an ambitious agenda of empire building, launching what its leaders acknowledged to be a preemptive war for "regime change" and "American interests," dispatching soldiers to the far corners of the earth and upping military spending to the highest levels in the history of humankind, old-fashioned Americanism had few tribunes daring enough to borrow from the patriotic lexicon of the anti-imperialists. A media that practiced stenography to power made no room for those who might note the emperor's state of undress. Television and radio studios were occupied by language police who monitored every utterance for deviation from the chorus for conflict. Even the most tepid questioning of what would turn out to be an empty brief for war led to the dismissal of the doubter as "disloyal," "duped," "inhumane," or, when the list of insults ran out, an "isolationist." Even the most progressive members of the Congress where John Quincy Adams, Abraham Lincoln, William Jennings Bryan, Robert M. La Follette, Jeannette Rankin, Wayne Morse, and Ernest Gruening once preached the gospels of anti-imperialism seemed, at once, afraid and embarrassed to speak the self-evident truths of the moment. Days, weeks, and months went by without mention of the fact that the Republic was behaving like an "empire."

When Robert Byrd, the ancient senator from West Virginia, made apt comparisons between the excesses of Roman military adventurers from the past and American military adventurers from the present, he was dismissed as the last nineteenth-century senator. Yet, modern innovations, cable television's C-SPAN network, and the Internet, in particular, dispatched Byrd's speeches to millions of Americans who heard something familiar, something that rang true—an echo from their past that made a sound purer than the cacophony of the present and that, for the most optimistic among them, held out the promise of a different future than George W. Bush imagined.

For those who cling to the thread of true history, it came as no great surprise that Byrd, who was born while World War I raged, would become a hero to antiwar protesters seventy years his junior. Though it had often been true that they were, as the historian Fred Harvey

Harrington noted, "too feeble" and "too few," anti-imperialists had always been a part of the American body politic. Though the movement itself would ebb and flow, sometimes turning the tide of U.S. foreign policy, sometimes failing to form much more than a ripple in seas dominated by the last great superpower, the anti-imperialist instinct had always been present. Even at the start.

The first European settlers to populate the colonies that clung to the eastern seaboard of the United States were frequently religious and political refugees. They imagined their experiments in communal living as "city-on-a-hill" models that would light the way of the world toward a moral ordering of affairs. They saw the monarchies of Europe, with their vast colonial empires, as corrupt and ultimately self-destructive. They sought a truer path, proclaiming when they took up arms against the British king, "We fight not for glory or for conquest." While that statement from the Continental Congress might not have been entirely true, it spoke to the image that early Americans had of their endeavor as both a political and moral alternative to the old empires of Europe. Thomas Jefferson, an imperfect anti-imperialist to be sure, offered a perfect enunciation of the vision fifty years after the revolution began, when he wrote, "May it be to the world, what I believe it will be, (to some parts sooner, to others later, but finally to all,) the signal of arousing men to burst the chains, under which monkish ignorance and superstition had persuaded them to bind themselves, and to assume the blessings and security of self-government. That form which we have substituted, restores the free right to the unbounded exercise of reason and freedom of opinion. All eyes are opened, or opening, to the rights of man. The general spread of the light of science has already laid open to every view. The palpable truth, that the mass of mankind has not been born with saddles on their backs, nor a favored few booted and spurred, ready to ride them legitimately, by the grace of god. These are grounds of hope for others. For ourselves, let the annual return of this day forever refresh our recollections of these rights, and an undiminished devotion to them."

The American way, at least at its best, would be to inspire by example rather than force. John Quincy Adams, when he was secretary of state, announced on July 4, 1821, "[America's] glory is not dominion, but liberty. Her march is the march of the mind. She has a spear and a shield: but the motto upon her shield is Freedom, Independence, Peace. This has been her declaration: this has been, as far as her necessary intercourse with the rest of mankind would permit, her practice." Adams, the great moralist of his age, did not declare against imperialism merely out of righteousness. He recognized, even at that early point in the history of the Republic, that while through the use of force, "she might become the dictatress of the world," the ultimate result of such endeavoring would mean that "she would be no longer the ruler of her own spirit . . ."

Adams's 1821 pronouncement regarding foreign policy, with its delicious language—"But she goes not abroad, in search of monsters to destroy."—and incredible pretense, remains arguably the greatest statement of the American anti-imperialist ethos. It is so, not because of its own influence across the ages but because it captures so many of the sentiments that would inspire the critics of expansion, entanglement, and empire over the ensuing two centuries. At the heart of the matter is a sense that meddling in the affairs of other lands—even if the intent is good—threatens both the spirit and the democracy of the United States.

The history of American anti-imperialism is in some senses incoherent, and in even more senses inconsistent. There is no pure pattern to follow, no easy staging that leads from a July 4, 1776, attack on the British military occupation of the American colonies down through the years to a July 4, 2004, Code Pink protest against the U.S. military occupation of Iraq. No political party, nor even any ideology, can be said to have defined the tradition across the country's history. Even individuals who at one point seemed so ably to express the ethos, as did the revolutionary Jefferson, at another point violated it, as did the expansionist Jefferson. This is not to suggest that there were no heroes across time—John Quincy Adams comes out looking pretty good, as do Jane Addams, Robert M. La Follette, Wayne Morse, Henry B. Gonzalez, John Conyers and, of course, Gore Vidal, to name but a few—but rather to remind readers that the heroes of one anti-imperialist moment have frequently turned out to be the villains of another.

When viewed through the prism of anti-imperialism, American history is quickly turned upside down. Battles that are now taught, at least in mainstream histories, as necessary, such as the Mexican War of 1846–1848 and World War I, are exposed as the ghastly excesses of territorial ambition and war profiteering that they were. The devastation that westward expansion imposed upon American Indians becomes all the more grotesque, because a reading of the congressional record prior to the "Trail of Tears" reveals that those in power knew, as Representative Theodore Frelinghuysen stated in a last attempt to avert the horror, that their actions, the removal of the Cherokee from Georgia and the Carolinas, would eventually be regarded as "cruel injustice" and "sin." The "acquisition" of Hawaii is exposed as theft. The Spanish-American War, like the 2003 invasion and occupation of Iraq, is a lie spun into blood and death.

There are no innocents here. The history of American expansion, entanglement, and empire does not reveal wrongs after the fact. Rather, it invites us to review the record of those wrongs as it was recorded in real time. What is remarkable is that each time America went searching abroad for monsters to destroy, each time she sought to make herself the dictatress of the world, there were voices, sometimes lonely, sometimes many, that cried out in dissent. Wise historians and philosophers will long debate whether the dissenters of any moment were Cassandras or clarions. But there can be no debate about the motivations of the *New York Evening Post*'s editorials against the War of 1812, or Freylinghuysen's opposition to Indian removals, Abraham Lincoln's "spot resolutions" in opposition to the Mexican War, Mark Twain's criticism of the occupation of the Philippines, Helen Keller's campaigning against U.S. entry into World War I, Langston Hughes's cry for the liberation of Haiti, William Fulbright's hearings on the Vietnam War, or Barbara Lee's vote against the Use-of-Force Resolution laid down by the Bush administration before the smoke of the September 11, 2001, terrorist attacks had cleared.

The primary motivation was not pacifism; while some of the most effective and consistent anti-imperialists were pacifists, they often found themselves allied with old soldiers who did not want to see a new generation of warriors die in corrupted combat.

Nor was it isolationism; although there has frequently been a nativist streak in anti-imperialist risings, the ablest anti-imperialists have invariably been progressive internationalists whose experiences beyond the borders of the United States allowed them to dismiss the deceits of American administrations.

Nor were anti-imperialists duped or motivated by traitorous intent; indeed, the instances of divided loyalty are so rare as to render the most common critique of the anti-imperialists into nothing more than the cheap shot it has always been.

The motivation that remained common across the centuries was patriotism. In struggle after struggle, those who have argued against expansion, entanglement, and empire acted—often at great personal and political cost to themselves—because they believed that in some spiritual, political, or practical sense, the Republic itself was endangered by the territorial desires, foreign intrigues, and militarism of misguided or immoral leaders. Imperialism, in whatever form it took, was viewed as a beast, a monster, a threat, a horror that had to be confronted lest it empty the treasury, subvert the democracy, and consume all that was good in the American endeavor. Such was the sentiment expressed by *New York Tribune* editor Horace Greeley when he rallied opposition to the Mexican war with an editorial that screamed, "People of the United States! Your rulers are precipitating you into a fathomless abyss of crime and calamity! Why sleep you thoughtless on its verge, as though this was not your business, or murder could be hid from the sight of God by a few flimsy rags called banners? Awake and arrest the work of butchery ere it shall be too late to preserve your souls from the guilt of wholesale slaughter!"

It is this patriotic impulse that most merits exploration—not simply to relive courageous fights, nor to restate "I told you so's," nor even to recapture the sheer poetic force of orators seeking to save their native land from an ignoble fate. The purpose of this book is to renew America's acquaintance with her better self and her better instincts. If Americans understand the opposition to expansion, entanglement, and empire as an act of love and loyalty, they will, necessarily, see debates about foreign policy in a radically different light. And that different light should guide us toward the restoration of what has ever been the most honorable of American traditions to its proper place in our national consciousness. That does not mean, of course, that the Fox News Channel will suddenly hire an "anti-imperialism consultant" to go up against its many military consultants, nor that CNN will be careful to balance every neoconservative advocate for military interventions abroad with an anti-imperialist who will ask, as George Washington did, "Why quit our own to stand upon foreign ground?"

Rather, what it means is that when an administration in Washington begins to rattle the sabers once more, when the old lies are dusted off to justify a new war, and when the dispatch of another generation of young Americans to another distant shore is imminent, those who choose to dissent will recognize that they do not stand alone in their opposition. They will, as anti-imperialists always have, recognize that their position, descended from Washington and Lincoln and La Follette and Rankin, is the patriotic stance, the American stance.

Anti-imperialism is, indeed, old-fashioned Americanism. It is as American as the Fourth of July parade in Blue River, and the apple pie and the fireworks, and the flag. And, if we understand it as such, if we recognize it as the truest patriotism, then anti-imperialism may also be the new Americanism.

ONE

We Fought Not for Conquest

Founding Principles

"We should have nothing to do with conquest.

—THOMAS JEFFERSON, *1791*

When dissenters from the impulse toward the American Empire held their annual gatherings in cities and towns across the United States in the early years of the twentieth century, they would meet on the anniversary of George Washington's birth. It was the accepted wisdom of the day that, in addition to having been "the father of his country," Washington was also the father of the anti-imperialist movement. The first president had given his ideological descendents ample evidence on which to base their claim. His 1793 proclamation of American neutrality in regards to European political and military conflicts explicitly rejected international entanglements, with Washington later explaining that, "The duty of holding a neutral conduct may be inferred, without anything more, from the obligation which justice and humanity impose on every nation, in cases in which it is free to act, to maintain inviolate the relations of peace and amity towards other nations." But it was Washington's Farewell Address, delivered in 1796, toward the end of his second presidential term, that became a touchstone for ensuing generations of anti-imperialists. Washington used his last great statement to the nation he had shepherded through the struggle to loose the grip of British colonial rule, "to warn against the mischiefs of foreign intrigue, to guard against the impostures of pretended patriotism." Washington saw great danger in any step that would "entangle our peace and prosperity in the toils of European ambition, rivalship, interest, humor, or caprice." But it was not just alliances with European states that worried him. The first president counseled that it should be "our true policy to steer clear of permanent alliances with any portion of the foreign world."

The commander of America's revolutionary armies did not want his country to follow the European course of collecting colonies and establishing spheres of influence that would ever need to be defended.

He warned that the new United States might "pay with a portion of its independence" for involving itself in "projects of hostility instigated by pride, ambition, and other sinister and pernicious motives." And, he asked a question that would echo across the ages as his presidential successors moved the country further and further from its founding principles, "Why quit our own to stand upon foreign ground?"

The principles that Washington discussed in his Farewell Address were not new concepts. They were, in fact, mainstream opinions shared by many, though surely not all, of his countrymen. A measure of pragmatism underpinned their broad acceptance. America was a new nation, rich in resources but sparsely populated and militarily weak. A career of empire seemed both hypocritical for the former colony, and impractical. America was divided, not just over questions of foreign allegiance and entanglement but with regards to her domestic course. New Englanders were already objecting to the practice of human bondage in the Southern states, and Jefferson, himself a slaveholder, acknowledged that he trembled at the thought of the rough justice that awaited a nation that countenanced the sin of slavery. While the Pennsylvania Quakers imagined cooperation and comity with the indigenous owners of the ground on which Europeans stood as newcomers, governors from Massachusetts to Georgia plotted violent removals of American Indians from their lands. Washington well recognized that the United States lacked the strength and unity to survive internal struggles over alignment with particular colonial powers, let alone the conflicts and costs associated with colonialism of its own.

But there was more than enlightened self-interest in play when Washington suggested that "our detached and distant situation invites and enables us to pursue a different course." From the beginnings of what would come to be referred to as "the American experiment," there was a sense that this endeavor ought to be about something nobler than the mere re-creation of European excesses on the new ground of the Western Hemisphere. John Winthrop's notion that an American settler might see his or her community "as a city on a hill," a model unto the world for the moral ordering of affairs, echoed across religious, ethnic, and regional lines. Among a certain rebellious element, it came to be accepted that Europe's potentates, with their subjects and colonies, represented a corrupt old order that would be replaced only by a shot heard around the world. The American revolutionaries promised that their challenge to the British king and crown would, in the words of their tribune, Tom Paine, "begin the world again." The revolution, which the Continental Congress pledged to fight neither "for glory or for conquest," did, in fact, inspire more revolts against colonial authorities. America's progression toward democracy—slowed, as it was, by the hypocrisy and intolerance of the founders—would, as well, provide a model for the systems that replaced the divine right of kings with the consent of the governed. That requirement of consent should, by its very nature, have rendered illegitimate any colonial or imperialist impulse. And, it seemed, many of the founders read it that way. Fifty years after independence was declared, its author, Jefferson, would renew the city-on-a-hill promise with a call to globalize the democratic revolution, saying, "May it be to the world, what I believe it will be (to some parts sooner, to others later, but finally to all): the signal of arousing men to burst the chains, under which monkish ignorance and superstition had persuaded them to bind themselves, and to assume the blessings and security of self-government."

Debates over the direction of the new nation would be central to the struggle to frame the Constitution. A healthy fear of concentrated power led to the erection of unprecedented constraints upon the executive's authority, with an eye, one delegate declared, toward "clogging rather than facilitating war." Yet, a substantial minority of the founders feared that the document did not guard sufficiently against the impulse toward empire, and they struggled without success to block its ratification.

When the forms of government were generally in place, Americans were free to begin defining the scope and character of their country's engagement with other nations. The great debates were over treaties and alliances—entanglements—with Jefferson seeking closer ties to France while John Adams proposed a special relationship with Britain. Washington's proclamation of American neutrality, though it would eventually be read more broadly, was initially penned with an eye toward easing these tensions. It succeeded in some measure, though the America of the 1790s was a land where a succession of foreign intrigues obsessed those who jockeyed for power in Washington's wake.

After Jefferson defeated Adams for the presidency in 1800, the debate over entanglement eased as a new debate over expansion opened. Jefferson's secret Louisiana Purchase negotiations to obtain French territories west of the Mississippi, which would double the size of the United States, opened a fierce debate about whether the city on a hill was becoming an empire. Jefferson himself worried that the Constitution made no provision for "incorporating foreign nations into our Union." Federalists in Congress, decrying the acquisition of what they identified as "colonies," asserted that the accumulation of new territories threatened to "quench the light" of liberty. As Jefferson's presidency gave way to Madison's, the Federalists grew increasingly critical of military adventures abroad and, with the American declaration of war against Britain in 1812, at home. Federalist opposition to the war, which they saw as an American-initiated attempt to seize parts of Canada, was so intense that, even as the British attacked Washington, Federalists in Congress argued for halting the war. New England Federalists debated seceding from the United States but the war ended before anything came of their efforts. Still, a precedent had been set for domestic debate about the morality of U.S. involvement in wars—even as the conflicts were pursued.

In the years following the War of 1812, there was little doubt that America would remain secure in her territory. But debates about entanglement and expansion continued. Indeed, as the fiftieth anniversary of the American Declaration of Independence approached in the 1820s, Jefferson, Daniel Webster, and young free-thinkers, such as Frances Wright, explored the place of America in the world. On the Fourth of July in 1821, Secretary of State John Quincy Adams would, in an address to Congress, deliver the most important statement of the era, and perhaps of all American history, on the subject: "Wherever the standard of freedom and Independence has been or shall be unfurled, there will her heart, her benedictions and her prayers be," Adams announced, "But she goes not abroad, in search of monsters to destroy."

For wee must Consider that wee shall be as a Citty upon a Hill, the eies of all people are uppon us.

—JOHN WINTHOP, *governor of the Massachusetts Bay Colony, framing the argument that the new settlements on the North America continent could and should inspire the world by their example, 1630.*

∞

I always consider the settlement of America with reverence and wonder, as the opening of a grand scheme and design by Providence for the illumination and emancipation of mankind all over the earth.

—JOHN ADAMS,
from Dissertation on the Canon and Feudal Law, *1765.*

∞

We fight not for glory or for conquest.

—CONTINENTAL CONGRESS, *"Causes of the Necessity of Taking Up Arms," a declaration by the Representatives of the United Colonies of North America, 1775.*

∞

He has combined with others to subject us to a jurisdiction foreign to our constitution, and unacknowledged by our laws; giving his Assent to their Acts of pretended Legislation.

—CONTINENTAL CONGRESS, *from the accounting of King George III's wrongs contained in the Declaration of Independence from the British Empire, 1776.*

∞

The executive should be able to repel and not to commence war.

> —ROGER SHERMAN, *Connecticut delegate to the Constitutional Convention, explaining the intent of a motion to deny the executive the power to "make war," 1787. The motion passed overwhelmingly.*

∽

I am for clogging rather than facilitating war.

> —GEORGE MASON,
> *Virginia delegate to the Constitutional Convention, 1787.*

∽

This system will not hurry us into war; it is calculated to guard against it. It will not be in the power of a single man, or a single body of men, to involve us in such distress; for the important part in declaring war is vested in the legislature at large.

> —JAMES WILSON, *Pennsylvania delegate to the Constitutional Convention, arguing for ratification of the document, 1787.*

∽

The whole powers of war being, by the Constitution of the United States, vested in Congress, the acts of that body alone can be resorted to as our guides.

> —SUPREME COURT CHIEF JUSTICE JOHN MARSHALL,
> *writing for the unanimous court in its ruling on the case of* Talbot v.
> Seeman, *1801. Before joining the high court, Marshall was a participant in the Virginia Ratifying Convention. In 1973, Supreme Court Justice Thurgood Marshall would observe that, "nothing in the one hundred seventy-two years since those words were written alters the fundamental constitutional postulate."*
> *Unfortunately, Congress was at the time enacting a War Powers Act that ensuing presidents would use as a tool to circumvent constitutional dictates regarding executive war making.*

∽

The framers did not view the title of commander in chief as confer-
ring control over the power to declare or instigate war. They per-
ceived it as amounting to "nothing more than the supreme command
and direction of the military and naval forces" so as to maintain civil
authority over them. In later years, presidents, students of the office,
and others would follow a far more expansive interpretation that
would, in their judgment, make the commander in chief clause "one
of the most important in the Constitution." Even so, most constitutional scholars hold to the original view. It states essentially that the
clause "vested in the president only the authority to repel sudden
attacks on the United States . . ."

—ALEXANDER DECONDE, *from* Presidential Machismo:
Executive Authority; Military Intervention, and Foreign Relations
(Northeastern University Press, 2000.)

∾

If there be one principle more deeply written than any other in the
mind of every American, it is that we should have nothing to do with
conquest.

—THOMAS JEFFERSON, *from a letter to William Short, 1791.*

∾

OBSERVE GOOD FAITH and justice towards all nations; cultivate
peace and harmony with all. Religion and morality enjoin this conduct; and can it be, that good policy does not equally enjoin it? It will
be worthy of a free, enlightened, and at no distant period, a great
nation, to give to mankind the magnanimous and too novel example
of a people always guided by an exalted justice and benevolence.
Who can doubt that, in the course of time and things, the fruits of
such a plan would richly repay any temporary advantages which
might be lost by a steady adherence to it? Can it be that Providence
has not connected the permanent felicity of a nation with its virtue?

The experiment, at least, is recommended by every sentiment which ennobles human nature. Alas! Is it rendered impossible by its vices?

In the execution of such a plan, nothing is more essential than that permanent, inveterate antipathies against particular nations, and passionate attachments for others, should be excluded; and that, in place of them, just and amicable feelings toward all should be cultivated. The nation which indulges toward another a habitual hatred or a habitual fondness is in some degree a slave. It is a slave to its animosity or to its affection, either of which is sufficient to lead it astray from its duty and its interest. Antipathy in one nation against another disposes each more readily to offer insult and injury, to lay hold of slight causes of umbrage, and to be haughty and intractable, when accidental or trifling occasions of dispute occur. Hence, frequent collisions, obstinate, envenomed, and bloody contests. The nation, prompted by ill-will and resentment, sometimes impels to war the government, contrary to the best calculations of policy. The government sometimes participates in the national propensity, and adopts through passion what reason would reject; at other times it makes the animosity of the nation subservient to projects of hostility instigated by pride, ambition, and other sinister and pernicious motives. The peace often, sometimes perhaps the liberty, of nations, has been the victim.

So, likewise, a passionate attachment of one nation for another produces a variety of evils. Sympathy for the favorite nation, facilitating the illusion of an imaginary common interest in cases where no real common interest exists, and infusing into one the enmities of the other, betrays the former into a participation in the quarrels and wars of the latter without adequate inducement or justification. It leads also to concessions to the favorite nation of privileges denied to others, which is apt doubly to injure the nation making the concessions; by unnecessarily parting with what ought to have been retained, and by exciting jealousy, ill-will, and a disposition to retaliate, in the parties from whom equal privileges are withheld. And, it gives to ambitious, corrupted, or deluded citizens (who devote themselves to the favorite nation), facility to betray or sacrifice the interests of their own country, without odium, sometimes even with popularity; gilding, with the appearances of a virtuous sense of obligation, a commendable deference for public opinion, or a laudable zeal for public good, the base or foolish compliances of ambition, corruption, or infatuation.

As avenues to foreign influence in innumerable ways, such attachments are particularly alarming to the truly enlightened and independent patriot. How many opportunities do they afford to tamper with domestic factions, to practice the arts of seduction, to mislead public opinion, to influence or awe the public councils? Such an attachment of a small or weak toward a great and powerful nation dooms the former to be the satellite of the latter.

Against the insidious wiles of foreign influence (I conjure you to believe me, fellow-citizens), the jealousy of a free people ought to be constantly awake, since history and experience prove that foreign influence is one of the most baneful foes of republican government. But that jealousy to be useful must be impartial; else it becomes the instrument of the very influence to be avoided, instead of a defense against it. Excessive partiality for one foreign nation and excessive dislike of another cause those whom they actuate to see danger only on one side, and serve to veil and even second the arts of influence on the other. Real patriots who may resist the intrigues of the favorite are liable to become suspected and odious, while its tools and dupes usurp the applause and confidence of the people to surrender their interests.

The great rule of conduct for us in regard to foreign nations is in extending our commercial relations, to have with them as little political connection as possible. So far, as we have already formed engagements, let them be fulfilled with perfect good faith. Here let us stop. Europe has a set of primary interests which to us have none; or a very remote relation. Hence, she must be engaged in frequent controversies, the causes of which are essentially foreign to our concerns. Hence, therefore, it must be unwise in us to implicate ourselves by artificial ties in the ordinary vicissitudes of her politics, or the ordinary combinations and collisions of her friendships or enmities.

Our detached and distant situation invites and enables us to pursue a different course. If we remain one people under an efficient government, the period is not far off when we may defy material injury from external annoyance; when we may take such an attitude as will cause the neutrality we may, at any time, resolve upon to be scrupulously respected; when belligerent nations, under the impossibility of making acquisitions upon us, will not lightly hazard giving us provocation; when we may choose peace or war, as our interest, guided by justice, shall counsel.

Why forego the advantages of so peculiar a situation? Why quit our own to stand upon foreign ground? Why, by interweaving our destiny with that of any part of Europe, entangle our peace and prosperity in the toils of European ambition, rivalship, interest, humor, or caprice?

It is our true policy to steer clear of permanent alliances with any portion of the foreign world; so far, I mean, as we are now at liberty to do it; for let me not be understood as capable of patronizing infidelity to existing engagements. I hold the maxim no less applicable to public than to private affairs, that honesty is always the best policy. I repeat it, therefore, let those engagements be observed in their genuine sense. But, in my opinion, it is unnecessary and would be unwise to extend them.

Taking care always to keep ourselves by suitable establishments on a respectable defensive posture, we may safely trust to temporary alliances for extraordinary emergencies.

Harmony, liberal intercourse with all nations, are recommended by policy, humanity, and interest. But even our commercial policy should hold an equal and impartial hand; neither seeking nor granting exclusive favors or preferences; consulting the natural course of things; diffusing and diversifying by gentle means the streams of commerce, but forcing nothing; establishing (with powers so disposed, in order to give trade a stable course, to define the rights of our merchants, and to enable the government to support them) conventional rules of intercourse, the best that present circumstances and mutual opinion will permit, but temporary, and liable to be from time to time abandoned or varied, as experience and circumstances shall dictate; constantly keeping in view that it is folly in one nation to look for disinterested favors from another; that it must pay with a portion of its independence for whatever it may accept under that character; that, by such acceptance, it may place itself in the condition of having given equivalents for nominal favors, and yet of being reproached with ingratitude for not giving more. There can be no greater error than to expect or calculate upon real favors from nation to nation. It is an illusion, which experience must cure, which a just pride ought to discard.

In offering to you, my countrymen, these counsels of an old and affectionate friend, I dare not hope they will make the strong and lasting impression I could wish; that they will control the usual current of the passions, or prevent our nation from running the course which has hitherto marked the destiny of nations. But, if I may even flatter myself that they may be productive of some partial benefit, some occasional good; that they may now and then recur to moderate the fury of party spirit, to warn against the mischiefs of foreign intrigue, to guard against the impostures of pretended patriotism; this hope will be a full recompense for the solicitude for your welfare, by which they have been dictated.

—GEORGE WASHINGTON, *Farewell Address, 1796. Washington's words were so influential that, more than a century later, American anti-imperialists gathered annually to celebrate the first president's birthday and to renew their commitment to the principle of avoiding foreign entanglements.*

In spite of all the claims and examples of patriotism, which ought by no means to be undervalued, the testimony of all ages forces us to admit that war is among the most dangerous of all enemies to liberty; and that the executive is the most favored by it, of all the branches of power.

> —JAMES MADISON, *February 23, 1799, "Political Reflections,"*
> *found in* The Papers of James Madison, *Vol.17 (University of*
> *Virginia Press, W. T. Hutchinson et al., editors, 1962–1991).*

∽

Peace, commerce, and honest friendship with all nations, entangling alliances with none . . .

> —THOMAS JEFFERSON, *first inaugural address, March 4, 1801.*

∽

The Constitution has made no provision for our holding foreign territory, still less for incorporating foreign nations into our Union.

> —THOMAS JEFFERSON, *letter to John Breckinridge explaining*
> *his concerns regarding the proposed annexation of the Louisiana*
> *Territory from France, August 12, 1803. Jefferson initially suggested*
> *that the Constitution be amended to allow for the purchase, but he*
> *eventually chose to pursue the deal without legal sanction. His*
> *decision provoked one of the first serious debates on expansionism.*
> *Critics accused him of steering the country onto a colonialist*
> *course like that of the British Empire against which the*
> *American revolutionaries had rebelled.*

∽

The purchase of the Louisiana Territory is sure to send the United States hurdling "like a comet into infinite space. In our wild career, we may jostle some other world out of its orbit, but we shall, in every event, quench the light of our own."

—FORMER FEDERALIST PARTY LEADER IN THE HOUSE OF REPRESENTATIVES, FISHER AMES to Christopher Gore, October 3, 1803.

∽

It is a colonial system of government. It is the first the United States has established. It is a bad precedent. The U.S. will, in time, have many colonies—precedents are therefore important.

—U.S. SENATOR WILLIAM PLUMER, *from a discussion of how to manage the Louisiana Purchase published in "Debates and Proceedings" in the eighth Congress, 1804.*

∽

And when we consider the present extent of the U.S., and that not ¹⁄₁₆ part of its territory is yet under occupation, the advantage of the acquisition, as it relates to actual settlement, appears too distant and remote to strike the mind of a sober politician with much force.

Should our own citizens, more enterprising than wise, become desirous of settling this country, and emigrate thither, it must not only be attended with all the injuries of a too widely dispersed population, but, by adding to the great weight of the western part of our territory, must hasten the dismemberment of a large portion of our country, or a dissolution of the government.

—NEW YORK HERALD, *editorial opposing the Louisiana Purchase, July 6, 1803.*

∽

The president of the United States cannot control the statute, nor dispense with its execution, and still less can he authorize a person to do what the law forbids. . . . Does he possess the power of making war? That power is exclusively vested in Congress.

> —SUPREME COURT JUSTICE WILLIAM PATERSON,
> *from his opinion in* United States v. Smith, *where he held that testimony from the secretary of state and the secretary of the navy was irrelevant to determining whether a U.S. Army colonel violated federal statutes by intriguing to aid a rogue expedition against the Spanish rulers of Venezuela, 1806. The defendant claimed that he acted at the behest of President Jefferson. But Patterson ruled that the Constitution gave Congress, not the president or his cabinet, sole authority over decisions regarding military endeavors abroad. Patterson knew something of the "original intent" of the founders; he had served as a delegate from New Jersey to the Constitutional Convention.*

∽

We have no need to league with the belligerents, we have only to defend ourselves from oppression.

> —AURORA GENERAL ADVERTISER,
> *newspaper editorial arguing for neutrality in conflicts between European states, July 31, 1809.*

∽

THE FOLLY OF JOINING THE ARMY

"Tricks upon Travellers," or "More Ways Than One to Kill a Cat."— Old saws. We are certainly now to have a war, for Congress have voted to have an army. But let me tell you, there is all the difference in the world between an army on paper, and an army in the field. An army on paper is voted in a whiff, but to raise an army, you must offer men

We send soldiers off to fight, little pay etc. for a "purpose." many times, they cannot find the actual "purpose" of war.

good wages. The wages proposed to be given to induce men to come forward and enlist for five years, leave their homes and march away to take Canada, is a bounty of sixteen dollars, and five dollars a month; and at the end of the war, if they can get a certificate of good behavior, one hundred sixty acres of wild land and three months' pay; for the purpose, I presume, of enabling the soldier to walk off and find it, if he can. Now I should really be glad to be informed, whether it is seriously expected that, in a country where a stout able-bodied man can earn fifteen dollars a month from May to November, and a dollar a day during mowing and harvesting, he will go into the army for a bounty of sixteen dollars, five dollars a month for five years, if the war should last so long, and one hundred sixty acres of wild land, if he happens to be on such good terms with his commanding officer as to obtain a certificate of good behavior? Let the public judge if such inducements as these will ever raise an army of twenty-five thousand men, or ever were seriously expected to do it? If not, can anything be meant more than "sound and fury signifying nothing?" This may be called humbugging on a large scale.

—NEW YORK EVENING POST, *editorial opposing war with Britain, which critics portrayed as an attempt by American expansionists to seize Canada, January 24, 1812.*

⚭

You have lately seen fifteen millions of dollars wasted in the purchase of a province we did not want, and never shall possess. And, will you spend thousands of millions in conquering a province which, were it made a present to us, would not be worth accepting? Our territories are already too large. The desire to annex Canada to the United States is as base an ambition as ever burned in the bosom of Alexander. What benefit will it ever be to the great body of the people, after their wealth is exhausted, and their best blood is shed in its reduction? "We wish to clear our continent of foreign powers." So did the Madman of Macedon wish to clear the world of his enemies, and such as would not bow to his sceptre. So does Bonaparte wish to clear Europe of all his enemies; yea, and Asia, too. Canada, if annexed to the United States, will furnish offices to a set of hungry villains, grown quite too numerous for our present wide limits; and that is all the benefit we ever shall derive from it.

—NEW YORK EVENING POST, *editorial, April 21, 1812.*

∽

WAR!

The universal sentiment against a British war which prevails among considerate men of all parties in this section of the Union, is accompanied by a natural, but perhaps a false security in the conviction of the impossibility of this event. With the exception of a few brawlers in the street, and of some office-holding editors, we can find none who seriously wish to promote this calamity. It is evident that under the circumstances of this country a declaration of war would be in effect a license and a bounty offered by our government to the British Fleet to scour our coasts—to sweep our remaining navigation from the ocean, to annihilate our commerce, and to drive the country, by a rapid declension, into the state of poverty and distress which attended the close of the revolutionary struggle. We are convinced of the absence of those exasperated feelings in the great body of the people which would impel them to such a conflict. We fathom the length and depth of the artificial excitement, which is attempted by men of desperate fortunes and character, and we are satisfied that, in their efforts to influence the public mind, they apply their blazing torches to a mountain of ice. Other considerations come in aid of our confidence. The proposed enemy is invulnerable to us, while we are on all sides open to assault. The conquest of Canada would be less useful to us than that of Nova-Zembla, and could not be so easily achieved. Our red brethren forgetful of the patriotic "talks" of their "father" Jefferson would pour down upon our frontier, and our black brethren would show themselves not less enamoured with the examples of liberty taught in St. Domingo than their masters are with those derived from its mother country. New Orleans and the Floridas would pass into the hands of the enemy. Our seaports would be under strict blockade, and the mouths of our rivers would be bridged with frigates. Besides the war would be interminable, or end in a surrender on our part of the objects of contention . . .

—COLUMBIAN CENTINEL (BOSTON), *editorial, May 20, 1812.*

❧

North of the Delaware, there is among all who do not bask or expect to bask in the executive sunshine but one voice for peace. South of that river, the general cry is, "Open war. O, peers!" There are not two hostile nations upon earth whose views of the principles and polity of a perfect commonwealth, and of men and measures, are more discordant than those of these two great divisions. There is but little of congeniality or sympathy in our notions or feelings; and this small residuum will be extinguished by this withering war.

The sentiment is hourly extending, and in these Northern states will soon be universal, that we are in a condition no better in relation to the South than that of a conquered people . . .

—COLUMBIAN CENTINEL (BOSTON), *editorial illustrating deep opposition of the New England states to the War of 1812, January 13, 1813. That opposition would, in some quarters, take the form of threats by leaders in New England states to try and secede from the United States rather than support a war of conquest.*

❧

MR. MADISON'S WAR

—NEW ENGLAND PHRASE FOR THE WAR OF 1812, *which was portrayed in much of the country as a war of presidential whim and expansionist sentiment, as opposed to necessity.*

Mr. Chairman:

After the best reflection which I have been able to bestow on the subject of the bill before you, I am of opinion that its principles are not warranted by any provision of the Constitution.

This bill . . . is an attempt to exercise the power of forcing the free men of this country into the ranks of an army, for the general purposes of war, under color of a military service. To this end, it commences with a classification, which is no way connected with the general organization of the militia, nor, to my apprehension, included within any of the powers which Congress possesses over them. . . .

Is this, Sir, consistent with the character of a free government? Is this civil liberty? Is this the real character of our Constitution? No, Sir, indeed it is not. The Constitution is libelled, foully libelled. The people of this country have not established for themselves such a fabric of despotism. They have not purchased at a vast expense of their own treasure and their own blood a Magna Charta to be slaves. Where is it written in the Constitution, in what article or section is it contained, that you may take children from the parents, and parents from their children, and compel them to fight the battles of any war, in which the folly or the wickedness of government may engage it? Under what concealment has this power lain hidden, which now for the first time comes forth, with a tremendous and baleful aspect, to trample down and destroy the dearest rights of personal liberty? Who will show me any constitutional injunction, which makes it the duty of the American people to surrender everything valuable in life, and even life itself, not when the safety of their country and its liberties may demand the sacrifice, but whenever the purposes of an ambitious and mischievous government may require it? . . .

—U.S. REPRESENTATIVE DANIEL WEBSTER, *speech to the House of Representatives opposing a proposal by Secretary of State James Monroe to allow for a national draft to raise a larger army to fight the British, December 9, 1814.*

What the terms of the peace are, we cannot tell; they will only be made known at Washington, by the dispatches themselves. But one thing I will venture to say now and before they are opened, and I will hazard my reputation upon the correctness of what I say, that when the terms are disclosed, it will be found that the government have not by this negociation obtained one single avowed object for which they involved the country in this bloody and expensive war.

—NEW YORK EVENING POST, *editorial headlined "Peace,"*
February 13, 1815.

∽

AND NOW, FRIENDS and countrymen, if the wise and learned philosophers of the elder world, the first observers of nutation and aberration, the discoverers of maddening ether and invisible planets, the inventors of Congreve rockets and Shrapnel shells, should find their hearts disposed to enquire what has America done for the benefit of mankind?

Let our answer be this: America, with the same voice which spoke herself into existence as a nation, proclaimed to mankind the inextinguishable rights of human nature, and the only lawful foundations of government. America, in the assembly of nations, since her admission among them, has invariably, though often fruitlessly, held forth to them the hand of honest friendship, of equal freedom, of generous reciprocity.

She has uniformly spoken among them, though often to heedless and often to disdainful ears, the language of equal liberty, of equal justice, and of equal rights.

She has, in the lapse of nearly half a century, without a single exception, respected the independence of other nations while asserting and maintaining her own.

She has abstained from interference in the concerns of others, even when conflict has been for principles to which she clings, as to the last vital drop that visits the heart. She has seen that probably for centuries to come, all the contests of that Aceldama the European world, will be contests of inveterate power, and emerging right. Wherever the standard of freedom and independence has been or shall be unfurled, there will her heart, her benedictions, and her prayers be. But she goes not abroad, in search of monsters to destroy.

She is the well-wisher to the freedom and independence of all.

She is the champion and vindicator only of her own.

She will commend the general cause by the countenance of her voice, and the benignant sympathy of her example.

She well knows that by once enlisting under other banners than her own, were they even the banners of foreign independence, she would involve herself beyond the power of extrication, in all the wars of interest and intrigue, of individual avarice, envy, and ambition, which assume the colors and usurp the standard of freedom. The fundamental maxims of her policy would insensibly change from liberty to force. . . .

She might become the dictatress of the world. She would be no longer the ruler of her own spirit. . . .

[America's] glory is not dominion, but liberty. Her march is the march of the mind. She has a spear and a shield, but the motto upon her shield is: Freedom, Independence, Peace. This has been her declaration. This has been, as far as her necessary intercourse with the rest of mankind would permit, her practice.

—SECRETARY OF STATE JOHN QUINCY ADAMS,
speech to the House of Representatives regarding America's role in the world, July 4, 1821.

Our first and fundamental maxim should be, never to entangle ourselves in the broils of Europe.

> —THOMAS JEFFERSON, *letter to President James Monroe*
> *regarding the Monroe Doctrine, October 24, 1823.*

∽

Are we, Sir, to go on a crusade, in another hemisphere, for the prop-
agation of two objects as dear and delightful to my heart as to that of
any gentleman in this, or in any other assembly—liberty and religion—and, in the name of those holy words, by this powerful spell,
is this nation to be conjured and beguiled out of the high way of
Heaven, out of its present comparatively happy state, into all the disastrous conflicts arising from the policy of European powers, with all
the consequences which flow from them?

> —JOHN RANDOLPH OF ROANOKE, *opposing the dispatch of*
> *U.S. agents to aid the Greek struggle for independence, 1824. (A*
> *member of the House of Representatives from 1799–1813, 1815–17,*
> *1819–25, 1827–29 and in 1832, Randolph served as a senator*
> *from 1825–27, and as minister to Russia in 1832.)*

∽

Too honest or too proud to feign
A love he never cherished,
Beyond Virginia's border line
His patriotism perished.
While others hailed in distant skies
Our eagle's dusty pinion,
He only saw the mountain bird
Stoop o'er his Old Dominion!

> —JOHN GREENLEAF WHITTIER, *"Randolph of Roanoke." This*
> *poem was written after the death of John Randolph,*
> *on May 24, 1833.*

∽

IF THE BLESSINGS of our political and social condition have not been too highly estimated, we cannot well overrate the responsibility and duty which they impose upon us. We hold these institutions of government, religion, and learning, to be transmitted, as well as enjoyed. We are in the line of conveyance, through which whatever has been obtained by the spirit and efforts of our ancestors is to be communicated to our children.

We are bound to maintain public liberty, and, by the example of our own systems, to convince the world that order and law, religion and morality, the rights of conscience, the rights of persons, and the rights of property, may all be preserved and secured, in the most perfect manner, by a government entirely and purely elective. If we fail in this, our disaster will be signal, and will furnish an argument, stronger than has yet been found, in support of those opinions which maintain that government can rest safely on nothing but power and coercion. As far as experience may show errors in our establishments, we are bound to correct them; and if any practices exist contrary to the principles of justice and humanity within the reach of our laws or our influence, we are inexcusable if we do not exert ourselves to restrain and abolish them.

—DANIEL WEBSTER, *"Discourse in Commemoration of the First Settlement of New England," delivered at Plymouth Rock to celebrate the two hundreth anniversary of the landing of the Pilgrims, December 22, 1820. Webster, a leading opponent of slavery, would frequently argue during his political career that the United States should remain a city on a hill, leading the world by example rather than force. The chief example, said Webster was "that prodigy of modern times, at once the wonder and the blessing of the world . . . the American Revolution." At the dedication of the Bunker Hill Monument on June 17, 1825, Webster declared the influence of the American Revolution to be universal, noting, "Europe, within the same period, has been agitated by a mighty revolution, which, while it has been felt in the individual condition and happiness of almost every man, has shaken to the centre her political fabric, and dashed against one another thrones which had*

*stood tranquil for ages. On this, our continent, our own example has
been followed, and colonies have sprung up to be nations.
Unaccustomed sounds of liberty and free government have reached
us from beyond the track of the sun; and at this moment the
dominion of European power in this continent, from the place where
we stand to the south pole, is annihilated forever."*

⚮

WHAT A SEASON of deep interest is the present! . . . What distinguishes the present from every other struggle in which the human race has been engaged, is, that the present is, evidently, openly and acknowledged, a war of class, and that this war is universal. It is no longer nation pitched against nation for the good pleasure and sport of kings and great captains, nor sect cutting the throats and roasting the carcasses of sect for the glory of God and satisfaction of priests, nor is it one army butchering another to promote the fortunes of their leaders—to pass from a James to a George or a Charles to a Louis Philip the privilege of coining laws, money and peers, and dividing the good things of the land among his followers.

No; it is now everywhere the oppressed millions who are making common cause against oppression; it is the ridden people of the earth who are struggling to throw from their backs the "booted and spurred" riders whose legitimate title to starve as well as to work them to death will no longer pass current; it is labor rising up against idleness, industry against money, justice against raw and against privilege.

And truly the struggle hath not come too soon. Truly there hath been oppression and outrage enough on the one side, and suffering and endurance enough on the other, to render the millions rather chargeable with excess of patience and overabundance of good nature than with too eager a spirit for the redress of injury, not to speak of recourse to vengeance.

It has been long clear to me that in every country the best feelings and the best sense are found with the laboring and useful classes, and the worst feelings and the worst sense with the idle and the useless. Until all classes shall be merged into one however by gradual but fundamental changes in the whole organization of society, much bad feeling must prevail everywhere . . .

> —FRANCES WRIGHT, *"The People at War," Free Enquirer, November 27, 1830. Wright was an early feminist who was associated with Robert Owen's utopian experiment at New Harmony, while the* Free Enquirer *was a radical journal of free thought, abolitionism, and broad social and economic reform. She is often credited with coining the phrase "class war."*

TWO

Traitors to Our Principles and Our Fame

The Indian Removal Debates and the Trail of Tears

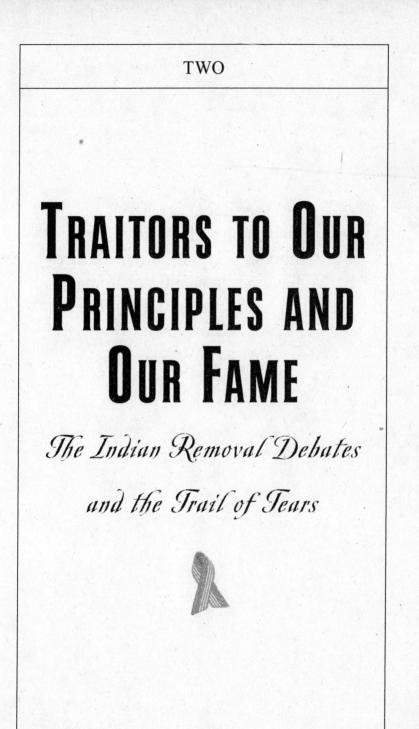

"We are denationalized;
we are disfranchised. We are deprived
of membership in the human family!
We have neither land nor home,
nor resting place that can be
called our own.

—CHIEF JOHN ROSS *of the Cherokee Nation, 1836*

The greatest lies of history begin with the words, "You have to understand the context of the times . . ." and rarely is the "context of the times" fabrication more frequently employed than in discussions of the treatment of American Indians. "If only the white settlers and their governors had better understood the nobility of the Native Americans," the lie goes, "then they might not have been so aggressive about robbing them of their lands and killing them off." But, of course, the political leaders of the United States knew from the start that the Indian tribes of the eastern United States had a better claim to the land on which the American experiment would play out than any European settler. And even if a calculus developed to "legitimize" particular displacements of tribes from their native lands, the first generations of American leaders recognized that the Indians had a right to demand the same treatment that was afforded foreign governments. In the early years of the Republic, it fell to the secretary of state, the cabinet member responsible for dealing with foreign governments, to discuss policies toward the tribes—including those that resided on land within the new American states. Secretary of State Thomas Jefferson made his position exceptionally clear. "I am of the opinion," wrote Jefferson in 1791, "that the Indians have a right to the occupation of their lands, independent of the states within those chartered limits they happen to be: that until they cede them by a treaty, no act of a state can give a right to such lands."

As was so often the case, however, Jefferson's words proved better than his countrymen's deeds. In the expansionist rush of the late eighteenth and early nineteenth centuries, Indians who had played a pivotal role in easing the entry of European settlers into their homelands were prodded with increasing force to abandon the soil to which they—not the Europeans—were native. In the 1790s, even tribes that had been allies of the American revolutionaries and friends to the new government found themselves pressured to sell off vast stretches of the territories that had always been theirs. The land struggles grew increasingly bitter, frequently erupting into outbursts of violence. Yet, some tribes were able to remain on their native lands. They maintained their sovereignty, as a new generation of tribal leaders developed their capacities as diplomats and political negotiators. They learned the political, legal, and political frameworks of their neighbors, and they won allies in the Congress and the courts. This would not, however, protect them from the rapacious excesses of expansionists—particularly in Southern states, such as Georgia and North Carolina.

The great stand against the expansionists was taken by the Cherokee Nation, which had established sophisticated political and economic structures on tribal lands surrounded by states such as Georgia, North Carolina, Alabama, and Tennessee. The relative wealth of the Cherokee, who had developed farms and ranches as part of an effort to clarify their claims to tribal lands in the southeast, gave them a measure of confidence that was evident in the 1823 declaration of the Cherokee General Council that, "It is the fixed and unalterable determination of this nation never again to cede one foot more of our land." In the mid 1820s, when state officials in Georgia backed moves by white settlers to seize Cherokee land, the tribe was able to turn to allies in the federal government. President John Quincy Adams, who had distinguished himself in the early years of the decade with his anti-imperialist opposition to those who would have America go abroad "in search of monsters to destroy," declared he would use federal force to prevent the expansionists from committing "acts of encroachment upon the terrotories secured by a solemn treaty to the Indians." But Adams's day was passing. Narrowly elected to the presidency in 1824, he would be swept from office in 1828. His replacement, Andrew Jackson, had earned his U.S. Army commission after leading a force that crushed the Creek Indian resistance in the Mississippi Territory and then led a ruthless war on Florida's Seminoles. A small "d" democrat who was appropriately critical of concentrated power, his presidency would do much to break the grip of the new nation's emerging elites on its governance. "Yet," as historian Sean Wilentz would note, "those advances went hand in hand with the continued subjugation of Native Americans and a determination not to disturb the slavery issue. Jackson stood for a more egalitarian America, but his vision of democracy stopped squarely at the color line." And, the Cherokee Nation fell on the wrong side of Jackson's color line.

Still, the Cherokee battled, aided by their white allies in Congress and the courts, to make real the promise of American righteousness. Their lawyers fought all the way to the U.S. Supreme Court, initially losing in the case of *Cherokee Nation v. State of Georgia* (1831), where the Supreme Court denied the tribe's right of appeal. A year later, however, in the case of *Worcester v. State of Georgia,* the high court declared that the "laws of Georgia can have no force" in Cherokee territory. That ruling, written by Chief Justice John Marshall, should have protected the Cherokee. But Jackson, in one of the most extraordinary rejections of judicial authority in American history, announced, "John Marshall has made his decision. Now let him enforce it." The presidential endorsement of state lawlessness provoked a national debate that would surge again and again in the Congress during the 1830s, inspiring debates that would touch frequently on the question—a constant in the dialogue about imperialism—of whether America's government was sacrificing morality in the pursuit of expansion. Maine Senator Peleg Sprague warned that, with its treatment of the Indians, America was imitating the "conquerors of kingdoms (who) lived in luxury upon their spoils," while New Jersey Congressman Theodore Frelinghuysen demanded, "Do the obligations of justice change with the color of the skin? Is it one of the prerogatives of the white man, that he may disregard the dictates of moral principles when an Indian shall be concerned?" Even a young congressman named Davy Crockett joined in the defense of the rights of the Indians, admitting that his stance would surely cost him his seat representing a Tennessee district but stating that, "I would sooner be honestly damned than hypocritically immortalized."

Frelinghuysen, Crockett, and their allies would not prevail. The removals of the Cherokee went ahead, with members of the tribe following a "Trail of Tears" that would, in the words of historian Wilcomb Washburn, become "an enduring symbol of white injustice toward the Indians." Over time, the court and congressional battles would be forgotten. The excuse of ignorance would be advanced on behalf of those who supported the removals, despite the fact that they were warned in their own era that they were doing "the work of war in time of peace" and that their actions would expose them "to the judgments of Heaven."

Your laws extend not into our country, nor ever did. You talk of the law of nature and the law of nations, and they both are against you. Indeed, much has been advanced on the want of what you term civilization among the Indians; and many proposals have been made to us to adopt your laws, your religion, your manners, and your customs. But we confess that we do not yet see the propriety, or practibility of such a reformation, and should be better pleased with beholding the good effect of these doctrines in your practices than with hearing you talk about them, or reading your papers to us upon such subjects.

You say: Why do not the Indians till the ground as we do? May we not, with equal propriety, ask, Why do white people not hunt and live as we do? You profess to think it no injustice to warn us not to kill our deer and other game for the mere love of waste; but it is very criminal in our young men if the chance to kill a cow or hog for their sustenance when they happen to be in your lands. We wish, however, to be at peace with you, and to do as we would be done by. We do not quarrel with you for killing an occasional buffalo, bear, or deer on our lands when you need one to eat, but you go much further. Your people hunt to gain a livelihood by it, They kill all our game; our young men resent the injury, and it is followed by bloodshed and war.

—CORN TASSEL, *July 1785. A Cherokee leader, Corn Tassel was addressing the Continental Congress of the United States.*

Almost every war between the Indians and the whites has been occasioned by some injustice of the latter towards the former.

—BENJAMIN FRANKLIN, *letter to a French associate, 1786.*

I am of the opinion . . . that the Indians have a right to the occupation of their lands, independent of the states within those chartered limits they happen to be: that until they cede them by a treaty, no act of a state can give a right to such lands; that neither under the present Constitution, nor the ancient confederation, had any state or person, a right to treat with the Indians, without the consent of the general government . . . that the government is determined to exert its energy for the patronage and protection of the rights of the Indians, and the preservation of peace between the United States and them; and that if any settlements are made on the lands not ceded to them, without the previous consent of the United States, the government will think itself bound, not only to declare to the Indians that such settlements are without the authority or protection of the United States, but to remove them also by force.

—SECRETARY OF STATE THOMAS JEFFERSON,
letter to Secretary of War Henry Knox, August 10, 1791.
Jefferson's letter set out the principles on which he felt the U.S.
should develop relations with Indians living within the
thirteen states and in territories to the west.

∽

Money, to us, is of no value, and to most of us unknown, and as no consideration whatever can induce us to sell the lands on which we get sustenance for our women and children, we hope we may be allowed to point out a mode by which your settlers may be easily removed, and peace thereby obtained. . . . We know that these settlers are poor, or they would never have ventured to live in a country which has been in continual trouble ever since they crossed the Ohio; divide, therefore, this large sum of money which you have offered to us, among these people, give to each also a portion of what you say you would give us annually over and above this very large sum of money, and we are persuaded they would most readily accept of it in lieu of the lands you sold to them, if you add also the great sums you must expend in raising and paying armies, with a view to force us to yield you our country, you will certainly have more than sufficient for the purposes of repaying these settlers for all their labor and improvements. You have talked to us about concessions. It appears strange that you should expect any from us, who have only been defending our just rights against your invasion. We want peace. Restore to us our country and we shall be enemies no longer . . . our only demand is the peaceable possession of a small part of our once great country. Look back and view the lands from whence we have been driven to this spot, we can retreat no further . . . we have therefore resolved, to leave our bones in this small space.

—SEVEN NATIONS, response to offer U.S. government commissioners money for land in Ohio, August 16, 1793. Despite the signal from Jefferson and a number of members of Congress that cordial relations should be developed with Indian tribes, tensions flared frequently. Invariably, those tensions were stoked by pressure on the Indians to leave their land in order to make way for the westward expansion of the U.S. During the presidencies of George Washington and John Adams, Indians grew increasingly distrustful of promises made by the U.S. government and its representatives.

∽

Brother Handsome Lake:

I have received the message in writing which you sent me through Captain Irvine, our confidential agent, placed near you for the purpose of communicating and transacting between us, whatever may be useful for both nations. I am happy to learn you have been so far favored by the divine spirit as to be made sensible to those things which are for your good and that of your people, and of those which are harmful to you, and particularly that you see the ruinous effects which the abuse of spirituous liquors have produced upon them. It has weakened their bodies, enervated their minds, exposed them to hunger, cold, nakedness, and poverty, kept them in perpetual broils, and reduced their population. . . .

You remind me, brother, of what I said to you, when you visited us last winter, that the lands you then held would remain yours, and should never go from you but when you should be disposed to sell. This I now repeat, and will ever abide by. We indeed are always ready to buy lands but we will never ask but when you wish to sell. . . . Go on them, brother, in the great reformation you have undertaken. Persuade our red brethren to be sober and to cultivate their lands, and their women to spin and weave for their families. You will soon see your women and children well fed and clothed, your men living happily in peace and plenty, and your numbers increasing from year to year. It will be a great glory to you to have been the instrument of so happy a change in your children's children, for generation to generation, will repeat your name with love and gratitude forever. In all the enterprises for the good of your people, you may count with confidence on the aid and protection of the United States, and on the sincerity and zeal with which I am myself animated in the furthering of this humane work. You are our brethren of the same land: We wish to see your prosperity as brethren should do.

Farewell.

—PRESIDENT THOMAS JEFFERSON, *letter to Handsome Lake, the Seneca chief and prophet, November 2, 1802. As president, Jefferson attempted to improve relations with the various Indian tribes, maintaining regular correspondence with Indian chiefs during his two terms in the White House.*

From the secretary at war you receive from time to time information and instructions as to our Indian affairs. These communications being for the public records are restrained always to particular objects and occasions. But this letter being unofficial, and private, I may with safety give you a more extensive view of our policy respecting the Indians, that you may the better comprehend the parts dealt out to you in detail through the official channel, and observing the system of which they make a part, conduct yourself in unison with it in cases where you are obliged to act without instruction. Our system is to live in perpetual peace with the Indians, to cultivate an affectionate attachment from them, by everything just and liberal

which we can [do] for them within the bounds of reason, and by giving them effectual protection against wrongs from our own people.
The decrease of game rendering their subsistence by hunting insufficient, we wish to draw them to agriculture, spinning, and weaving.

—PRESIDENT THOMAS JEFFERSON, *letter to William Henry
Harrison, who was then serving as governor of the Indiana
Territory, February 27, 1803.*

∽

You want by your distinctions of Indian tribes, in allotting to each a
particular, to make them war with each other. You never see an Indian
endeavor to make the white people do this. You are continually driving the red people, when at last you will drive them onto the great
lake, where they can neither stand nor work.

Since my residence at Tippecanoe, we have endeavored to level all
distinctions, to destroy village chiefs, by whom all mischiefs are
done. It is they who sell the land to the Americans. Brother, this land
that was sold, and the goods that was given for it, was only done by
a few. . . . In the future we are prepared to punish those who propose
to sell land to the Americans. If you continue to purchase them, it
will make war among the different tribes, and, at last I do not know
what will be the consequences among the white people.

Brother, I wish you would take pity on the red people and do as I
have requested. If you will not give up the land and do cross the
boundary of our present settlement, it will be very hard, and produce
great trouble between us.

The way, the only way to stop this evil is for the red men to unite in
claiming a common and equal right in the land, as it was at first, and
should be now—for it was never divided, but belongs to all. No tribe
has the right to sell, even to each other, much less to strangers. . . . Sell
a country! Why not sell the air, the great sea, as well as the earth? Did
not the Great Spirit make them all for the use of his children?

How can we have confidence in the white people? When Jesus Christ came upon the earth you killed him and nailed him to the cross.

> —TECUMSEH, *1810, explaining to Governor William Henry Harrison why Indians objected to the practice of U.S. representatives buying property from individual Indians or small tribal groupings and then claiming that the deals ended all Indian claims on those lands.*

∾

It is the fixed and unalterable determination of this nation never again to cede one foot more of our land.

> —CHEROKEE GENERAL COUNCIL, *signaling opposition to moves by state and federal officials to force the Cherokee off land in western Georgia, North Carolina, Alabama, and Tennessee, 1823.*

∾

[We declare that:] The Cherokee are not foreigners, but the original inhabitants of America, and that they now stand on the soil of their own territory, and they cannot recognize the sovereignty of any state within the limits of their territory.

> —CHEROKEE GENERAL COUNCIL, *message delivered by a delegation sent to Washington to object to encroachment of their sovereignty and territory by officials of the state of Georgia, 1826. Georgia was pressing claims against the Cherokee in order to gain control of the mineral-rich lands on which members of the tribe resided.*

∾

In the present instance, it is my duty to say, that, if the legislature and executive of the State of Georgia should persevere in acts of encroachment upon the territories secured by a solemn treaty to the Indians, and the laws of the Union remain unaltered, a super-added obligation, even higher than that of human authority, will compel the executive of the United States to enforce the laws, and fulfill the duties of the nation, by all the force committed for that purpose to his charge.

> —PRESIDENT JOHN QUINCY ADAMS, *message to Congress indicating that he saw it as his duty to prevent encroachment by Georgia on the territory of the Cherokee, February 5, 1827. Adams's position, and the stances of congressional leaders, such as Daniel Webster, slowed the efforts of those who sought to remove the Cherokee and other tribes from regions east of the Mississippi River. But the issue became increasingly volatile, as Southerners stoked anti-Indian and expansionist sentiments.*

₝ℓ₞

I am glad, Mr. Chairman, that this measure is thus brought forward, and that it stands before us in its proper form and nakedness, stripped of the pretence of disinterested humanity, which has around it. It is now presented in its true character, as a measure, not for the benefit of the Indians—not for their civilization and preservation—but for our interest, and only our interest. This appropriation is asked, as the means to effect measures for the removal of the Indians out of the limits of our states and territories, that they may, by our aid, trail their bodies into the wilderness, and die where our delicacy and our senses may not be offended by their unburied carcasses. . . .

We are told, Sir, that this is a measure necessary for the happiness and preservation of the Indian—that we must adopt it, or they will perish, and become extinct as a people. I do not believe this is the only way in which we can save the Indians, or promote their happiness. In my opinion, this measure would effect more rapidly their extinction. Instead of being entitled, "An act for the preservation and civilization of the Indian tribes within the United States," it should be called a scheme for their speedy extermination. . . . We are told by one of our sovereign states, while urging upon us her claims to the Indian country within her limits, that it belongs to her, and that she must and she will have it; that we are bound, at all hazards, "and without regard to terms, to procure it." Shall we be told that Congress is to disregard the right of the Indians? That the lands on which they now reside shall be taken from them "without regard to terms?" That it is the interest—the determination—the settled policy of the United States, "at all hazards," to drive them from their country and homes? I hope not, Sir; for the honor of my country, I hope not.

—U.S. REPRESENTATIVE JOHN WOODS, *of Ohio, arguing against a proposal to fund an Indian removal program that would force the Cherokee and other tribes from their lands in the east and dispatch them to regions west of the Mississippi, February 1828. Later that year, with the defeat of President John Quincy Adams by Andrew Jackson, foes of Indian removal lost their ally in the White House. As Jackson indicated his support for removal, the issue moved to the center of the national debate.*

∝

[We] have done so much to destroy the Indians, and so little to save them; and that, before another step is taken, there should be the most thorough deliberation, on the part of all our constituted authorities, lest we act in such a manner as to expose ourselves to the judgments of Heaven.

—JEREMIAH EVARTS, *from* Essays on the Present Crisis in the Condition of the American Indians, *1829.*

∝

Our fathers . . . successfully and triumphantly contended for the very rights and privileges that our Indian neighbors now implore us to protect and preserve to them. Sir, this thought invests the subject under debate with most singular and momentous interest. We, whom God has exalted to the very summit of prosperity—whose brief career forms the brightest page in history; the wonder and praise of the world; Freedom's hope and her consolation (are) about to turn traitors to our principles and our fame—about to become the oppressors of the feeble, and to cast away our birthright. . . . Sir, the question has ceased to be, What are our duties? An inquiry much more embarrassing is forced upon us: How shall we most plausibly, and with the least possible violence break our faith?

> —U.S. REPRESENTATIVE THEODORE FRELINGHUYSEN,
> *April 9, 1830. In one of the most widely reported speeches of the day, the New Jersey Whig uttered these words during an extended House debate on the Indian Removal Bill. The bill passed despite the passionate remarks from Frelinghuysen, whose speech gave voice within the Capitol to growing public concern that the United States was acting immorally in its relations with the Indians. His national reputation grew during the ensuing debates over Indian removal and, in 1844, Frelinghuysen was chosen as the Whig candidate for vice president.*

∽

More than a year ago we were officially given to understand by the secretary of war, that the president could not protect us against the laws of Georgia. . . . Finding that relief could not be obtained from the chief magistrate, and not doubting that our claim to protection was just, we made an application to Congress. . . . But, just at the close of the (congressional) session, an act was passed, by which a half million of dollars was appropriated toward effecting a removal of Indians. . . . Thus have we realized, with heavy hearts, that our supplication has not been heard; that the protection heretofore experienced is now to be with held; that the guaranty, in consequence of which our fathers laid aside their arms and ceded the best portions of their country, means nothing; and that we must either emigrate to an unknown region and leave the pleasant land to which we have the strongest attachment, or submit to the legislation of a state, which has already made our people outlaws. . . .

But in the midst of our sorrows, we do not forget our obligations to our friends and benefactors. It was with sensations of inexpressible joy that we have learned that the voice of thousands, in many parts of the United States, has been raised in our behalf, and numerous memorials offered in our favor, in both houses of congress. To those numerous friends, who have thus sympathized with us in our low estate, we tender our grateful acknowledgements. In pleading our cause, they have pleaded the cause of the poor and defenceless throughout the world . . .

The people of the United States will have the fairness to reflect, that all the treaties between them and the Cherokee were made, at the solicitation, and for the benefit, of the whites; that valuable considerations were given for every stipulation, on the part of the United States; that it is impossible to reinstate the parties in their former situation; that there are now hundreds of thousands of citizens of the United States residing upon lands ceded by the Cherokee in these very treaties; and that our people have trusted their country to the guaranty of the United States. If this guaranty fails them, in what can they trust, and where can they look for protection? We wish to remain on the land of our fathers. We have a perfect and original right to remain without interruption or molestation. The treaties with us, and laws of the United States made in pursuance of treaties, guaranty our residence and our privileges, and secure us against intruders. Our only request is, that these treaties may be fulfilled, and these laws executed. It is under a sense of the most pungent feelings that we make this, perhaps our last appeal to the good people of the United States. It cannot be that the community we are addressing, remarkable for its intelligence and religious sensibilities, and preeminent for its devotion to the rights of man, will lay aside this appeal.

—CHEROKEE GENERAL COUNCIL, *public appeal addressed to the people of the United States, July 17, 1830.*

⚬

Resolved, that we view the Indian Question, at present so much agitated in the United States, as being not merely of a political, but of a moral nature—inasmuch as it involves the maintenance or violation of the faith of our country—and as demanding, therefore, the most serious consideration of all American citizens, not only as patriots, but as Christians.

Resolved, that we regard the present crisis of affairs, relating to the Cherokee Nation, as calling for the sympathies, and prayers, and aid, of all benevolent people throughout the United States.

—SAMUEL WORCESTER, ISAAC PROCTOR, JOHN THOMPSON, AND OTHER MISSIONARIES, *statement that referred to the land on which the Cherokee lived as having been "given them" by "He who rules the destinies of nations," December 29, 1830. The intervention of white religious leaders on behalf of the Cherokee so agitated Georgia officials that they had Worcester, Proctor, and Thompson arrested.*

༄

The last point which we shall notice in the conduct of the administration . . . perhaps the most important of all, as far as concerns the principles involved, is that of our relations with the Indian tribes, and particularly that portion of the Cherokees situated within the territorial limits of Georgia. A series of solemn treaties concluded successively by all the administrations of the general government since the period of its establishment, guaranteed to these Indians the possession of their lands without interference or intrusion from any quarter, their right of governing themselves according to their own laws within those limits, and their character of sovereign states. An act of Congress passed in the year 1802, authorized and required the president to protect the Indians in the rights guaranteed to them by those treaties, if necessary, by the employment of military force.

In open violation to all these solemn engagements the state of Georgia has extended her jurisdiction, over the territory and persons of the Cherokee situated within her limits, interrupted them in the possession of their dwellings and plantations, and attempted to deprive them of the character of distinct communities; while the president, instead of protecting the Indians against these acts of wholly unauthorized violence, has openly countenanced the pretentions of Georgia, and instead of employing the armed force of the United States, in their defence, has actually withdrawn that force at the instance of the offending party, from the scene of action, and left the unoffending natives entirely at the mercy of their enemies.

The recent inhuman and unconstitutional outrages committed under the authority of Georgia upon the persons of several unoffending citizens heretofore residing as missionaries within the territory of the Cherokees, constitutes, perhaps, the most unjustifiable portion of these proceedings. They have received, like the rest, the countenance and approbation of the general executive. Few examples can be found, even in the history of barbarous communities, in which the sacred character of a minister of religion has furnished so slight a protection against disrespect and violence.

—NATIONAL REPUBLICAN PARTY, *"Address to the People of the United States," December 1831. The Republicans nominated the chief congressional critic of Indian removal, Henry Clay, as their challenger to President Andrew Jackson. Clay's vice presidential running mate was John Sergeant, who had served as a lawyer for the Cherokee Nation when the tribe sued in the U.S. Supreme Court to block Georgia's actions. Jackson was reelected, however, and the fate of the Cherokee appeared to be sealed.*

∽

The state of Georgia is about to perpetrate one of the most shameless and atrocious depredations that was ever committed in times of peace, upon any nation or people. Without awaiting the extinguishment of the Indian title, as pledged by the general government to that state, without regard to the most solemn treaties, guaranteeing forever to the Cherokee the occupancy of their lands, her governor has fixed upon the twenty-second instant, as the day, when she will commence drawing for our lands and gold mines by a lottery system. While we have submitted to one calamity, another and another, like the billows of an angry sea, has rolled upon us. Still our position has not been moved, nor not even by the appointment of that day when Georgian honor was to be run through a sporting wheel to enable her to seize our lands. We have looked forward to the crisis, when the President of the United States would be moved by public opinion to the execution of our treaties and would restore to us the rights affirmed to us by the Supreme Court. But the president continues to withhold his fostering care of these rights, and refuses to fulfill in good faith our treaties with him.

—THE PHOENIX, *editorial, December 1832.*

∽

And then, as to those who desire to remain on this side of the river, I ask again, are we powerless? Can we afford them no redress? Must we sit still, and see the injury they suffer, and extend no hand to relieve them? It were strange, indeed, were such the case. Why have we guaranteed to them the enjoyment of their own laws? Why have we pledged to them protection? Why have we assigned them limits of territory? Why have we declared that they shall enjoy their homes in peace, without molestation from any? If the United States government has contracted these serious obligations, it ought, before the Indians were reduced by our assurances to rely upon our engagement, to have explained to them its want of authority to make the contract. Before we pretend to Great Britain, to Europe, to the civilized world, that such were the rights we would secure to the Indians, we ought to have examined the extent and the grounds of our own rights to do so. But is such, indeed, our situation? No, sir. Georgia has shut her courts against these Indians. What is the remedy? To open ours. Have we not the fight? What says the Constitution? "The judicial power shall extend to all cases in law and arising under this Constitution, the laws of the United States, and treaties made, or which shall be made, under their authority."

—SENATOR HENRY CLAY, *speech to Congress where he called once more for congressional or judicial intervention to prevent the removal of the Cherokee, the Seminole, and other tribes from the eastern states, January 24, 1835. Clay declared that "the rights of the Indians have been trampled upon" and referred to the Indians facing removal as "the most oppressed of all" humans. His speech ignited a national furor over the removals that would continue for three years. The Cherokee, under the leadership of John Ross, repeatedly sought to reopen the congressional debate, finally delivering petitions signed by more than fifteen thousand Cherokee to Washington. After the election of 1836, in which a Democrat, Martin Van Buren, narrowly won, their political options were effectively exhausted.*

∽

I would sooner be honestly damned than hypocritically immortalized.

—U.S. REPRESENTATIVE DAVY CROCKETT, *of Tennessee, response to public criticism of his support in Congress for the rights of the Cherokee Nation, 1834. Crockett lost his seat in Congress at least in part because of his passionate advocacy on behalf of the Indians of the eastern U.S.*

∽

The newspapers now inform us that, in December, 1835, a treaty contracting for the exchange of all the Cherokee territory was pretended to be made by an agent on the part of the United States with some persons appearing on the part of the Cherokees; that the fact afterward transpired that these deputies did by no means represent the will of the nation; and that (the administration and the Congress) are contracting to put this active nation into carts and boats, and to drag them over mountains and rivers to a wilderness at a vast distance beyond the Mississippi. . . .

You, Sir, will bring down that renowned chair in which you sit into infamy if your seal is set to this instrument of perfidy; and the name of this nation, hitherto the sweet omen of religion and liberty, will stink to the world . . .

—RALPH WALDO EMERSON, *from a letter to President Martin Van Buren, April 23, 1838. Emerson was one of many leading intellectual, political, and religious leaders who sought to prevent the removals from going forward—and, later, from being completed. But Van Buren gave the order that April for the military to implement the removal program. After more than a decade of intense national debate regarding their fate, the Indians found themselves on the Trail of Tears.*

The Cherokees are nearly all prisoners. They had been dragged from their houses and encamped at the forts and military places, all over the nation. Multitudes were allowed no time to take anything with them except the clothes they had on. Females are driven on foot before the bayonets of brutal men. . . . It is the work of war in time of peace.

—EVAN JONES, *June 16, 1838, from "The Trail Where They Cried," published by the* Cherokee Observer *(April 8, 1998). Jones, a Baptist minister, traveled in the Cherokee country of the southeast U.S. on the eve of the tribe's forced removal.*

We are now about to take our kind farewell to our native land, the country that the Great Spirit gave our Fathers, we are on the eve of leaving that country that gave us birth . . . we bid farewell to it and all we hold dear.

—CHARLES HICK, *November 4, 1838, from accounts published in the* Cherokee Phoenix *newspaper. The* Phoenix *has been the newspaper on the Cherokee Nation for more than 175 years. Hick was a vice chief of the Cherokee Nation.*

The removal of the Cherokee Indians from their lifelong homes in the year 1838 found me a young man in the prime of life and a private soldier in the American army. Being acquainted with many of the Indians and able to fluently speak their language, I was sent as interpreter into the Smoky Mountain Country in May, 1838, and witnessed the execution of the most brutal order in the history of American warfare. I saw helpless Cherokees arrested and dragged from their homes, and driven at the bayonet point in the stockades. And, in the chill of a drizzling rain on an October morning, I saw them loaded like cattle or sheep in six hundred and forty-five wagons and started toward the west.

One can never forget the sadness and solemnity of that morning. Chief John Ross led in prayer and when the bugle sounded and the wagons started rolling many of the children rose to their feet and waved their little hands good-bye to their mountain homes, knowing they were leaving them forever.

—PRIVATE JOHN G. BURNETT, *recalling his service in*
Abraham McClellan's Company, 2nd Regiment, 2nd Brigade,
Mounted Infantry, Cherokee Indian Removal, 1838–1839.

✆

Americans like to pretend that they have no imperial past. Yet they have shown expansionist tendencies since colonial days. . . . Overland expansion, often at the expense of Mexicans and Indians, was a marked feature of American history right through the period of the Civil War, by which time the United States had reached its continental proportions.

—WARREN ZIMMERMANN, First Great Triumph:
How Five Americans Made Their Country a World Power
(New York: Farrar Straus and Giroux, 2002).

THREE

ROME THOUGHT AS YOU NOW THINK

Challenging the Annexation

of Texas and the Theft

of Mexican Lands

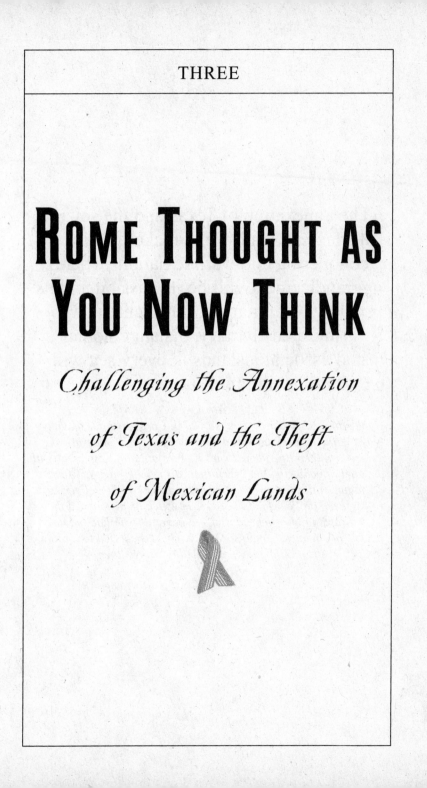

"[The annexation of Texas and the seizure of Mexican land would make the U.S. a] conquering and warlike nation [where] aggrandizement will be its passion and its policy. A military government, a large army, a costly navy, distant colonies and associate islands in every sea will follow in rapid succession . . .

—U.S. REP. JOHN QUINCY ADAMS,
the nation's sixth president, served in Congress after leaving the White House and was a militant foe of U.S. imperialism. He accused then President James K. Polk of launching a war with the goal of achieving the "perfidious dismemberment of Mexico." Adams collapsed on the floor of the House while delivering a speech on February 21, 1848, in which he denounced the awarding of commendations to generals who had led a "war of conquest" against Mexico. He was carried to a room just off the floor and died two days later.

The linkage between American expansionism
and the spread of slavery, which had long been understood by the
most astute campaigners against the sin of human bondage, became
increasingly evident in the 1830s and 1840s as the United States
engaged in bitter debates over the annexation of Texas and the seizure
by force of Mexican land from what is now New Mexico to
California. The antislavery campaigner Frederick Douglass would
make the connection explicitly when he observed, "The purchase of
Louisiana, the annexation of Texas, the war with the Seminoles, and
the war with Mexico, were all measures commenced and carried on
for the purpose of giving prosperity and perpetuity to slavery, and for
maintaining the sway of the slave power over the republic." And, his
view was not that of the radical abolitionists alone.

After his defeat for the presidency in 1828, John Quincy Adams
became the only president in American history to return to Congress.
There, he was referred to as "Old Man Eloquent." And his eloquence,
like that of his comrades, Abraham Lincoln and Daniel Webster, was
employed in the struggle to avert the spread of slavery. Antislavery
sentiment would lead Adams and his allies to become the most outspoken foes of the expansionist enterprises of President James K.
Polk—a man who might reasonably be described as the George W.
Bush of the 1840s. Polk was a Manifest Destiny man, a rabid expansionist whose passion was to extend America's reach to the Pacific.
That passion made Polk a popular man in the South, where slaveholders believed, with good reason, that expansion would add more
slave states to the Union—tipping the balance of power in favor of
the practice that underpinned their economic and political strength.
But Polk faced passionate opposition in the antislavery hotbeds of
New England, Ohio, and Illinois.

Historian James Rawley suggests that "the election of 1844 was virtually a referendum on westward expansion," with Polk arguing for annexation of Texas, then an independent "republic" that permitted slaveholding and a policy of belligerence toward Mexico, while his Whig opponent, Henry Clay, fresh from the congressional battles against the forced removal of the Cherokee Nation from the southeastern states, opposed annexation and challenged the expansionist view. A third candidate, the antislavery campaigner James Birney, took enough votes from Clay to elect Polk.

Before the first year of Polk's presidency was finished, Texas had been admitted to the Union as a slave state. By May of 1846, the United States had declared war on Mexico. A war fever was whipped up by the partisan press, yet Adams and the Whigs in Congress continued to express their opposition. Challenging the Polk administration's claims that the Mexicans had provoked the fight, Lincoln introduced his "spot resolutions," demanding to know the precise spot where injury had been done to Americans or their interests. Abolitionist Charles Sumner declared, "A war of conquest is bad; but the present war has darker shadows. It is a war for the extension of slavery over a territory which has already been purged by Mexican authority from this stain and curse." Newspaper editor Horace Greeley warned that the American experiment itself was endangered, asking, "Have the histories of the ruin of Greek and Roman liberty consequent on such extensions of empire by sword no lesson for us?" And, Henry David Thoreau, who went to jail rather than pay taxes to support the war, urged its opponents to "cast your whole vote, not a strip of paper merely, but your whole influence."

The opponents of the Mexican War did not succeed in preventing Polk's imperial dream from being realized. Nor did they slow the growth of what Douglass referred to as "the slave power." Between 1840 and 1860, the slave population of the United States grew from 2,487,355 to 3,953,760. The anti-imperialist Whigs would recognize the need for a new party that would defend the Republic against the excesses of the expansionists and the slavers. In the 1850s, they would organize under the Republican banner a party that would force a fight over America's original sins. Well into the twentieth century, the Republican Party would be home to the heirs of Adams and

Lincoln, many of whom summoned their memory as they campaigned against newer and in some senses darker imperialisms.

John Quincy Adams would not survive to see the Whigs give way to the Republicans. Adams, who had promised as a young man that America would never seek to become "the dictatress of the world" would die complaining that his country was surrendering its moral authority in order to become a "conquering and warlike nation (where) aggrandizement will be its passion and its policy. A military government, a large army, a costly navy, distant colonies and associate islands in every sea will follow in rapid succession. . . ."

I proceed now to a consideration of what is to me the strongest argument against annexing Texas to the United States. This measure will extend and perpetuate slavery. . . .

By this act, slavery will be perpetuated in the Old States as well as spread over new. It is well-known, that the soil of some of the old states has become exhausted by slave cultivation. . . . It is by slave-breeding and slave-selling that these states subsist. . . . By annexing Texas, we shall not only create [slavery] where it does not exist, but breathe new life into it, where its end seemed to be near. States, which might and ought to throw it off, will make the multiplication of slaves their great aim and chief resource.

—REVEREND WILLIAM ELLERY CHANNING, *letter to then-U.S. Senator Henry Clay, 1837. Channing's letter has been credited by some historians with having convinced Clay to use his influence to oppose efforts to annex Texas and launch a war with Mexico.*

ODE, INSCRIBED TO WILLIAM H. CHANNING

Though loth to grieve
The evil time's sole patriot,
I cannot leave
My buried thought
For the priest's cant,
Or statesman's rant.

If I refuse
My study for their politique,
Which at the best is trick,
The angry muse
Puts confusion in my brain.

But who is he that prates
Of the culture of mankind,
Of better arts and life?
Go, blind worm, go,
Behold the famous States
Harrying Mexico
With rifle and with knife.

Or who, with accent bolder,
Dare praise the freedom-loving mountaineer,
I found by thee, O rushing Contoocook!
And in thy valleys, Agiochook!
The jackals of the negro-holder.

The God who made New Hampshire
Taunted the lofty land
With little men.
Small bat and wren
House in the oak.
If earth fire cleave
The upheaved land, and bury the folk,
The southern crocodile would grieve.

Virtue palters, right is hence,
Freedom praised but hid;
Funeral eloquence
Rattles the coffin-lid.

What boots thy zeal,
O glowing friend,
That would indignant rend
The northland from the south?
Wherefore? To what good end?
Boston Bay and Bunker Hill
Would serve things still:
Things are of the snake.

The horseman serves the horse,
The neat-herd serves the neat,
The merchant serves the purse,
The eater serves his meat;
'Tis the day of the chattel,
Web to weave, and corn to grind,
Things are in the saddle,
And ride mankind.

There are two laws discrete
Not reconciled,
Law for man, and law for thing;
The last builds town and fleet,
But it runs wild,
And doth the man unking.

'Tis fit the forest fall,
The steep be graded,
The mountain tunnelled,
The land shaded,
The orchard planted,
The globe tilled,
The prairie planted,
The steamer built.

Live for friendship, live for love,
For truth's and harmony's behoof;
The state may follow how it can,
As Olympus follows Jove.
Yet do not I implore
The wrinkled shopman to my sounding woods,
Nor bid the unwilling senator
Ask votes of thrushes in the solitudes.
Every one to his chosen work.
Foolish hands may mix and mar,
Wise and sure the issues are.
Round they roll, till dark is light,
Sex to sex, and even to odd;
The over-God,
Who marries Right to Might,
Who peoples, unpeoples,
He who exterminates
Races by stronger races,
Black by white faces,
Knows to bring honey
Out of the lion,
Grafts gentlest scion
On Pirate and Turk.

The Cossack eats Poland,
Like stolen fruit;
Her last noble is ruined,
Her last poet mute;
Straight into double band
The victors divide,
Half for freedom strike and stand,
The astonished muse finds thousands at her side.

—RALPH WALDO EMERSON, *"Ode, Inscribed to William H. Channing,"* Early Poems of Ralph Waldo Emerson *(Thomas Y. Crowell & Co., New York, 1899). Emerson wrote this poem in 1846 as a denunciation of war with Mexico. The poet and essayist warned that America was eating into foreign territory much "as the man*

swallows arsenic, which brings him down in turn." (William Henry
Channing was a social reformer, a slavery foe, and the nephew of
William Ellery Channing.)

∞

TO FANEUIL HALL

MEN!—if manhood still ye claim,
 If the Northern pulse can thrill;
Roused by wrong or stung by shame,
 Freely, strongly still,
Let the sounds of traffic die:
 Shut the mill-gate, eave the stall,
 Throng to Faneuil Hall!

Wrongs which freemen never brooked,
 Dangers grim and fierce as they,
Which, like couching lions, looked
 On your fathers' way,
These your instant zeal demand,
 Shaking with their earthquake-call
Every rood of Pilgrim land,
 Ho, to Faneuil Hall!

From your capes and sandy bars,
 From your mountain-ridges cold,
Through whose pines the westering stars
 Stoop their crowns of gold,
Come, and with your footsteps wake
 Echoes from that holy wall;
Once again, for Freedom's sake,
 Rock your fathers' hall!

Up, and tread beneath your feet
 Every cord by party spun:
Let your hearts together beat

As the heart of one.
Banks and tariffs, stocks and trade,
  Let them rise or let them fall:
Freedom asks your common aid,
  Up, to Faneuil Hall!

Up, and let each voice that speaks
  Ring from thence to Southern plains,
Sharply as the blow which breaks
  Prison bolts and chains!
Speak as well becomes the free:
  Dreaded more than steel or ball,
Shall your calmest utterance be,
  Heard from Faneuil Hall!

Have they wronged us? Let us then
  Render back nor threats nor prayers;
Have they chained our free-born men?
  Let us unchain theirs!
Up, your banner leads the van,
  Blazoned, "Liberty for all!"
  Up, to Faneuil Hall!

> —JOHN GREENLEAF WHITTIER, *"To Faneuil Hall," published
> in* The Void of Freedom *(1846). Whittier was a bitter foe of the
> annexation of Texas as a slave state, and a critic of war with
> Mexico, which he viewed as a scheme to expand slavery. Boston's
> Faneuil Hall was the great gathering place for opponents of slavery,
> who focused their energy in the mid-1840s on seeking to prevent
> expansion of the United States to include territories that
> could become slave states.*

There must be some limit to the extent of our territory, if we would make our institutions permanent.

—U.S. SENATOR DANIEL WEBSTER, *arguing against war with Mexico, December 1845. A foe of the annexation of Texas since 1837, he resigned as President John Tyler's secretary of state in protest against Tyler's moves to annex the Republic. Like many New Englanders, Webster feared that expansion of the United States would open the way for the extension of slavery.*

ᴄᴏ

OUR COUNTRY, RIGHT OR WRONG!

This is the spirit in which a portion of the press, which admits that our treatment of Mexico has been ruffianly and piratical, and that the invasion of her territory by General Taylor is a flagrant outrage, now exhorts our people to rally in all their strength, to lavish their blood and treasure in the vindictive prosecution of War on Mexico. We protest against such a course. . . .

We can easily defeat the armies of Mexico, slaughter them by the thousands, and pursue them perhaps to their capital; we can conquer and "annex" their territory; but what then? Have the histories of the ruin of Greek and Roman liberty consequent on such extensions of empire by sword no lesson for us? Who believes that a score of victories over Mexico, the "annexation" of half her provinces, will give us more liberty, a purer morality, a more prosperous industry, than we now have? . . . Is not life miserable enough, comes not death soon enough, without resort to the hideous enginery of war?

People of the United States! Your rulers are precipitating you into a fathomless abyss of crime and calamity! Why sleep you thoughtless on its verge, as though this was not your business, or murder could be hid from the sight of God by a few flimsy rags called banners? Awake and arrest the work of butchery ere it shall be too late to preserve your souls from the guilt of wholesale slaughter!

—HORACE GREELEY, *editorial,* New York Tribune, *May 12, 1846.*

Even Christian ministers urge on the people to join in the slaughter.
. . . They adopt and advocate the current phrases—"Our country, may
she be right, but our country right or wrong. Go it blind, boys.
However unjustifiable the war, now it has begun we must fight it
through." . . . The president involves us in war—an unjust and unjustifiable war—yet we sustain him, right or wrong. Have not people a
right to judge? . . . Why, how much short does this come to the doctrine that the king can do no wrong? . . . The president says that our
country has been invaded. Now, if I understand the matter, that is just
a plain, plump lie.

> —OWEN LOVEJOY, *letter regarding the war with Mexico, June
> 23, 1846. This letter was written during his campaign for Congress
> from Illinois on the Liberty Party ticket. The brother of slain
> abolitionist newspaper editor Elijah Lovejoy, Owen Lovejoy
> campaigned against war with Mexico and the annexation of Texas.
> He was eventually elected to the U.S. House, serving during the
> administration of President Abraham Lincoln, who said,
> "Lovejoy was the best friend I had in Congress."*

∽

What is the territory, Mr. President, which you propose to wrest from
Mexico? It is consecrated to the heart of the Mexican by many a well-
fought battle with his old Castilian master. His Bunker Hills, and
Saratogas, and Yorktowns are there. The Mexican can say, "There I bled
for liberty! and shall I surrender that consecrated home of my affections
to the Anglo-Saxon invaders? What do they want with it? They have
Texas already. They have possessed themselves of the territory between
the Nueces and the Rio Grande. What else do they want? . . .

Sir, had one come and demanded Bunker Hill of the people of
Massachusetts, had England's lion ever showed himself there, is there
a man over thirteen and under ninety who would not have been ready
to meet him; is there a river on this continent that would not have run
red with blood; is there a field but would have been piled high with the
unburied bones of slaughtered Americans before these consecrated
battlefields of liberty should have been wrested from us? But this

same American goes into a sister republic and says to poor, weak Mexico, "Give up your territory; you are unworthy to possess it. I have got one-half already, all I ask of you is to give up the other!"

Why, says the chairman of this committee on foreign relations, it is the most reasonable thing in the world! We ought to have the Bay of San Francisco. Why? Because it is the best harbor on the Pacific! It has been my fortune, Mr. President, to have practised a good deal in criminal courts in the course of my life, but I never yet heard a thief arraigned for stealing a horse plead that it was the best horse that he could find in the country! We want California. What for? Why, says the senator from Michigan, we will have it; and the senator from South Carolina, with a very mistaken view, I think, of policy, says you can not keep our people from going there.

Let them go and seek their happiness in whatever country or clime it pleases them. All I ask of them is, not to require this government to protect them with that banner consecrated to war waged for principles—eternal, enduring truth. Sir, it is not meet that our old flag should throw its protecting folds over expeditions for lucre or for land. But you still say you want room for your people . . . Alexander, too, the mighty "Macedonian madman," when he wandered with his Greeks to the plains of India and fought a bloody battle on the very ground where recently England and the Sikhs engaged in strife for "room," was no doubt in quest of some California there. Many a Monterey had he to storm to get "room."

Sir, he made quite as much of that sort of history as you ever will. Mr. President, do you remember the last chapter in that history? It is soon read. Oh! I wish we could but understand its moral. Ammon's son (so was Alexander named), after all his victories, died drunk in Babylon! The vast empire he conquered to "get room" became the prey of the generals he had trained; it was disparted, torn to pieces, and so ended. Sir, there is a very significant appendix; it is this: The descendants of the Greeks—of Alexander's Greeks—are now governed by a descendant of Attila!

Sir, I have read in some account of your Battle of Monterey, of a lovely Mexican girl, who, with the benevolence of an angel in her bosom and the robust courage of a hero in her heart, was busily engaged during the bloody conflict, amid the crash of falling houses, the groans of the dying, and the wild shriek of battle, in carrying, water to slake the burning thirst of the wounded of either host. While bending over a wounded American soldier a cannon-ball struck her and blew her to atoms! Sir, I do not charge my brave, generous-hearted countrymen who fought that fight with this. No, no! We who send them— we who know that scenes like this, which might send tears of sorrow "down Pluto's iron cheek," are the invariable, inevitable attendants on war—we are accountable for this. And this—this is the way we are to be made known to Europe. This—this is to be the undying renown of free, republican America! "She has stormed a city—killed many of its inhabitants of both sexes—she has room!" . . .

Mr. President, this uneasy desire to augment our territory has depraved the moral sense and blunted the otherwise keen sagacity of our people. What has been the fate of all nations who have acted upon the idea that they must advance! Our young orators cherish this notion with a fervid but fatally mistaken zeal. They call it by the mysterious name of "destiny." "Our destiny," they say, "is onward," and hence they argue, with ready sophistry, the propriety of seizing upon any territory and any people that may lie in the way of our "fated" advance. Recently these progressives have grown classical; some assiduous student of antiquities has helped them to a patron saint. They have wandered back into the desolate Pantheon, and there, among the polytheistic relics of that "pale mother of dead empires," they have found a god whom these Romans, centuries gone by, baptized "Terminus."

Sir, I have heard much and read somewhat of this gentleman Terminus. Alexander, of whom I have spoken, was a devotee of this divinity. We have seen the end of him and his empire. It was said to be an attribute of this god that he must always advance and never recede. So both republican and imperial Rome believed. It was, as they said, their destiny. And for a while it did seem to be even so. Roman Terminus did advance. Under the eagles of Rome he was carried from his home on the Tiber to the farthest East on the one hand, and to the far West, among the then barbarious tribes of western Europe, on the other.

But at length the time came when retributive justice had become "a destiny." The despised Gaul calls out the condemned Goth, and Attila with his Huns answers back the battle-shout to both. The "blue-eyed nations of the North," in succession or united, pour forth their countless hosts of warriors upon Rome and Rome's always-advancing god Terminus. And now the battle-ax of the barbarian strikes down the conquering eagle of Rome. Terminus at last recedes, slowly at first, but finally he is driven to Rome, and from Rome to Byzantium. Whoever would know the further fate of this Roman deity, so recently taken under the patronage of American democracy, may find ample gratification of his curiosity in the luminous pages of Gibbon's *Decline and Fall.*

Such will find that Rome thought as you now think, that it was her destiny to conquer provinces and nations, and no doubt she sometimes said, as you say, "I will conquer a peace," and where now is she, the mistress of the world? The spider weaves his web in her palaces; the owl sings his watch-song in her towers. Teutonic power now lords it over the servile remnant, the miserable memento of old and once omnipotent Rome . . .

[Likewise,] the mighty Napoleon, who has resolved on universal dominion, he, too, is summoned to answer for the violation of that ancient law, "Thou shalt not covet anything which is thy neighbor's." How is the mighty fallen! He, beneath whose proud footstep Europe trembled, he is now an exile at Elba, and now finally a prisoner on the rock of St. Helena, and there, on a barren island, in an unfrequented sea, in the crater of an extinguished volcano, there is the death bed of the mighty conqueror. All his annexations have come to that! His last hour is now come, and he, the man of destiny, he who had rocked the world as with the throes of an earthquake, is now powerless, still—even as a beggar, so he died. On the wings of a tempest that raged with unwonted fury, up to the throne of the only power that controlled him while he lived, went the fiery soul of that wonderful warrior, another witness to the existence of that eternal decree that they who do not rule in righteousness, shall perish from the earth. He has found "room" at last.

And France,—she, too, has found "room." Her "eagles" now no longer scream along the banks of the Danube, the Po, and the Borysthenes. They have returned home, to their old eyrie, between the Alps, the Rhine, and the Pyrenees. So it shall be with yours. You may carry them to the loftiest peaks of the Cordilleras, they may wave with insolent triumph in the halls of the Montezumas, the armed men of Mexico may quail before them, but the weakest hand in Mexico, uplifted in prayer to the god of justice, may call down against you a power in the presence of which the iron hearts of your warriors shall be turned into ashes.

> —U.S. SENATOR THOMAS CORWIN, *of Ohio, leading*
> *Congressional opposition to the U.S. invasion of Mexico,*
> *February 11, 1847.*

∽

Slavery follows in the rear of our armies. Shall the war power of our government be exerted to produce such a result? Shall this government depart from its neutrality on this question, and lend its power and influence to plant slavery in these territories?

> —U.S. REP. DAVID WILMOT, *speech to the House opposing*
> *the war with Mexico and the spread of slavery, February 8, 1847.*

∽

Sir, we are in the midst of a war, not waged at home in defense of our soil, but waged a thousand miles off, and in the heart of the territories of another government. Of that war no one yet sees the end, and no one counts the cost. It is not denied that this war is now prosecuted for the acquisition of territory; at least, if any deny it, others admit it, and all know it to be true.

> —U.S. SENATOR DANIEL WEBSTER, *during a debate on the*
> *expanding war with Mexico, March 1847.*

∽

A war of conquest is bad; but the present war has darker shadows. It is a war for the extension of slavery over a territory which has already been purged by Mexican authority from this stain and curse. . . .

The slaveholders of the country—who are not supposed to exceed two hundred thousand or at most three hundred thousand in numbers—by the spirit of union which animates them, by the strong sense of a common interest, and by the audacity of their leaders, have erected themselves into a new "estate," as it were, under the Constitution. Disregarding the sentiments of many of the great framers of that instrument, who notoriously considered slavery as temporary, they proclaim it a permanent institution; and, with a strange inconsistency, at once press its title to a paramount influence in the general government, while they deny the right of that government to interfere, in any way, with its existence. According to them, it may never be restrained or abolished by the general government, though it may be indefinitely extended.

—CHARLES SUMNER, *from* Report on the War with Mexico, *(April 1847). A leading Whig foe of war with Mexico and the extension of slavery, Sumner was later elected to the U.S. Senate, where he emerged as the chamber's leading advocate for the end of slavery.*

∽

Whereas the President of the United States, in his message of . . . December 7, 1847, [declares] that "the Mexican Government refused even to hear the terms of adjustment which he [our minister of peace] was authorized to propose, and finally, under wholly unjustifiable pretexts, involved the two countries in war, by invading the territory of the State of Texas, striking the first blow, and shedding the blood of our citizens on our own soil."

And whereas this House is desirous to obtain a full knowledge of all the facts which go to establish whether the particular spot on which the blood of our citizens was so shed was or was not at that time our own soil: Therefore,

Resolved by the House of Representatives, that the President of the United States be respectfully requested to inform this House—

1. Whether the spot on which the blood of our citizens was shed, as in his messages declared, was or was not within the territory

of Spain, at least after the treaty of 1819, until the Mexican revolution.

2. Whether that spot is or is not within the territory which was wrested from Spain by the revolutionary Government of Mexico.

3. Whether that spot is or is not within a settlement of people, which settlement has existed ever since long before the Texas revolution, and until its inhabitants fled before the approach of the United States Army.

4. Whether that settlement is or is not isolated from any and all other settlements by the Gulf and the Rio Grande on the south and west, and by wide uninhabited regions on the north and east.

5. Whether the people of that settlement, or a majority of them, or any of them, have ever submitted themselves to the government or laws of Texas or the United States, by consent or compulsion, either by accepting office, or voting at elections, or paying tax, or serving on juries, or having process served upon them, or in any other way.

6. Whether the people of that settlement did or did not flee from the approach of the United States Army, leaving unprotected their homes and their growing crops, before the blood was shed, as in the messages stated; and whether the first blood, so shed, was or was not shed within the enclosure of one of the people who had thus fled from it.

7. Whether our citizens, whose blood was shed, as in his message declared, were or were not, at that time, armed officers and soldiers, sent into that settlement by the military order of the president, through the secretary of war.

8. Whether the military force of the United States was or was not sent into that settlement after General (Zachary) Taylor had more than once intimated to the War Department that, in his opinion, no such movement was necessary to the defence or protection of Texas.

—ABRAHAM LINCOLN, *"Spot Resolutions," December 22, 1847. This resolution was introduced in the U.S. House to challenge President James K. Polk's assertion that the U.S. invasion of Mexico was not a war of conquest but a legitimate response to provocation*

*by Mexico. Polk had just asked for ten more regiments and new
volunteers, arguing that the larger force was needed to secure
Mexico's surrender on terms generous to the United States.*

∽

As to the mode of terminating the war, and securing peace, the president is equally wandering and indefinite. First, it is to be done by a more vigorous prosecution of the war in the vital parts of the enemy's country; and, after apparently, talking himself tired, on this point, the president drops down into a half-despairing tone, and tells us that "with a people distracted and divided by contending factions, and a government subject to constant changes, by successive revolutions, the continued success of our arms may fail to secure a satisfactory peace." Then he suggests the propriety of wheedling the Mexican people to desert the counsels of their own leaders, and trusting in our protection, set up a government from which we can secure a satisfactory peace; telling us, that, "this may become the only mode of obtaining such a peace." But soon he falls into doubt of this too and then drops back onto the already half-abandoned ground, of more vigorous prosecution. All this shows that the president is, in no wise, satisfied with his own positions. First he takes up one, and in attempting to argue us into it, he argues himself out of it then seizes another, and goes through the same process; and then, confused at being able to think of nothing new, he snatches up the old one again, which he has some time before cast off. His mind, tasked beyond its power, is running hither and thither, like some tortured creature on a burning surface, finding no position on which it can settle down and be at ease. Again, it is a singular omission in this message, that it, no where intimates when the president expects the war to terminate. At its beginning, General (Winfield) Scott was, by this same president, driven into disfavor, if not disgrace, for intimating that peace could not be conquered in less than three or four months. But now, at the end of about twenty months, during which time our arms have given us the most splendid successes—every department, and every part, land and water, officers and privates, regulars and volunteers, doing all that men could do, and hundreds of things which it had ever before been thought men could not do. After all this, this same president gives us a long message, without showing us, that, as to the end, he himself, has, even an imaginary conception. As I have before said, he knows not where he is. He is a bewildered, confounded, and miserably perplexed man. God grant he may be able to show, there is not something about his conscience, more painful than all his mental perplexity.

—U.S. REPRESENTATIVE ABRAHAM LINCOLN, *speech to the House in response to President Polk's charge that Mexico had started the hostilities, January 12, 1848. Lincoln, a Whig, would not allow the Democratic president to suggest that the war was necessary, or legitimate.*

❧

[We] are summoned to fresh warlike operations; to create a new army of thirty thousand men for the further prosecution of the war; to carry the war, in the language of the president, still more dreadfully into the vital parts of the enemy, and to press home, by fire and sword, the claims we make and the grounds which we insist upon, again our fallen, prostrate, I had almost said, our ignoble enemy.

—U.S. SENATOR DANIEL WEBSTER, *speech to Congress, March 23, 1848. Webster objected to the absurdity of the Senate's vote to authorize sending more troops and spending more money on a war that had supposedly ended with a peace treaty that the Senate ratified on March 10. Webster asked, "What is the object of bringing these new regiments into the field? . . . There is no army to fight . . . Mexico is prostrate. . . . Are we going to cut the throats of her people? Are we to thrust the sword deeper and deeper into the 'vital parts' of Mexico?"*

❧

I am against all accession of territory to form new states . . . according to my conscientious conviction, we are now fixing on the

Constitution of the United States, and its frame of government, a monstrosity, a disfiguration, an enormity!

—U.S. SENATOR DANIEL WEBSTER, *objecting to suggestions that regions seized from Mexico could quickly become states, March 23, 1848.*

∽

I would like to hold up to you a picture; not drawn by an American pen or pencil, but by a foreigner. I want to show you how you look abroad in the delectable business of kidnapping and slave-driving.

Sometimes since—I think it was in the December number of *Punch,*—I saw an excellent pictorial description of America. What think you it was? It was entitled, "Brother Jonathan." It was a long, lean, gaunt, shrivelled looking creature, stretched out on two chairs, and his legs resting on the prostrate bust of Washington; projecting from behind was a cat-o'-nine-tails knotted at the ends; around his person he wore a belt in which were stuck those truly American implements—a bowie knife, dirk, and revolving pistol; behind him was a whipping post, with a naked woman tied to it, and a strong-armed American citizen in the act of scourging her livid flesh with a cowskin. [At his feet was another group;—a sale going on of human cattle—and around the auctioneer's table were gathered the respectability,—the religion represented in the person of the clergy,—of America, buying them for export to the goodly city of New Orleans.] Little further on there was a scene of branding—a small group of slaves tied hand and foot, while their patriotic and philanthropic masters were burning their name into their quivering flesh. Further on, there was a drove of slaves, bound for New Orleans. Above these and several other scenes illustrative of the character of our institutions, waved the star-spangled banner. Still further back in the distance was the picture of the achievements of our gallant army in Mexico, shooting, stabbing, hanging, destroying property, and massacring the innocent with the innocent, not with the guilty, and over all this was a picture of the Devil himself, looking down with Satanic satisfaction on passing events.

Here I conceive to be a true picture of America, and I hesitate not to say that this description falls far short of the real facts, and of the aspect we bear to the world around us.

—FREDERICK DOUGLASS, *speech to the American Anti-Slavery Society, May 9, 1848.*

∽

FREE DEMOCRAT PARTY PLATFORM RESOLUTIONS:

SIXTEENTH. That every nation has a clear right to alter or change its own government, and to administer its own concerns in such manner as may best secure the rights and promote the happiness of the people; and foreign interference with that right is a dangerous violation of the law of nations, against which all independent governments should protest, and endeavor by all proper means to prevent; and especially A is it the duty of the American government, representing the chief republic of the world, to protest against, and by all proper means to prevent, the intervention of kings and emperors against nations seeking to establish for themselves republican or constitutional governments.

SEVENTEENTH. That the independence of Haiti ought to be recognized by our government, and our commercial relations with it placed on the footing of the most favored nations.

—FREE DEMOCRAT PARTY, *from the 1852 platform on which John P. Hale, a veteran leader of the antislavery contingent in Congress sought the presidency. Hale won more than one hundred fifty thousand votes and later helped form the Republican Party.*

∽

The purchase of Louisiana, the annexation of Texas, the war with the Seminoles, and the war with Mexico, were all measures commenced and carried on for the purpose of giving prosperity and perpetuity to slavery, and for maintaining the sway of the slave power over the republic. Any man who doubts this has only to read Jay's "View of the Action of the Federal Government," and his "Review of the Mexican War," to have his doubts entirely removed.

—FREDERICK DOUGLASS, *October 14, 1852, speaking to a convention of the antislavery Free Democrat Party. The Jay referred to here is abolitionist William Jay, who argued that the Mexican-American War was immoral because it was launched against "a people . . . who were utterly incapable of acting on the offensive against us."*

∽

You remember I was an old Whig, and whenever the Democratic Party tried to get me to vote that the war had been righteously begun by the president, I would not do it.

—ABRAHAM LINCOLN, *recalling his opposition in the Lincoln-Douglas debate at Ottawa, Illinois, August 21, 1858. Lincoln always defended his stance in opposition to what he saw as a war of conquest.*

FOUR

NOW, LET US ANNEX THE ISLANDS

Queen Liliʻuokalani, Mr. Dole,

and the Taking of Hawaii

> "We must annex those people.
> We can afflict them with our wise and
> beneficent government.
> —MARK TWAIN

John Quincy Adams's warning that an America bent on conquest would soon seek to acquire "distant colonies and associate islands in every sea" was prescient. Within a decade of his death in 1848, southern slave owners would be agitating in Congress for the acquisition of Caribbean islands, including Cuba, where they hoped to establish a slave-based economy. Little came of those initiatives, but in short order the imperial reach of the United States would stretch halfway across the Pacific.

Before the Civil War, U.S. business interests began investing in what were then referred to as the Sandwich Islands. By the late 1880s, they were in control not merely of the lucrative sugar industry but much of the rest of the economic and political life of what native islanders referred to as Hawaii. And they wanted, desperately, to have "their" islands annexed by the United States. So feverish was their desire that a visiting author, Mark Twain, parodied it in his essay, "The Sandwich Islands," that satirically announced, "We must annex those people. We can afflict them with our wise and beneficent government. We can introduce the novelty of thieves, all the way up from street-car pickpockets to municipal robbers and government defaulters, and show them how amusing it is to arrest them and try them and then turn them loose—some for cash and some for 'political influence.'"

Unfortunately for the merchants, the native islanders had different ideas. They wanted to maintain their independence and they wanted to be governed not by distant colonial overlords, or the local chamber of commerce, but by the Hawaiian royal family.

In the late 1880s, Sanford Dole, a cousin of the founder of the Dole Pineapple Company, and other businessmen succeeded in asserting their will over a weak monarch. But when a new member of the royal family, Queen Lili'uokalani, came to power in 1891, she challenged their power grab. Lili'uokalani advocated the principle of "Hawaii for Hawaiians" and sought a more equitable distribution of the wealth that was being taken from the islands. Dole and his tiny band of business buccaneers were not amused. They first formed the Annexation Club to demand U.S. intervention. When it was not forthcoming, they organized a "Committee of Safety"—using the classic imperialist dodge of suggesting that a resource-rich independent land was not safe for business exploitation. In 1893, the Committee of Safety proved that the danger came not from the Hawaiians but from the business community. They launched a "revolution" and, with the support of U.S. Marines called in by a U.S. minister who was friendly to their enterprise, forced Lili'uokalani to abdicate.

Dole immediately petitioned for annexation. Unfortunately for the merchants, Lili'uokalani knew a thing or two about lobbying. She demanded that the new American president, Grover Cleveland, investigate the injustice. Cleveland did and determined that the local U.S. minister had called in the U.S. Marines without requesting permission from anyone but the man in the mirror. "Thus it appears that Hawaii was taken possession of by the United States forces without the consent or wish of the government of the islands, or of anybody else so far as shown, except the United States minister," declared Cleveland, who promptly ordered the U.S. flag removed from above the government building in Honolulu and withdrew the troops who were protecting Dole from the real Hawaiians. That should have been the end of it, but Dole and his minions hired mercenaries and declared themselves rulers of the short-lived Republic of Hawaii.

They then waited until the administration changed in Washington. With the election of a business-friendly Republican president, William McKinley, the dirty deal was resubmitted for congressional consideration. After anti-imperialists, such as South Dakota's R. F. Pettigrew, blocked the annexation in the Senate, the land grab was finally approved by a joint resolution of the Congress and Hawaii became a U.S. colony, er, territory.

At the close of the twentieth century, however, Hawaiian representatives in Congress won a rare admission of imperial overreach. In 1993, both houses of Congress approved and President William Jefferson Clinton signed a resolution that apologized "to Native

Hawaiians on behalf of the people of the United States for the overthrow of the Kingdom of Hawaii on January 17, 1893 . . . and the
deprivation of the rights of Native Hawaiians to self-determination."

The Annexation of Hawaii marks a turning point in the history of the
United States. For the first time, the American people secured possession of territory lying outside of the mainland of North America.
For the first time the United States acquired territory lying within the
tropics. The annexation of Hawaii was the first imperialistic act after
the annexation of Texas, more than fifty years before. It was the first
imperialistic act since the capitalists of the North had succeeded the
slave-owners of the South as the masters of American public life.

—SCOTT NEARING, The American Empire, 1921.

Now, let us annex the islands. Think how we could build up that
whaling trade! (Though under our courts and judges it might soon be
as impossible for whaleships to rendezvous there without being fleeced
and "pulled" by sailors and pettifoggers as it now is in San Francisco—
a place the skippers shun as they would rocks and shoals.) Let us
annex. We could make sugar enough there to supply all America,
perhaps, and the prices would be very easy with the duties removed.
And then we would have such a fine halfway house for our Pacific-
plying ships; and such a convenient supply depot and such a commanding sentry box for an armed squadron; and we could raise cotton
and coffee there and make it pay pretty well, with the duties off and
capital easier to get at. And then we would own the mightiest volcano
on earth—Kilauea! Barnum could run it—he understands fires now.
Let us annex, by all means. We could pacify Prince Bill and other
nobles easily enough—put them on a reservation. Nothing pleases a
savage like a reservation—a reservation where he has his annual hoes,
and Bibles and blankets to trade for powder and whisky—a sweet

Arcadian retreat fenced in with soldiers. By annexing, we would get all those fifty thousand natives cheap as dirt, with their morals and other diseases thrown in. No expense for education; they are already educated. No need to convert them; they are already converted. No expense to clothe them, for obvious reasons.

We must annex those people. We can afflict them with our wise and beneficent government. We can introduce the novelty of thieves, all the way up from streetcar pickpockets to municipal robbers and government defaulters, and show them how amusing it is to arrest them and try them and then turn them loose—some for cash and some for "political influence." We can make them ashamed of their simple and primitive justice. We can do away with their occasional hangings for murder, and let them have Judge Pratt to teach them how to save imperiled Avery-assassins to society. We can give them some Barnards to keep their money corporations out of difficulties. We can give them juries composed entirely of the most simple and charming leatherheads. We can give them railway corporations who will buy their legislatures like old clothes, and run over their best citizens and complain of the corpses for smearing their unpleasant juices on the track. In place of harmless and vaporing Harris, we can give them Tweed. We can let them have Connolly; we can loan them Sweeny; we can furnish them some Jay Goulds who will do away with their old-time notion that stealing is not respectable. We can confer Woodbull and Claflin on them. And George Francis Train. We can give them lecturers! I will go myself.

We can make that little bunch of sleepy islands the hottest corner on earth, and array it in the moral splendor of our high and holy civilization. Annexation is what the poor islanders need. "Shall we to men benighted, the lamp of life deny?"

—MARK TWAIN, *from "The Sandwich Islands: Concluding Views
of Mark Twain," published in the* New York Tribune*, January 9,
1873. Twain had spent several months on the Sandwich (Hawaiian)
Islands as a reporter for the* Sacramento Union *newspaper. Twain
frequently wrote columns and delivered speeches satirizing
proposals to annex the islands.*

I, Lili'uokalani, by the grace of God and under the Constitution of the Hawaiian Kingdom, Queen, do hereby solemnly protest against any and all acts done against myself and the constitutional government of the Hawaiian Kingdom by certain persons claiming to have established a provisional government of and for this kingdom. That I yield to the superior force of the United States of America, whose minister plenipotentiary, His Excellency John L. Stevens, has caused United States troops to be landed at Honolulu and declared that he would support the said provisional government.

Now, to avoid any collision of armed forces, and perhaps the loss of life, I do, under this protest and impelled by said forces, yield my authority until such time as the government of the United States shall, upon the facts being presented to it, undo the action of its representative and reinstate me in the authority which I claim as the constitutional sovereign of the Hawaiian Islands.

—QUEEN LILI'UOKALANI, *letter to Sanford Dole and others composing the provisional government of the Hawaiian Islands, January 17, 1893.*

∽

To the Senate and House of Representatives:

It appears that Hawaii was taken possession of by the United States forces without the consent or wish of the government of the islands, or of anybody else so far as shown, except the United States minister.

Therefore the military occupation of Honolulu by the United States on the day mentioned was wholly without justification, either as an occupation by consent or as an occupation necessitated by dangers threatening American life and property . . .

—PRESIDENT GROVER CLEVELAND, *December 18, 1893. Cleveland, a Democrat, brought a halt to moves to annex Hawaii and ordered a congressional examination of the role the U.S. military played in the takeover of Hawaii by American and European businessmen. Cleveland's actions slowed the rush to annex Hawaii, but the congressional inquiry was thwarted by Republican advocates for expansion.*

To His Excellency Albert J. Willis,
U.S. Envoy Extraordinary Minister Plenipotentiary:

Sir, Having in mind the amicable relations hitherto existing between the government which you here represent and the government of Hawai'i, as evidenced by many years of friendly intercourse, and being desirous of bringing to the attention of your government the facts here following, I, Lili'uokalani, by the grace of God, and under the Constitution of the Hawaiian Kingdom, Queen, do hereby solemnly protest that I am now and have continuously been, since the twentieth day of January A.D. 1891, the constitutional sovereign of the Hawaiian Kingdom; that on the seventeenth day of January A.D. 1893—in the words of the president of the United States himself— "By an act of war, committed with the participation of a diplomatic representative of the United States, and without authority of Congress, the government of a feeble but friendly and confiding people has been overthrown. A substantial wrong has thus been done which a due regard for our national character as well as the rights of the injured peoples requires we should endeavor to repair;" that on said date I and my government prepared a written protest against any and all acts done against myself and the constitutional government of the Hawaiian Kingdom by certain persons claiming to have established a provisional government of and for this kingdom, that said protest was forwarded to the president of the United States, also to Sanford B. Dole, vice chairman of the executive council of the said provisional government, and was by the latter duly acknowledged; that in response to said protest, the president of the United States sent a special commissioner in the person of Honorable James H. Blount to Honolulu to make an accurate, full, and impartial investigation of the facts attending the subversion of the constitutional government of Hawai'i and the installment in its place of the provisional government; that said commissioner arrived in Honolulu on the twenty-ninth day of March, A.D. 1893 and fulfilled his duties with untiring diligence and with care, tact, and fairness; that said commissioner found that the government of Hawai'i surrendered its authority under a threat of war, until such time only as the government of the United States, upon the facts being presented to it should reinstate the constitutional sovereign, and the provisional government was created to exist until terms of union with the United States of America have been negotiated and agreed upon, also that but for the lawless occupation of Honolulu under false pretexts by the United States forces and but for the United States minister's recognition of the provisional government when the United States forces were its sole support, and constituted its only military strength, I, and my government would never have yielded to the provisional government, even for a time, and for the sole purpose of submitting my case to the enlightened justice of the United States, or for any purpose; also that the great wrong done to this feeble but independent state by an abuse of the authority of the United States should be undone by restoring the legitimate government.

That since the happening of said events, the executive and the Congress of the United States have formally declined the overtures of the said provisional government for the annexation of the Hawaiian Islands to the United States. That notwithstanding said facts, said provisional government has continued to exercise the functions of government in this kingdom to the present date, and that its course, from the time of its inception to the present, has been marked by a succession of arbitrary, illiberal, and despotic acts, and by the enactment and enforcement of pretended "laws" subversive of the first principles of free government and utterly at variance with the traditions, history, habits, and wishes of the Hawaiian people.

That said provisional government has now recently convened and is now holding what it is pleased to term a constitutional convention, composed of nineteen (19) self-appointed members being the president and executive and advisory councils of said provisional government, and eighteen (18) delegates elected by less than 10 percent (10%) of the legal voters of the kingdom, consisting almost entirely of aliens, and chiefly of such aliens as have no permanent home or interest in Hawai'i, and which said convention is now considering a draft of a constitution . . . submitted for its approval by the executive council of said provisional government consisting of the president and ministers thereof.

That it is the expressed purpose of the said provisional government to promulgate such constitution as shall be approved by said convention without submitting it to a vote of the people, or of any of the people, and to thereupon proclaim a government under such constitution, and under the name of the Republic of Hawai'i.

That the said provisional government has not assumed a republican or other constitutional form, but has remained a mere executive council or oligarchy, set up without the consent of the people; that it has not sought to find a permanent basis of popular support, and has given no evidence of an intention to do so; that its representatives assert that the people of Hawai'i are unfit for popular government and frankly avow that they can be best ruled by arbitrary or despotic power, and that the proposed constitution so submitted by said executive council of the provisional government for the approval of said convention does not provide for or contemplate a free, popular, or republican form of government but does contemplate and provide for a form of government of arbitrary and oligarchical powers, concentrated in the hands of a few individuals irresponsible to the people, or to the representatives of the people, and which is opposed to all modern ideas of free government.

Wherefore, I, the constitutional sovereign of the Hawaiian Kingdom on behalf of myself and the people of my said kingdom do hereby again most solemnly protest against the acts aforesaid and against any and all other acts done against myself, my people, and the constitutional government of the Hawaiian Kingdom, and I do hereby most earnestly request that the government represented by you will not extend its recognition to any pretended government of the Hawaiian Islands under whatever name it may apply for such recognition, other than the constitutional government so deposed as aforesaid, except such government shall show its title to exist by the will of the people of Hawai'i, expressed at an election wherein the whole people shall have had an opportunity, unembarrassed by force, and undeterred by fear or fraud to register their preferences as to the form of government under which they will live.

With assurances of my esteem, I am, Sir,

—LILI'UOKALANI OF HAWAII, *letter formally protesting her removal as Queen, June 20, 1894. With strong support from the Hawaiian people, Lili'uokalani would press her protests until the Congress approved annexation of Hawaii in 1898. Encouraged by*

the supportive words of President Grover Cleveland, she argued her
cause aggressively, but was repeatedly undermined by business
interests in Hawaii and the U.S., and by their allies in Congress.

∾

I, Lili'uokalani of Hawaii, by the will of God named heir apparent on
the tenth day of April, A.D. 1877, and by the grace of God, Queen of
the Hawaiian Islands on the seventeenth day of January, A.D. 1893,
do hereby protest against the ratification of a certain treaty, which, so
I am informed, has been signed at Washington by Messieurs Hatch,
Thurston, and Kinney, purporting to cede those Islands to the territory and dominion of the United States. I declare such a treaty to be
an act of wrong toward the native and part-native people of Hawaii,
an invasion of the rights of the ruling chiefs, in violation of international rights both toward my people and toward friendly nations with
whom they have made treaties, the perpetuation of the fraud whereby
the constitutional government was overthrown, and, finally, an act of
gross injustice to me.

Because the official protests made by me on the seventeenth day
of January, 1893, to the so-called provisional government was signed
by me, and received by said government with the assurance that the
case was referred to the United States of America for arbitration.

Because that protest and my communications to the United States
government immediately thereafter expressly declare that I yielded
my authority to the forces of the United States in order to avoid
bloodshed, and because I recognized the futility of a conflict with so
formidable a power.

Because the president of the United States, the secretary of state,
and an envoy commissioned by them reported in official documents
that my government was unlawfully coerced by the forces, diplomatic
and naval, of the United States; that I was at the date of their investigations the constitutional ruler of my people.

Because neither the above-named commission nor the government
which sends it has ever received any such authority from the regis-
tered voters of Hawaii, but derives its assumed powers from the

so-called committee of public safety, organized on or about the seventeenth day of January, 1893, said committee being composed largely of persons claiming American citizenship, and not one single Hawaiian was a member thereof, or in any way participated in the demonstration leading to its existence.

Because my people, about forty thousand in number, have in no way been consulted by those, three thousand in number, who claim the right to destroy the independence of Hawaii. My people constitute four-fifths of the legally qualified voters of Hawaii, and excluding those imported for the demands of labor, about the same proportion of the inhabitants.

Because said treaty ignores, not only the civic rights of my people, but, further, the hereditary property of their chiefs. Of the four million acres composing the territory said treaty offers to annex, one million or nine hundred fifteen thousand acres has in no way been heretofore recognized as other than the private property of the constitutional monarch, subject to a control in no way differing from other items of a private estate.

Because it is proposed by said treaty to confiscate said property, technically called the crown lands, those legally entitled thereto, either now or in succession, receiving no consideration whatever for estates, their title to which has been always undisputed, and which is legitimately in my name at this date.

Because said treaty ignores, not only all professions of perpetual amity and good faith made by the United States in former treaties with the sovereigns representing the Hawaiian people, but all treaties made by those sovereigns with other and friendly powers, and it is thereby in violation of international law.

Because, by treating with the parties claiming at this time the right to cede said territory of Hawaii, the government of the United States receives such territory from the hands of those whom its own magistrates (legally elected by the people of the United States, and in office in 1893) pronounced fraudulently in power and unconstitutionally ruling Hawaii.

Therefore, I, Lili'uokalani of Hawaii, do hereby call upon the president of that nation, to whom alone I yielded my property and my authority, to withdraw said treaty (ceding said Islands) from further consideration. I ask the honorable Senate of the United States to decline to ratify said treaty, and I implore the people of this great and good nation, from whom my ancestors learned the Christian religion, to sustain their representatives in such acts of justice and equity as may be in accord with the principles of their fathers, and to the Almighty Ruler of the universe, to him who judgeth righteously, I commit my cause.

Done at Washington, District of Columbia, United States of America, this seventeenth day of June, in the year eighteen hundred and ninety-seven.

—LILI'UOKALANI OF HAWAII, June 17, 1897. This official protest to the treaty of annexation was lodged shortly after William McKinley became president, replacing Grover Cleveland. Mr. McKinley did not share Cleveland's distaste for imperialism. The new president was known to be sympathetic to the annexation initiative, which was pushed by white business leaders on the islands and their U.S. partners. McKinley's tenure has been referenced by George W. Bush's chief political advisor, Karl Rove, as a model for the Bush presidency.

༄

[In] Hawai'i—the best beloved, the most richly endowed of all Mother Nature's beautiful family, the old, old struggle for Anglo-Saxon supremacy is going on.

The centuries-old tragedy is being repeated upon a stage small comparatively, but with a perfection of gorgeous setting and characters whose classical simplicity gives strength to the impersonation. The only new phase in the old drama is that this time a republic is masquerading in the despot's role. The United States, founded upon the belief that a just government can exist only by the consent of the governed, is calmly making up for the bloody fifth act—preparing to take a nation's life with all the complacent assurance of an old time stage villain.

For Hawaii has not asked for annexation. There are one hundred thousand people on the islands. Of these, not 3 percent have declared for annexation. To the natives the loss of nationality is hateful, aberrant. It is the old battle—the white man against the brown; might against right; strength against weakness; power and intellect and art against docility, inertia, and simplicity.

And the result?

"I tell the natives that work for me," said a man suffering from an acute attack of annexation mania to me, "you might as well walk out into the sea and attempt to push out the incoming waves with your two uplifted hands as to try to prevent what's coming."

"It's purely a question of conquest, I admit," he went on. "We are stronger and we'll win. It's a survival of the fittest."

The strongest memory I have of the islands is connected with the hall of the Salvation Army at Hilo, on the island of Hawai'i. It's a crude little place, which holds about three hundred people, I should think. The rough, uncovered rafters show above, and the bare walls are relieved only by Scripture admonitions in English and Hawaiian. . . .

As I entered, the bell on the foreign church, up on one of the beautiful Hilo hills, was striking ten. The place was packed with natives, and outside stood a patient crowd unable to enter. It was a women's meeting, but there were many men present. . . .

The women who presided had said a few words to the people, when all at once I saw a thousand curious eyes turned upon me.

"What is it?" I asked the interpreter. "What did she say?"

He laughed. "A reporter is here," she says. She says to the people, "Tell how you feel. Then the Americans will know. Then they may listen."

A remarkable scene followed. One by one, men and women rose and in a sentence or two in the rolling, broad-voweled Hawaiian made a fervent profession of faith.

"My feeling," declared a tall, broad-shouldered man, whose dark eyes were alight with enthusiasm. "This is my feeling: I love my country and I want to be independent—now and forever."

"And my feeling is the same," cried a stout, bold-faced woman, rising in the middle of the hall. "I love this land. I don't want to be annexed."

"This birthplace of mine I love as the American loves his. Would he wished to be annexed to another, greater land?"

"I am strongly opposed to annexation. How dare the people of the United States rob a people of their independence?"

"I want the American government to do justice. America helped to dethrone Lili'uokalani. She must be restored. Never shall we consent to annexation!"

"My father is American; my mother is pure Hawaiian. It is my mother's land I love. The American nation has been unjust. How could we ever love America?"

"Let them see their injustice and restore the monarchy!" cried an old, old woman, whose dark face framed in its white hair was working pathetically.

"If the great nations would be fair they would not take away our country. Never will I consent to annexation!"

"Tell America I don't want annexation. I want my queen," said the gentle voice of a woman.

"That speaker is such a good woman," murmured the interpreter. "A good Christian, honest, kind, and charitable."

"I am against annexation—myself and all my family."

"I speak for those behind me," shouted a voice from far in the rear. "They cannot come in—they cannot speak. They tell me to say, No annexation. Never."

"I am Kauhi of Kalaoa. We call it middle Hilo. Our club has three hundred members. They have sent me here. We are all opposed to annexation. All! All!"

He was a young man. His open coat showed his loose dark shirt; his muscular body swayed with excitement. He wore boots that came above his knees. There was a large white handkerchief knotted about his throat, and his fine head, with its intelligent eyes, rose from his shoulders with a grace that would have been deerlike were it not for its splendid strength.

"I love my country and oppose annexation," said a heavy-set, gray-haired man with a good, clear profile. "We look to America as our friend. Let her not be our enemy!"

"Hekipi, a delegate to Moloka'i to the league, writes: 'I honestly assert that the great majority of Hawaiians on Moloka'i are opposed to annexation. They fear that if they become annexed to the United States they will lose their lands. The foreigners will reap all the benefit and the Hawaiians will be put in a worst position than they are today.'"

"I am a mail carrier. Come with me to my district." A man who was sitting in the first row rose and stretched out an appealing hand.

"Come to my district. I will show you two thousand Hawaiians against annexation."

"I stand—we all stand—to testify to our love of our country. No flag but the Hawaiian flag. Never the American!"

There was cheering at this, and the heavy, sober, brown faces were all aglow with excited interest.

—MIRIAM MICHELSON, *from an article, "Many Thousands of Native Hawaiians Sign a Protest to the United States Government Against Annexation," San Francisco Call, September 30, 1897.*

∽

Imperialism is a state of mind, not alone a series of acts. It assumes that there are two grades of human beings: those who are entitled to rule and those who must submit to be ruled, and that the latter may be utilized for the benefit and profit of the former. It assumes various forms, and sometimes covers itself with a cloak of religious cant, but at the bottom it is always the same greed of gain. True anti-imperialism denies the right of any set of men or any people to assume authority over any other people. It denies the right to decide for that people what shall be its political status in the world until it has reached its political majority, through the only means a people can reach it—self-government and responsibility. It denies the right of this nation to annex Hawaii, for instance, until the people of Hawaii, by means of self-government, are fitted to become citizens of the United States; and not then, unless both the people of Hawaii and the people of the United States desire the union. It denies that the question of Hawaii or Puerto Rico has been settled in the court of morals, unless we admit that it is no part of the law to restore stolen goods to their owner.

—THOMAS MOTT OSBORNE, *from an address to the convention of the National Party in New York City, September 5, 1900. A noted reformer and political figure, Osborne was one of the few prominent figures to continue to raise the Hawaii question after the annexation was completed.*

∽

I remember the argument that was used when there was talk about the annexation of the Sandwich Islands to America. They said that if we did not take them, England would be going around picking up everything and taking possession of it. They said we must annex the Sandwich Islands and thus save them from the domination of an empire; and now what have they got? We have thought too highly of our country. We have been too boastful of it. We have become too much infected with the pride of it, and have thought we were better, a little better, than the other nations.

    —MARY ASHTON LIVERMORE, *November 30, 1903, at the Annual Meeting of the New England Anti-Imperialist League. A suffragist and abolitionist campaigner from before the time of the Civil War, Livermore was the editor of the* Agitator *and other publications that campaigned for social justice at home and abroad.*

∾

Sovereignty of Hawai'i was formally transferred to the United States at ceremonies at 'Iolani Palace on August 12, 1898. Sanford Dole spoke as the newly appointed governor of the Territory of Hawai'i. The Hawaiian anthem, "Hawai'i Pono'i"—with words written by King Kalakaua—was played a[s] the Hawaiian flag was lowered, and replaced by the American flag and "The Star-Spangled Banner." The Hawaiian people had lost their land, their monarchy, and now their independence.

    —PAT PITZER, *from "The Overthrow of the Monarchy," published in* Spirit of Aloha, *May 1994.*

∾

The overthrow of the Hawaiian monarchy . . . was a hostile act, an armed takeover of a legitimate government that was an established member of the community of nations.

> —GOVERNOR JOHN WAIHEE, *of Hawaii, January 16, 1993.*
> *During the five-day centennial commemoration of the overthrow of Hawaii's last Queen, Waihee ordered that the U.S. flag not be flown over state buildings. Hauling down the stars and stripes was, Waihee said, "an appropriate reminder" of the role the U.S. played in the overthrow of a sovereign government.*

∞

Whereas, prior to the arrival of the first Europeans in 1778, the Native Hawaiian people lived in a highly organized, self-sufficient, subsistent social system based on communal land tenure with a sophisticated language, culture, and religion;

Whereas, from 1826 until 1893, the United States recognized the independence of the Kingdom of Hawaii, extended full and complete diplomatic recognition to the Hawaiian government, and entered into treaties and conventions with the Hawaiian monarchs to govern commerce and navigation. . . .

Whereas, on January 14, 1893 . . . the United States minister assigned to the sovereign and independent Kingdom of Hawaii conspired with a small group of non-Hawaiian residents of the Kingdom of Hawaii, including citizens of the United States, to overthrow the indigenous and lawful government of Hawaii. . . .

Whereas, without the active support and intervention by the United States diplomatic and military representatives, the insurrection against the government of Queen Lili'uokalani would have failed for lack of popular support and insufficient arms.

Whereas, in a message to Congress on December 18, 1893, President Grover Cleveland reported fully and accurately on the illegal acts of the conspirators, described such acts as an "act of war, committed with the participation of a diplomatic representative of the United States and without authority of Congress", and acknowledged that by such acts the government of a peaceful and friendly people was overthrown . . . President Cleveland further concluded that a "substantial wrong has thus been done which a due regard for our national character as well as the rights of the injured people requires we should endeavor to repair" and called for the restoration of the Hawaiian monarchy.

Whereas, the indigenous Hawaiian people never directly relinquished their claims to their inherent sovereignty as a people or over their national lands to the United States, either through their monarchy or through a plebiscite or referendum. . . .

Now, therefore, be it

Resolved by the Senate and House of Representatives of the United States of America in Congress assembled,

•apologizes to Native Hawaiians on behalf of the people of the United States for the overthrow of the Kingdom of Hawaii on January 17, 1893 . . . and the deprivation of the rights of Native Hawaiians to self-determination;
•expresses its commitment to acknowledge the ramifications of the overthrow of the Kingdom of Hawaii, in order to provide a proper foundation for reconciliation between the United States and the Native Hawaiian people; and
•urges the President of the United States to also acknowledge the ramifications of the overthrow of the Kingdom of Hawaii and to support reconciliation efforts between the United States and the Native Hawaiian people.

—PUBLIC LAW 103–150, *signed by President William Jefferson Clinton, November 23, 1993. The Senate passed the resolution 65–34. The House passed it by a voice vote.*

FIVE

IMPERIALISM IS A STATE OF MIND

Spain, Cuba, and the

Betrayal of the Declaration

of Independence

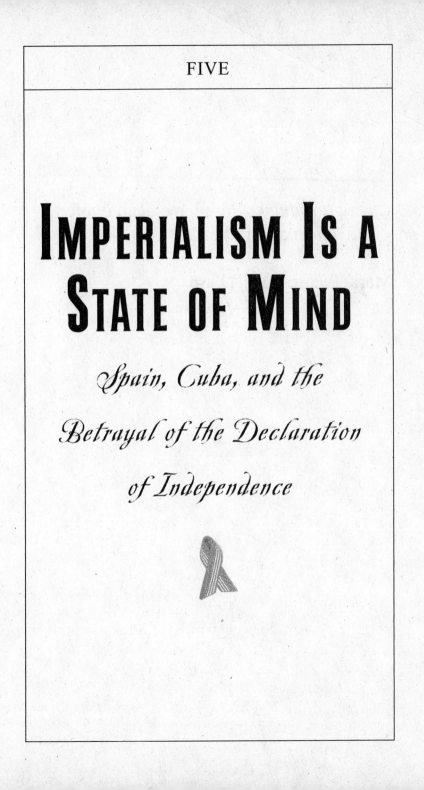

Chicago Tribune: 'You have been quoted here as an anti-imperialist.'

Mark Twain: 'Well, I am.'

—MARK TWAIN,
October 15, 1900

At the close of the nineteenth century, the United States was a vast, rich country that in less than one hundred years had, through wars, hard bargains, and foreign intrigues, extended its reach across the Western Hemisphere from the Atlantic seaboard where it was founded to the far shores of the Pacific. Its diplomats had purchased Alaska from the Russians and stolen Hawaii from the Hawaiians. But, as was already well-known to the British Empire builders against whom the first Americans had revolted, the urge for expansion would grow more and more difficult to satisfy. As the fading monarchs of Europe struggled to retain control of their increasingly restless colonies, those who believed that the turn of the calendar would herald the beginning of "the American century" urged the United States to embark on a career of empire. To realize their country's economic, military, and political potential, Teddy Roosevelt, Henry Cabot Lodge, Alfred Thayer Mahan, and the other twisted champions of American imperialism preached, the United States would need new markets for its manufactured goods. It would need island "protectorates" to serve as coal stations for its great steamers. It would require other lands to fill the status that it had refused in 1776: that of the empire's colony. The time had come for a bit of what Secretary of State John Hay would describe as "land piracy." The United States, Hay informed the territorially inclined Roosevelt, was ready for "a splendid little war." After all, America was now a country strong enough and ambitious enough to satisfy its wildest dreams of expansion.

The rapidly withering Spanish Empire, which was struggling to avert rebellions in its colonies of Cuba and the Philippines, was ripe for the plucking. A U.S. battleship, the USS *Maine*, was dispatched in January of 1898 to the harbor at Havana, where one of its magazines exploded. For the families of 266 seamen whose lives were lost, it was a tragedy. But for the fevered imperialists in Washington and New York, it was an opportunity that would be seized upon. Though the explosion was almost certainly caused by spontaneous combustion aboard the ship, the sensationalist headline writers of the Hearst and Pulitzer press faked up a fantasy of Spanish bombs. "Remember the *Maine*" became a battle cry every bit as resonant in the media of its day as would, 105 years later, be the charge that a dictator in distant Iraq was accumulating weapons of mass destruction that threatened America.

By April, Roosevelt was dressed in "Rough Rider" cowboy drag and sailing toward Santiago.

The great Harvard professor Charles Eliot Norton observed the grotesque mutation of the *Maine* lie into a political prerogative for the expansionist administration of President William McKinley. Norton objected to the nineteenth-century spin that would lead the country into an unjust war of conquest. "And now of a sudden, without cool deliberation, without prudent preparation," Norton concluded, "the nation is hurried into war, and America, she who more than any other land was pledged to peace and goodwill on earth, unsheathes her sword, compels a weak and unwilling nation to a fight, rejecting without due consideration her [Spain's] earnest and repeated offers to meet every legitimate demand of the United States. It is a bitter disappointment to the lover of his country; it is a turning back from the path of civilization to that of barbarism."

Norton's horror at his country's initiation of a war for conquest, and at the brutal occupation of the Caribbean and Pacific Islands that were quickly plucked from Spain's crown of empire, was shared by a great legion of anti-imperialists that included industrialist Andrew Carnegie, labor leaders Eugene Victor Debs and Samuel Gompers, social reformer Jane Addams, Republican Senator George Frisbie Hoar, Democratic presidential candidate William Jennings Bryan, and African-American newspaper editors who would question why America was being called to "take up the white man's burden." The breadth of the movement was remarkable and, at times, troubling. Gathered under the anti-imperialist banner were visionary internationalists and ugly nativists, those who sympathized with the plight of the Cubans and Filipinos and those who believed that the skin color of the islanders ought to disqualify them from American citizenship.

Yet, at the head of the movement were men and women who, for the most part, expressed a liberal and optimistic vision echoing Abraham Lincoln's pronouncement that "no man is good enough to govern another man without that other's consent." The dissenters ceded no patriotic ground to the jingoistic flag wavers of the imperialist camp. "We hold that the policy known as imperialism is hostile to liberty and tends toward militarism, an evil from which it has been our glory to be free. We regret that it has become necessary in the land of Washington and Lincoln to reaffirm that all men, of whatever race or color, are entitled to life, liberty, and the pursuit of happiness. We maintain that governments derive their just powers from the consent of the governed. We insist that the subjugation of any people is 'criminal aggression' and open disloyalty to the distinctive principles of our government," read the manifesto of the American Anti-Imperialist League. It added, "Whether the ruthless slaughter of the Filipinos shall end next month or next year is but an incident in a contest that must go on until the Declaration of Independence and the Constitution of the United States are rescued from the hands of their betrayers."

The campaign that developed to oppose the Spanish-American War and the occupations of Cuba and the Philippines, had much more in common with the antiwar and anti-interventionist movements of the late twentieth century than with the antiexpansionist campaigns of the mid-nineteenth century. The anti-imperialists developed their own organizations and networks, with the Chicago-based Anti-Imperialist League taking the lead. The movement had its celebrity backers, particularly Mark Twain. And, it focused on the explicitly political work of building coalitions, influencing Congress, and shaping the programs of the dominant political parties. The anti-imperialists had success with the Democrats, who wrote a 1900 platform, declaring, "We assert that no nation can long endure half republic and half empire, and we warn the American people that imperialism abroad will lead quickly and inevitably to despotism at home."

The movement succeeded, as well, in creating a new language of opposition to the American Empire that was more thoughtful and detailed in its expression. And, the anti-imperialists found new avenues for complaint, particularly involving the media. The Spanish-American War was the first modern war for Americans, in the sense that it was reported almost immediately in the rapid-fire editions of popular newspapers. Citizens were invited to cheer on soldiers in battles that were not yet finished. In this circumstance, the worst abuses of journalism—stenographic reportage of official pronouncements, jingoism, and the frequent failure of analysis—overwhelmed the truth. And, while the anti-imperialists did successfully stir a national debate over ratification of the Treaty of Paris that settled the war in America's favor, they did not prevail. McKinley defeated Bryan's anti-imperialist campaign in the election of 1900. And, upon McKinley's death by assassination in 1901, the most fearsome of the expansionist politicians, Teddy Roosevelt, succeeded to the presidency. For all the frustrations experienced of their immediate struggle, however, the anti-imperialists had asked questions that would echo through the decades to come, as America played the "great game" of empire in a manner that would frequently confirm Carl Schurz's dire warning that a democracy "cannot long play the king over subject populations without creating within itself ways of thinking and habits of action most dangerous to its own vitality."

THE CONQUEST OF THE UNITED STATES BY SPAIN

The American people believe that they have a free country, and we are treated to grandiloquent speeches about our flag and our reputation for freedom and enlightenment. The common opinion is that we have these things because we have chosen and adopted them, because they are in the Declaration of Independence and the Constitution. We suppose, therefore, that we are sure to keep them and that the follies of other people are things which we can hear about with complacency. People say that this country is like no other; that its prosperity proves its exceptionality, and so on. These are popular errors which in time will meet with harsh correction. The United States is in a protected situation. It is easy to have equality where land is abundant and where the population is small. It is easy to have prosperity where a few men have a great continent to exploit. It is easy to have liberty when you have no dangerous neighbors and when the struggle for existence is easy. There are no severe penalties, under such circumstances, for political mistakes. Democracy is not then a thing to be nursed and defended, as it is in an old country like France. It is rooted and founded in the economic circumstances of the country. The orators and constitution-makers do not make democracy. They are made by it. This protected position, however, is sure to pass away. As the country fills up with population, and the task of getting a living out of the ground becomes more difficult, the struggle for existence will become harder and the competition of life more severe. Then liberty and democracy will cost something, if they are to be maintained.

Now what will hasten the day when our present advantages will wear out and when we shall come down to the conditions of the older and densely populated nations? The answer is: war, debt, taxation, diplomacy, a grand governmental system, pomp, glory, a big army and navy, lavish expenditures, political jobbery—in a word, imperialism. In the old days, the democratic masses of this country, who knew little about our modern doctrines of social philosophy, had a sound instinct on these matters, and it is no small ground of political disquietude to see it decline. They resisted every appeal to their vanity in the way of pomp and glory which they knew must be paid for. They dreaded a public debt and a standing army. They were narrow-minded and went too far with these notions, but they were, at least, right, if they wanted to strengthen democracy.

The great foe of democracy now and in the near future is plutocracy. Every year that passes brings out this antagonism more distinctly. It is to be the social war of the twentieth century. In that war, militarism, expansion, and imperialism will all favor plutocracy. In the first place, war and expansion will favor jobbery, both in the dependencies and at home. In the second place, they will take away the attention of the people from what the plutocrats are doing. In the third place, they will cause large expenditures of the people's money, the return for which will not go into the treasury, but into the hands of a few schemers. In the fourth place, they will call for a large public debt and taxes, and these things especially tend to make men unequal, because any social burdens bear more heavily on the weak than on the strong, and so make the weak weaker and the strong stronger. Therefore expansion and imperialism are a grand onslaught on democracy.

The point which I have tried to make in this lecture is that expansion and imperialism are at war with the best traditions, principles, and interests of the American people, and that they will plunge us into a network of difficult problems and political perils, which we might have avoided, while they offer us no corresponding advantage in return. . . .

Yet there are people who are boasting of their patriotism, because they say that we have taken our place now amongst the nations of the earth by virtue of this war. My patriotism is of the kind which is outraged by the notion that the United States never was a great nation until in a petty three months' campaign it knocked to pieces a poor, decrepit, bankrupt old state like Spain. To hold such an opinion as that is to abandon all American standards, to put shame and scorn on all that our ancestors tried to build up here, and to go over to the standards of which Spain is a representative.

—WILLIAM GRAHAM SUMNER,— *speech to the Phi Beta Kappa Society of Yale University, January 16, 1899. Sumner a professor of political and social science at Yale, was one of the most respected academics of his time. His passionate condemnation of the American conquest of former Spanish territories caused a national outcry, not least because he suggested that the United States was becoming a colonial power. This speech, printed in pamphlet form, was one of the most widely distributed attacks on imperialism in the late nineteenth and early twentieth centuries.*

∞

And now of a sudden, without cool deliberation, without prudent preparation, the nation is hurried into war, and America, she who more than any other land was pledged to peace and goodwill on earth, unsheathes her sword, compels a weak and unwilling nation to a fight, rejecting without due consideration her [Spain's] earnest and repeated offers to meet every legitimate demand of the United States. It is a bitter disappointment to the lover of his country; it is a turning back from the path of civilization to that of barbarism.

"There never was a good war," said Franklin. There have indeed been many wars in which a good man must take part. . . . But if a war be undertaken for the most righteous end, before the resources of peace have been tried and proved vain to secure it, that war has no defense. It is a national crime. The plea that the better government of Cuba, and the relief of the *reconcentrados*, could only be secured by war is the plea either of ignorance or of hypocrisy.

But the war is declared; and on all hands we hear the cry that he is no patriot who fails to shout for it, and to urge the youth of the country to enlist, and to rejoice that they are called to the service of their native land. The sober counsels that were appropriate before the war was entered upon must give way to blind enthusiasm, and the voice of condemnation must be silenced by the thunders of the guns and the hurrahs of the crowd.

Stop! A declaration of war does not change the moral law. "The Ten Commandments will not budge" at a joint resolve of Congress. . . . No! The voice of protest, of warning, of appeal is never more needed than when the clamor of fife and drum, echoed by the press and too often by the pulpit, is bidding all men fall in and keep step and obey in silence the tyrannous word of command. Then, more than ever, it is the duty of the good citizen not to be silent, and spite of obliquity, misrepresentation, and abuse, to insist on being heard, and with sober counsel to maintain the everlasting validity of the principles of the moral law.

—CHARLES ELIOT NORTON, *speech delivered in Cambridge, Massachusetts, June 23, 1898. The popular Harvard professor of history of the fine arts, caused a huge controversy when he urged young men not to enlist in what he described as an immoral war.*

❧

To the Editor of the *Transcript*:

. . . We are now openly engaged in crushing out the sacredest thing in this great human world—the attempt of a people long enslaved to attain to the possession of itself, to organize its laws and government, to be free to follow its internal destinies according to its own ideals. ["War," said Moltke, "aims at destruction, and at nothing else."] And splendidly are we carrying out war's ideal. We are destroying the lives of these islanders by the thousand, their villages and their cities; for surely it is we who are solely responsible for all the incidental burnings that our operations entail. . . .

It is horrible, simply horrible. Surely there cannot be many born and bred Americans who, when they look at the bare fact of what we are doing, the fact taken all by itself, do not feel this, and do not blush with burning shame at the unspeakable meanness and ignominy of the trick? . . .

The issue is perfectly plain at last. We are cold-bloodedly, wantonly, and abominably destroying the soul of a people who never did us an atom of harm in their lives. It is bald, brutal piracy, impossible to dish up any longer in the cold pot-grease of President McKinley's cant at the recent Boston banquet—surely as shamefully evasive a speech, considering the right of the public to know definite facts, as can often have fallen even from a professional politician's lips. The worst of our imperialists is that they do not themselves know where sincerity ends and insincerity begins. Their state of consciousness is so new, so mixed of primitively human passions and, in political circles, of calculations that are anything but primitively human; so at variance, moreover, with their former mental habits—and so empty of definite data and contents—that they face various ways at once, and their portraits should be taken with a squint. One reads the President's speech with a strange feeling—as if the very words were squinting on the page.

The impotence of the private individual, with imperialism under full headway as it is, is deplorable indeed. But every American has a voice or a pen, and may use it. So, impelled by my own sense of duty, I write these present words. One by one we shall creep from cover, and the opposition will organize itself. If the Filipinos hold out long enough, there is a good chance (the canting game being already pretty well played out, and the piracy having to show itself henceforward naked) of the older American beliefs and sentiments coming to their rights again, and of the administration being terrified into a conciliatory policy towards the native government.

The programme for the opposition should, it seems to me, be radical. The infamy and iniquity of a war of conquest must stop.

—WILLIAM JAMES, *from a letter to the* Boston Evening Transcript, *February 26, 1899. Perhaps the leading American thinker of the day, James was an active foe of the U.S. occupation of the Philippines from the time of the Spanish-American War until his death in 1910.*

∽

THE LUST FOR EMPIRE

. . . If at any time hereafter [pro-imperialism senators] shall seek to put [their] theories into practice by reducing to subjection a distant people, dwelling in the tropics, aliens in blood, most of them Moslem in faith, incapable to speak or comprehend our language, or to read or to write any language, to whom the traditions and the doctrines of civil liberty are unknown, it will be time to point out what terrible results and penalties this departure from our constitutional principles will bring upon us. . . .

But the question with which we now have to deal is whether Congress may conquer and may govern, without their consent and against their will, a foreign nation, a separate, distinct, and numerous people, a territory not hereafter to be populated by Americans, to be formed into American states and to take its part in fulfilling and executing the purposes for which the Constitution was framed, whether it may conquer, control, and govern this people, not for the general welfare, common defense, more perfect union, more blessed liberty of the people of the United States, but for some real or fancied benefit to be conferred against their desire upon the people so governed or in discharge of some fancied obligation to them, and not to the people of the United States. . . .

My proposition, summed up in a nutshell, is this: I admit you have the right to acquire territory for constitutional purposes, and you may hold land and govern men on it for the constitutional purpose of a seat of government or for the constitutional purpose of admitting it as a state. I deny the right to hold land or acquire any property for any purpose not contemplated by the Constitution. The government of foreign people against their will is not a constitutional purpose but a purpose expressly forbidden by the Constitution. . . .

Now, I claim that under the Declaration of Independence you cannot govern a foreign territory, a foreign people, another people than your own; that you cannot subjugate them and govern them against their will, because you think it is for their good, when they do not; because you think you are going to give them the blessings of liberty. You have no right at the cannon's mouth to impose on an unwilling people your Declaration of Independence and your Constitution and your notions of freedom and notions of what is good . . .

—U.S. SENATOR GEORGE FRISBIE HOAR,
addressing the Senate, 1899. One of the great Congressional statements on the role of the U.S. in the world, the full address can be found in the Congressional Record, *fifty-fifth Congress, third session, p. 495.*

∽

When I think of my party, whose glory and whose service to liberty are the guide of my life, crushing out this people in their effort to establish a republic, and hear people talking about giving them good government and that they are better off than they ever were under Spain, I feel very much as if I had learned that my father or some other honored ancestor had been a slave trader in his time and had boasted that he had introduced a new and easier kind of handcuffs or fetters to be worn by the slaves during the horrors of the Middle Passage.

—GEORGE FRISBIE HOAR, *from his autobiography,*
Autobiography of Seventy Years, *1903. Hoar led the loyal*

*opposition within the Republican Party as President William
McKinley, a Republican, embarked on a career of empire after 1898.
Many other prominent Republicans abandoned McKinley and, in
some cases, the party, over the issue of imperialism.*

✧

If we [adopt a colonial system], we shall transform the government
of the people, for the people, and by the people, for which Abraham
Lincoln lived, into a government of one part of the people, the strong,
over another part, the weak. Such an abandonment of a fundamental
principle as a permanent policy may at first seem to bear only upon
more or less distant dependencies, but it can hardly fail in its ultimate
effects to disturb the rule of the same principle in the conduct of
democratic government at home. And I warn the American people
that a democracy cannot so deny its faith as to the vital conditions of
its being—it cannot long play the king over subject populations
without creating within itself ways of thinking and habits of action
most dangerous to its own vitality. . . .

We must stop at the beginning, before taking Porto Rico [sic]. If
we take that island, not even to speak of the Philippines, we shall
have placed ourselves on the inclined plane, and roll on and on, no
longer masters of our own will, until we have reached the bottom.
And where will that bottom be? Who knows?

—CARL SCHURZ, *"American Imperialism," a convocation
address at the University of Chicago, January 4, 1899. Schurz, a
German immigrant, was one of the leading liberal reformers in the
United States from the 1850s to the early years of the twentieth
century. He helped Abraham Lincoln build the Republican Party.
He served as Lincoln's ambassador to Spain, as a general in the
Union Army during the Civil War, and as a Republican U.S. senator
from Missouri. Schurz split with expansionist forces within the
Republican Party, however, and endorsed the presidential candidacy
of Democrat William Jennings Bryan, who ran on an
anti-imperialist platform in 1900.*

✧

Here are our "Manifest Destiny" men who tell us that whether it be right or not, we must take and keep the Philippines because "destiny" so wills it. We have heard this cry of Manifest Destiny before, especially when, a half century ago, the slave power demanded the annexation of Cuba and Central America to strengthen the slave power. The cry of destiny is most vociferously put forward by those who want to do a wicked thing and to shift the responsibility. The destiny of a free people lies in its intelligent will and its moral strength. When it pleads destiny, it pleads the baby act. Nay, worse; the cry of destiny is apt to be the refuge of evil intent and of moral cowardice.

Here are our "burden" men, who piously turn up their eyes and tell us with a melancholy sigh, that all this conquest business may be very irksome, but that a mysterious Providence has put it as a "burden" upon us, which, however sorrowfully, we must bear; that this burden consists in our duty to take care of the poor people of the Philippines; and that in order to take proper care of them we must exercise sovereignty over them; and that if they refuse to accept our sovereignty, we must—Alas! Alas!—kill them, which makes the burden very solemn and sad.

But cheer up, brethren! we may avoid that mournful way of taking care of them by killing them, if we simply recognize their right to take care of themselves, and gently aid them in doing so. Besides, you may be as much mistaken about the decrees of Providence as before our civil war the Southern Methodist bishops were who solemnly insisted that Providence willed the Negroes to remain in slavery.

Next there are our "flag" men, who insist that we must kill the Filipinos fighting for their independence to protect the honor of the stars and stripes. I agree that the honor of our flag sorely needs protection. We have to protect it against desecration by those who are making it an emblem of that hypocrisy which seeks to cover a war of conquest and subjugation with a cloak of humanity and religion; an emblem of that greed which would treat a matter involving our national honor, the integrity of our institutions, and the peace and character of the republic as a mere question of dollars and cents; an emblem of that vulgar lust of war and conquest which recklessly tramples upon right and justice and all our higher ideals; an emblem of the imperialistic ambitions which mock the noblest part of our history and stamp the greatest national heroes of our past as hypocrites or fools. These are the dangers threatening the honor of our flag, against which it needs protection, and that protection we are striving to give it.

Now, a last word to those of our fellow citizens who feel and recognize as we do that the Philippine war of subjugation is wrong and cruel, and that we ought to recognize the independence of those people, but who insist that, having begun that war, we must continue it until the submission of the Filipinos is complete. I detest, but I can understand, the jingo whose moral sense is obscured by intoxicating dreams of wild adventure and conquest, and to whom bloodshed and devastation have become a reckless sport. I detest even more, but still I can understand the cruel logic of those to whom everything is a matter of dollars and cents and whose greed of gain will walk coolly over slaughtered populations. But I must confess, I cannot understand the reasoning of those who have moral sense enough to recognize that this war is criminal aggression—who must say to themselves that every drop of blood shed in it by friend or foe is blood wantonly and wickedly shed, and that every act of devastation is barbarous cruelty inflicted upon an innocent people—but who still maintain that we must go on killing and devastating, and driving our brave soldiers into a fight which they themselves are cursing, because we have once begun it. This I cannot understand. Do they not consider that in such a war, which they themselves condemn as wanton and iniquitous, the more complete our success, the greater will be our disgrace? . . .

Have we not the example of England before us, who, after a seven years' war against the American colonists, recognized their independence? Indeed, the example of England teaches us a double lesson. England did not, by recognizing American independence, lose her position in the world and her chances of future greatness; on the contrary, she grew in strength. And, secondly, England would have retained, or won anew, the friendship of the Americans if she had recognized American independence more promptly, before appearing to have been forced to do so by humiliating defeats. Will our friends who are for Philippine independence, but also for continuing to kill those who fight for it, take these two lessons to heart?

Some of them say that we have here to fulfill some of the disagreeable duties of patriotism. Patriotism! Who were the true patriots of England at the time of the American Revolution? King George and Lord North, who insisted upon subjugation? Or, Lord Chatham and Edmund Burke, who stood up for American rights and American liberty? . . .

I am pleading for the cause of American honor and self-respect, American interests, American democracy—aye, for the cause of the American people against an administration of our public affairs which has wantonly plunged this country into an iniquitous war; which has disgraced the republic by a scandalous breach of faith to a people struggling for their freedom whom we had used as allies; which has been systematically seeking to deceive and mislead the public mind by the manufacture of false news; which has struck at the very foundation of our constitutional government by an executive usurpation of the war power; which makes sport of the great principles and high ideals that have been and should ever remain the guiding star of our course; and which, unless stopped in time, will transform this government of the people, for the people, and by the people, into an imperial government cynically calling itself republican—a government in which the noisy worship of arrogant might will drown the voice of right; which will impose upon the people a burdensome and demoralizing militarism, and which will be driven into a policy of wild and rapacious adventure by the unscrupulous greed of the exploiter—a policy always fatal to democracy. . . .

I confidently trust that the American people will prove themselves . . . too wise not to detect the false pride, or the dangerous ambitions, or the selfish schemes which so often hide themselves under that deceptive cry of mock patriotism: "Our country, right or wrong!" They will not fail to recognize that our dignity, our free institutions, and the peace and welfare of this and coming generations of Americans will be secure only as we cling to the watchword of true patriotism: "Our country—when right to be kept right; when wrong to be put right."

—CARL SCHURZ, *"The Policy of Imperialism," an address to the Chicago Anti-Imperialism Conference, October 17, 1899. Schurz used this speech, which formed the basis for a broadly distributed pamphlet, to link the struggle against empire abroad with the fight*

against slavery at home. He also inserted a critique of the media,
which members of the growing anti-imperialist movement saw as a
willing accomplice of expansionists in government. In 1900, the
National Liberty Congress of Anti-Imperialists would declare that,
"We believe that the greatest safeguard of liberty is a free press,
and we demand that the censorship in the Philippine Islands which
keeps from the American people the knowledge of what is done in
their name be abolished. We are entitled to know the truth,
and we insist that the powers which the president holds in trust
for us shall be not used to suppress it."

∽

THE NATIONAL EMBLEM

The flag is a national emblem and is obedient to the national will. It was made for the people, not the people for the flag. When the American people want the flag raised, they raise it; when they want it hauled down, they haul it down. The flag was raised upon Canadian soil during the war of 1812 and it was hauled down when peace was restored. The flag was planted upon Chapultepec during the war with Mexico and it was hauled down when the war was over. The morning papers announce that General Lee ordered the flag hauled down in Cuba yesterday, because it was raised too soon. The flag will be raised in Cuba again on the first of January, but the president declares in his message that it will be hauled down as soon as a stable government is established. Who will deny to our people the right to haul the flag down in the Philippines, if they so desire, when a stable government is established there?

Our flag stands for an indissoluble union of indestructible states. Every state is represented by a star and every territory sees in the Constitution a star of hope that will some day take its place in the constellation. What is there in the flag to awaken the zeal or reflect the aspirations of vassal colonies which are too good to be cast away, but not good enough to be admitted to the sisterhood of states?

Shall we keep the Philippines and amend our flag? Shall we add a new star—the blood-star, Mars—to indicate that we have entered upon a career of conquest? Or shall we borrow the yellow, which in

1896 was the badge of gold and greed, and paint Saturn and his rings, to suggest a carpetbag government, with its schemes of spoliation? Or shall we adorn our flag with a Milky Way composed of a multitude of minor stars representing remote and insignificant dependencies?

No, a thousand times better that we haul down the stars and stripes and substitute the flag of an independent republic than surrender the doctrines that give glory to "Old Glory." It was the flag of our fathers in the years that are gone, It is the flag of a reunited country today; let it be the flag of our nation in the years that are to come. Its stripes of red tell of the blood that was shed to purchase liberty; its stripes of white proclaim the pure and Heaven-born purpose of a government which derives its just powers from the consent of the governed. The mission of that flag is to float—not over a conglomeration of commonwealths and colonies—but over "the land of the free and the home of the brave;" and to that mission it must remain forever true—forever true.

—WILLIAM JENNINGS BRYAN, *speech in Lincoln, Nebraska, December 23, 1898. Bryan, a former congressman and Democratic nominee for president in 1896, 1900, and 1908, embraced the anti-imperialist message with increasing fervor between the elections of 1896 and 1900. His supporters were particularly angry with attempts by the McKinley administration to associate the flag with the cause of conquest in the Pacific and the Caribbean. Bryan sought in dozens of speeches during the period to identify imperialism as an affront to American values, telling a Minnesota crowd in 1899 that, "In commemoration of the fact that France was our ally in securing independence the citizens of that nation joined with the citizens of the United States in placing in New York harbor an heroic statue representing liberty enlightening the world. What course shall our nation pursue? Send the Statue of Liberty back to France and borrow from England a statue of William the Conqueror? Or shall our nation so act as to enable the American people to join with the Filipinos in placing in the harbor of Manila a statue of liberty enlightening the Orient?"*

⚯

Even if it could be shown that England's sovereignty over India had brought blessings to the Indian people and advantage to the inhabitants of Great Britain, we could not afford to adopt the policy. A monarchy can engage in work which a republic dare not undertake. A monarchy is constructed upon the theory that authority descends from the king and that privileges are granted by the crown to the subjects. Of course, the ruling power recognizes that it owes a duty to the people but, while the obligation is binding upon the conscience of the sovereign, it cannot be enforced by the subject.

—WILLIAM JENNINGS BRYAN, *"British Rule in India,"*
New York Journal, *January 22, 1899. Many critics of the U.S. occupation of former Spanish colonies warned that the United States must not follow the course of the British Empire against which the American revolutionaries of 1776 revolted.*

The Bible tells us that Ahab, the king, wanted the vineyard of Naboth and was sorely grieved because the owner thereof refused to part with the inheritance of his fathers. Then followed a plot, and false charges were preferred against Naboth to furnish an excuse for getting rid of him.

"Thou shalt not covet!" "Thou shalt not bear false witness!" "Thou shalt not kill"—three commandments broken, and still a fourth, "Thou shalt not steal," to be broken in order to get a little piece of ground! And what was the result? When the king went forth to take possession, Elijah, that brave old prophet of the early days, met him and pronounced against him the sentence of the Almighty: "In the place where the dogs licked the blood of Naboth shall the dogs lick thy blood, even thine."

Neither his own exalted position nor the lowly station of his victim could save him from the avenging hand of outraged justice. His case was tried in a court where neither wealth, nor rank, nor power can shield the transgressor.

Wars of conquest have their origin in covetousness; and the history of the human race has been written in characters of blood because rulers have looked with longing eyes upon the lands of others.

Covetousness is prone to seek the aid of false presence to carry out its plans, but what it cannot secure by persuasion it takes by the sword. . . .

We cannot afford to enter upon a colonial policy. The theory upon which a government is built is a matter of vital importance. The national idea has a controlling influence upon the thought and character of the people. Our national idea is self-government, and unless we are ready to abandon that idea forever we cannot ignore it in dealing with the Filipinos. . . .

The fruits of imperialism, be they bitter or sweet, must be left to the subjects of monarchy. This is the one tree of which the citizens of a republic may not partake. It is the voice of the serpent, not the voice of God, that bids us eat.

—WILLIAM JENNINGS BRYAN, *speech titled "Naboth's Vineyard," which he gave to state chairs of the Populist and Democratic parties gathered in Denver, Colorado, January 17, 1899. Like many opponents of empire, Bryan argued that it was immoral for the United States to seize distant lands. Bryan identified Manifest Destiny with sin, declaring in a Chicago speech earlier in 1899 that, "When the desire to steal becomes uncontrollable in an individual he is declared to be a kleptomaniac and is sent to an asylum; when the desire to grab land becomes uncontrollable in a nation we are told that the 'currents of destiny are flowing through the hearts of men' and that the American people are entering upon 'a manifest mission.' Shame upon a logic which locks up the petty offender and enthrones grand larceny. Have the people returned to the worship of the Golden Calf? Have they made unto themselves a new commandment consistent with the spirit of conquest and the lust for empire? Is 'thou shalt not steal upon a small scale' to be substituted for the law of Moses? Awake, o, ancient Law-Giver, awake! Break forth from shine unmarked sepulchre and speed thee back to cloud-crowned Sinai; commune once more with the God of our fathers and proclaim again the words engraver upon the tables of stone—the law that was, the law that is today—the law that neither individual nor nation can violate with impunity."*

To the Workers of America:

We desire to call attention to the manifest folly of contributing even in the slightest degree to the warlike feeling so prevalent in the country. We admit fully the unjust character of the Spanish administration of Cuba, but we deny that war between Spain and the United States can be in any way conducive to the best interests of mankind. . . .

The inhuman conditions which exist in Cuba have been primarily produced by that greed which gets in its work wherever man has the power to oppress his fellows. The cruelty exhibited in Cuba is no peculiarity of the Spanish race; within the last few weeks instances of cruelty to Negroes have occurred in this country which equal, if they do not surpass, anything which has occurred in Cuba. Honesty compels us to acknowledge that it is not the Spanish race especially, but the human race at large, that is cruel, and that our crusade in this matter should begin at home. We see every day the vast injustice prevailing in our own land, the hopeless toil, the wretched poverty, the armies of unemployed, and until we remove these beams from our own eyes should not presume to take the mote from our brother's.

—WILLIAM DEAN HOWELLS, CHARLES FREDERICK
ADAMS, JOSEPHINE SHAW LOWELL, BISHOP HENRY
CODMAN POTTER, BOLTON HALL, AND OTHERS.
An appeal to the Central Labor Union of New York City that was an.
early expression of opposition to war with Spain, April 17, 1898.

∽

A "foreign war as a cure for domestic discontent" has been the device of tyrants and false counselors from time immemorial, but it has always led to a Waterloo, a Sedan, to certain decadence and often utter ruin. In our country we are perhaps too powerful to incur outside disaster; but we shall certainly court worse evils at home if we try to benumb the nation's sense of justice and love of right, and prevent it from striving earnestly to correct all proved errors. . . .

If we attempt to force upon the natives of the Philippines our rule, and compel them to conform to our more or less rigid mold of government, how many lives shall we take? Of course, they will seem cheap, because they are poor laborers. They will be members of the majority in the Philippines, but they will be ruled and killed at the convenience of the very small minority there, backed up by our armed land and sea forces. The dominant class in the islands will ease its conscience because the victims will be poor, ignorant, and weak. When innocent men can be shot down on the public highway as they were in Lattimer, Pennsylvania, and Virden, Illinois, men of our own flesh and blood, men who help to make this homogenous nation great, because they dare ask for humane conditions at the hands of the moneyed class of our country, how much more difficult will it be to arouse any sympathy, and secure relief for the poor semi-savages in the Philippines, much less indignation at any crime against their inherent and natural rights to life, liberty, and the pursuit of happiness?

—SAMUEL GOMPERS, *"Imperialism—Its Danger and Wrongs,"*
a speech to the Chicago Peace Jubilee, October 18, 1898. In the
same speech, Gompers, the president of the American Federation of
Labor, expressed concern that the acquisition of distant territories
would encourage immigration from Asia, asking, "If these new
islands are to become ours, it will be either under the form of
territories or states. Can we hope to close the floodgates of
immigration from the hordes of Chinese and the semisavage races
coming from what will then be part of our own country?" Gompers
was by no means the only anti-imperialist who expressed nativist
and racist sentiments. However, more radical labor leaders were
clearer in their expressions of solidarity with the workers of the
Philippines and other Asian lands.

✑

APPEAL TO THE COLONIAL DAMES AND DAUGHTERS
OF THE AMERICAN REVOLUTION

Daughters of the American Revolution! Colonial Dames of America!
Why sit ye all the day idle?

While the principles for which ye Ancestors fought are violated, ye Constitution declared obsolete and ye sacred document, ye Declaration of Independence, spurned with contempt by those in power, who have sworn to protect and be governed by them.

Did ye ancestors transmit to ye no spark of rebellion?

Are ye degenerates? That ye "sit at ease in Zion" vainly posing as "patriotic women," while the fundamental principles which made ye organization possible, and for which ye ancestors laid down their lives at Bunker Hill, Lexington, Saratoga, and Yorktown, suffering worse than death at Valley Forge, trampling the frozen snows with bare and bleeding feet for ye nation's independence.

Do ye know why the tea was thrown overboard into Boston Harbor?

Can ye tell the real reason why the farmers sprang to arms at Concord and Lexington, and "fired the shot which was heard around the world"?

Is the spirit of Samuel Adams extinct among ye, that "ye sit all the day idle," while those in power turn their backs upon Washington, Jefferson, Clay, Webster, and Lincoln and form unholy and unconstitutional "alliances with European powers"? And ye republican institutions destroyed one by one, by the ruler of this (so-called) republic? Who has arrogated to himself greater powers than are possessed by the czar of Russia, sultan of Turkey or dowager empress of China.

Do ye know and care not?

To idly declare ye "are not in politics" is cowardly evasion of a duty peculiarly yours. Your silence is only commendable when there can be an honest difference of opinion, but when the principles of American independence are trampled under foot and republican institutions tottering and ye nation "facing the greatest peril in its history," the loudest and firmest protest should come from the descendants of the American revolutionists. There should be no "Tories" among ye grand dames and daughters of those brave old republicans who died that ye might live, and warned ye that "eternal vigilance is the price of liberty."

Are ye vigilant?

Have ye recognized the oppressive and tyrannical spirit of King George when it reared its venemous head upon American soil at the capital of this republic?

Can ye be longer blinded?

Go forth, ye dames and daughters, reason among yeselves.

Is ye Constitution and Declaration of Independence true or false?

Were ye ancestors right or wrong?

Have ye builded and stood upon a lie?

If it is true—and all ye pride of ancestry rests upon it—are ye not dishonored before the world if ye government departs from it?

Rise up, proud dames and daughters, protest! Protest loudly or go down forever in dishonor unworthy ye noble ancestors, not deserving ye titles "patriotic women," "daughters of the American revolution," "colonial dames of America."

Minorca Stearns Fitts, President
C. D. M. Springer, Secretary
Helen E. Kane, Treasurer

> —ILLINOIS WOMEN'S ANTI-IMPERIALIST LEAGUE, *letter, September 29, 1900. Women played a prominent role in anti-imperialist activism of the late nineteenth and early twentieth centuries, with Josephine Shaw Lowell serving as a national vice president of the Anti-Imperialist League.*

∽

PLATFORM OF THE AMERICAN
ANTI-IMPERIALIST LEAGUE

We hold that the policy known as imperialism is hostile to liberty and tends toward militarism, an evil from which it has been our glory to be free. We regret that it has become necessary in the land of Washington and Lincoln to reaffirm that all men, of whatever race or color, are entitled to life, liberty, and the pursuit of happiness. We maintain that governments derive their just powers from the consent of the governed. We insist that the subjugation of any people is "criminal aggression" and open disloyalty to the distinctive principles of our government.

We earnestly condemn the policy of the present national administration in the Philippines. It seeks to extinguish the spirit of 1776 in those islands. We deplore the sacrifice of our soldiers and sailors, whose bravery deserves admiration even in an unjust war. We denounce the slaughter of the Filipinos as a needless horror. We protest against the extension of American sovereignty by Spanish methods.

We demand the immediate cessation of the war against liberty, begun by Spain and continued by us. We urge that Congress be promptly convened to announce to the Filipinos our purpose to concede to them the independence for which they have so long fought and which of right is theirs.

The United States has always protested against the doctrine of international law which permits the subjugation of the weak by the strong. A self-governing state cannot accept sovereignty over an unwilling people. The United States cannot act upon the ancient heresy that might makes right. . . .

We deny that the obligation of all citizens to support their government in times of grave national peril applies to the present situation. If an administration may with impunity ignore the issues upon which it was chosen, deliberately create a condition of war anywhere on the face of the globe, debauch the civil service for spoils to promote the adventure, organize a truth-suppressing censorship, and demand of all citizens a suspension of judgment and their unanimous support while it chooses to continue the fighting, representative government itself is imperiled . . .

—THE AMERICAN ANTI-IMPERIALIST LEAGUE, *October 1899. Formed after the U.S. occupied Cuba, Puerto Rico, and the Philippine Islands, the American Anti-Imperialist League campaigned with particular fervor against the role the U.S. military was playing in the Philippines, where American troops were*

suppressing an independence movement. The league attracted broad
support from opponents of expansionism and empire, including Mark
Twain, Henry James, and Andrew Carnegie. A membership appeal
circulated a month after this platform statement was adopted, which
declared, "We are in full sympathy with the heroic struggles for
liberty of the people in the Spanish Islands, and therefore we protest
against depriving them of their rights by an exchange of masters.
Only by recognizing their rights as free men are all their interests
protected. Expansion by natural growth in thinly settled contiguous
territory, acquired by purchase for the expressed purpose of ultimate
statehood, cannot be confounded with, or made analogous to, foreign
territory conquered by war and wrested by force from a weak enemy.
A beaten foe has no right to transfer a people whose consent has not
been asked, and a free republic has no right to hold in subjection a
people so transferred. No American, until today, has disputed these
propositions; it remains for the new Imperialism to set up the law of
might and to place commercial gain and a false philanthropy above
the sound principles upon which the Republic was based. In defence
of its position it has already urged the fallacy of the Declaration of
Independence and proclaimed a wisdom superior to that of the
framers of the Constitution. As solemnly as a people could, we
announced the war to be solely for humanity and freedom, without a
thought, desire, or purpose of gain to ourselves; all that we sought
has been accomplished in Cuba's liberation. Shall we now prove false
to our declaration and seize by force islands thousands of miles away
whose peoples have not desired our presence and whose will we have
not asked?"

∽

TWO BURDENS

With all due respect for the alleged genius of one Rudyard Kipling, his latest conglomeration of rot about the "white man's burden" makes us very, very tired. It has ever been the dark races who have borne the world's burdens both in the heat of day and the travail of the night. The white man has never had a burden that was not self-imposed, sometimes through a temporary wave of indignation or charity, but more frequently through greed of gold and territory.

Might has been made to pose for right and the weak and untutored
peoples have had burdens forced upon them at the mouth of the cannon or point of the bayonet. The white man's burden is a myth. The
black man's burden is a crushing, grinding reality. Let us have done
with cant and hypocrisy.

—COLORED AMERICAN, *editorial, March 18, 1899. This article
expressed the general outrage of African-Americans at English writer
Kipling's poem, "The White Man's Burden," a defense of imperialism
that suggested that white Europeans had a responsibility to colonize
Africa, India, and other regions. Kipling's poem, which was
published approvingly by American daily newspapers that supported
the U.S. conquest of Cuba, Puerto Rico, and the Philippines, was
parodied in the African-American press of the day.*

THE WHITE MAN'S BURDEN

"Take up the white man's burden!"
He's borne for many years,
With hardened hearts for justice
And a smile for the orphans tears.

"Take up the white man's burden!"
And go to the Southern land
Where cities and towns are governed,
By a fiendish, lawless band.

"Take up the white man's burden!"
That causes the heart to quake
As we read again with horror,
Of those burnings at the stake,

Of white caps riding in the night,
And burning black men's homes,
Of the inmates shot as they rush out
And the awful dying groans,

Of crimes that would outnumber
Those in the foreign Isle,
Committed by heathen people
"Half devil and half child."

Then free those Filipinos people,
From the accursed rule of Spain,
And put on them the shackels
Of a haughtier nation's reign.

With "Judas" acts in every form,
Conceivable by man,
And the thirst for blood, and greed for gold
Is surely the white man's plan.

Oh! Wait not until the Martyr dies
Before bears the crown,
But sing his praises to the skies
And the burden help lay down.

> —ALICE SMITH-TRAVERS, *"The White Man's Burden,"*
> *in the* Freeman, *March 4, 1899. The* Freeman *was a*
> *nationally circulated weekly newspaper.*

∞

THE BLACK MAN'S BURDEN

Pile on the Black Man's burden,
'Tis nearest at your door;
Why heed long-bleeding Cuba
Or dark Hawaii's shore?
Halt ye your fearless armies
Which menace feeble folks,
Who fight with clubs and arrows
And brook your rifle smokes.

Pile on the Black Man's burden,
His wail with laughter drown,
You've sealed the Red Man's problem
And now take up the Brown.
In vain ye seek to end it
With bullets, blood or death—
Better by far defend it
With honor's holy breath.

Pile on the Black Man's burden
His back is broad though sore;
What though the weight oppress him,
He's borne the like before.
Your Jim-Crow laws and customs,
And fiendish midnight deed,
Though winked at by the nation,
Will some day trouble breed.

Pile on the Black Man's burden,
At length 'twill heaven pierce;
Then on you or your children
Will reign God's judgement fierce.
Your battleships and armies
May weaker ones appall,
But God Almighty's justice
They'll not disturb at all.

> —H.T. JOHNSON, *"The Black Man's Burden,"* Voice of Missions,
> *April 1, 1899. This was the official publication of the Missionary
> Department of the African Methodist Episcopal Church.*

∽

It is about time for the ministers of the A. M. E. Church, who, in the aggregate, are the most progressive, enlightened, and racial of the Africanite ministry of the world, with the highest regard for all other denominations, to begin to tell the young men of our race to stay out of the United States Army. If it is a white man's government, and we grant it is, let him take care of it.

The Negro has no flag to defend. There is not a star in the flag of this nation, out of the forty odd, that the colored race can claim, nor is there any symbol signalized in the colors of the flag that he can presume to call his, unless it would be the stripes, and the stripes are now too good for him . . .

—"THE NEGRO SHOULD NOT ENTER THE ARMY,"
Voice of Missions, *May 1, 1899.*

∽

To the Honorable William McKinley,
President of the United States

Sir:

We, colored people of Massachusetts in mass meeting assembled to consider our oppressions and the state of the country relative to the same, have resolved to address ourselves to you in an open letter, notwithstanding your extraordinary, your incomprehensible silence on the subject of our wrongs in your annual and other messages to Congress, as in your public utterances to the country at large. We address ourselves to you, Sir, not as suppliants, but as of right, as American citizens, whose servant you are, and to whom you are bound to listen, and for whom you are equally bound to speak, and upon occasion to act, as for any other body of your fellow-countrymen in like circumstances. We ask nothing for ourselves at your hands, as chief magistrate of the republic, to which all American citizens are not entitled. We ask for the enjoyment of life, liberty, and the pursuit of happiness equally with other men. We ask for the free and full exercise of all the rights of American freemen, guaranteed to us by the Constitution and laws of the Union, which you were solemnly sworn to obey and execute. We ask you for what belongs to us by the high sanction of Constitution and law, and the Democratic genius of our institutions and civilization. These rights are everywhere throughout the South denied to us, violently wrested from us by mobs, by lawless legislatures, and nullifying conventions, combinations, and conspiracies, openly, defiantly, under your eyes, in your constructive and actual presence. And we demand, which is a part of our rights, protection, security in our life, our liberty, and in the pursuit of our individual and social happiness under a government which we are bound to defend in war, and which is equally bound to furnish us in peace protection, at home and abroad. . . .

Are crying national transgressions and injustices more "injurious and menacing" to the Republic, as well as "shocking to its sentiments of humanity," when committed by a foreign state, in foreign territory, against a foreign people, than when they are committed by a portion of our own people at home? . . . Shall it be said that the federal government, with arms of Briareus, reaching to the utmost limits of the habitable globe for the protection of its citizens, for the liberation of alien islanders and the subjugation of others, is powerless to guarantee to certain of its citizens at home their inalienable right to life, liberty, and the pursuit of happiness, because those citizens happen to be Negroes residing in the southern section of our country? Do the colored people of the United States deserve equal consideration with the Cuban people at the hands of your administration, and shall they, though late, receive it? If, Sir, you have the disposition, as we know that you have the power, we are confident that you will be able to find a constitutional way to reach us in our extremity, and our enemies also, who are likewise enemies to great public interests and national tranquillity.

—ARCHIBALD H. GRIMKE, ET AL, *"Open Letter to President McKinley by Colored People of Massachusetts," October 3, 1899. This was one of several letters sent to McKinley by African-American groups, many associated with the Colored National League, that questioned why the president seemed to be more concerned with "ending the oppression" of foreigners than that of the victims of Southern racism.*

⚭

You ask me about what is called imperialism. Well, I have formed views about that question. I am at the disadvantage of not knowing whether our people are for or against spreading themselves over the face of the globe. I should be sorry if they are, for I don't think that it is wise or a necessary development. As to China, I quite approve of our government's action in getting free of that complication. They are withdrawing, I understand, having done what they wanted. That is quite right. We have no more business in China than in any other country that is not ours. There is the case of the Philippines. I have tried hard, and yet I cannot for the life of me comprehend how we got into that mess. Perhaps we could not have avoided it—perhaps it was inevitable that we should come to be fighting the natives of those islands—but I cannot understand it, and have never been able to get at the bottom of the origin of our antagonism to the natives. I thought we should act as their protector—not try to get them under our heel. We were to relieve them from Spanish tyranny to enable them to set up a government of their own, and we were to stand by and see that it got a fair trial. It was not to be a government according to our ideas, but a government that represented the feeling of the majority of the Filipinos, a government according to Filipino ideas. That would have been a worthy mission for the United States. But now—why? We have got into a mess, a quagmire from which each fresh step renders the difficulty of extrication immensely greater. I'm sure I wish I could see what we were getting out of it, and all it means to us as a nation.

> —MARK TWAIN, New York World, *October 6, 1900. Twain was in Great Britain when he made these comments. Long a critic of American empire, he had been sympathetic to U.S. efforts to end Spanish dominion over the Philippines and other colonies, but as it became clear that the U.S. was itself becoming a colonial power, he corrected his stance.*

⁂

I left these shores, at Vancouver, a red-hot imperialist. I wanted the American eagle to go screaming into the Pacific. It seemed tiresome and tame for it to content itself with the Rockies. Why not spread its wings over the Philippines, I asked myself? And I thought it would be a real good thing to do.

I said to myself, here are a people who have suffered for three centuries. We can make them as free as ourselves, give them a government and country of their own, put a miniature of the American Constitution afloat in the Pacific, start a brand new republic to take its place among the free nations of the world. It seemed to me a great task to which we had addressed ourselves.

But I have thought some more, since then, and I have read carefully the Treaty of Paris, and I have seen that we do not intend to free, but to subjugate the people of the Philippines. We have gone there to conquer, not to redeem.

We have also pledged the power of this country to maintain and protect the abominable system established in the Philippines by the Friars.

It should, it seems to me, be our pleasure and duty to make those people free, and let them deal with their own domestic questions in their own way. And so I am an anti-imperialist. I am opposed to having the eagle put its talons on any other land.

—MARK TWAIN, *"Mark Twain Home, An Anti-Imperialist,"* New
York Herald, *October 15, 1900.*

∾

When the government of the United States, in entering upon the war with Spain, proclaimed that its only object was the liberation of Cuba, denying all desire for national gain, its statement, although strictly true, was discredited by the civilized world, and the conduct of the administration during the past two years has, unhappily, justified the cynical distrust with which that declaration of unselfishness was received. The United States, in consequence, stands now convicted not only as a "criminal aggressor," but as a hypocritical aggressor, and the only way in which the fair name of our country can be restored is by the repudiation of the acts of the present administration by the people at the polls.

—JOSEPHINE SHAW LOWELL, *"Two Reasons in Favor of the
Election of William Jennings Bryan,"* City and State,
September 13, 1900.

We assert that no nation can long endure half republic and half empire, and we warn the American people that imperialism abroad will lead quickly and inevitably to despotism at home.

—DEMOCRATIC PARTY PLATFORM, *1900.*

℘

Mr. Chairman and Members of the Notification Committee:

. . . When the president, supported by a practically unanimous vote of the House and Senate, entered upon a war with Spain for the purpose of aiding the struggling patriots of Cuba, the country, without regard to party, applauded.

Although the Democrats realized that the administration would necessarily gain a political advantage from the conduct of a war which in the very nature of the case must soon end in a complete victory, they vied with the Republicans in the support which they gave to the president. When the war was over and the Republican leaders began to suggest the propriety of a colonial policy, opposition at once manifested itself.

When the president finally laid before the Senate a treaty which recognized the independence of Cuba, but provided for the cession of the Philippine Islands to the United States, the menace of imperialism became so apparent that many preferred to reject the treaty and risk the ills that might follow rather than take the chance of correcting the errors of the treaty by the independent action of this country. . . .

If it is right for the United States to hold the Philippine Islands permanently and imitate European empires in the government of colonies, the Republican Party ought to state its position and defend it, but it must expect the subject races to protest against such a policy and to resist to the extent of their ability.

The Filipinos do not need any encouragement from Americans now living. Our whole history has been an encouragement not only to the Filipinos, but to all who are denied a voice in their own government. If the Republicans are prepared to censure all who have used language calculated to make the Filipinos hate foreign domination, let them condemn the speech of Patrick Henry. When he uttered that passionate appeal, "Give me liberty or give me death," he expressed a sentiment which still echoes in the hearts of men.

Let them censure Jefferson; of all the statesmen of history none have used words so offensive to those who would hold their fellows in political bondage. Let them censure Washington, who declared that the colonists must choose between liberty and slavery. Or, if the statute of limitations has run again the sins of Henry and Jefferson and Washington, let them censure Lincoln, whose Gettysburg speech will be quoted in defense of popular government when the present advocates of force and conquest are forgotten. . . .

Those who would have this nation enter upon a career of empire must consider not only the effect of imperialism on the Filipinos, but they must also calculate its effects upon our own nation. We cannot repudiate the principle of self-government in the Philippines without weakening that principle here.

Lincoln said that the safety of this nation was not in its fleets, its armies, or its forts, but in the spirit which prizes liberty as the heritage of all men, in all lands, everywhere, and he warned his countrymen that they could not destroy this spirit without planting the seeds of despotism at their own doors.

Even now we are beginning to see the paralyzing influence of imperialism. Heretofore this nation has been prompt to express its sympathy with those who were fighting for civil liberty. While our sphere of activity has been limited to the Western Hemisphere, our sympathies have not been bounded by the seas. We have felt it due to ourselves and to the world, as well as to those who were struggling for the right to govern themselves, to proclaim the interest which our people have, from the date of their own independence, felt in every contest between human rights and arbitrary power.

Three-quarters of a century ago, when our nation was small, the struggles of Greece aroused our people, and Webster and Clay gave eloquent expression to the universal desire for Grecian independence. In 1896, all parties manifested a lively interest in the success of the Cubans, but now when a war is in progress in South Africa, which must result in the extension of the monarchical idea, or in the triumph of a republic, the advocates of imperialism in this country dare not say a word in behalf of the Boers. . . .

Our opponents, conscious of the weakness of their cause, seek to confuse imperialism with expansion, and have even dared to claim Jefferson as a supporter of their policy. Jefferson spoke so freely and used language with such precision that no one can be ignorant of his views. On one occasion he declared, "If there be one principle more deeply rooted than any other in the mind of every American, it is that we should have nothing to do with conquest." And again he said, "Conquest is not in our principles; it is inconsistent with our government."

The forcible annexation of territory to be governed by arbitrary power differs as much from the acquisition of territory to be built up into states as a monarchy differs from a democracy. The Democratic Party does not oppose expansion when expansion enlarges the area of the republic and incorporates land which can be settled by American citizens, or adds to our population people who are willing to become citizens and are capable of discharging their duties as such.

The acquisition of the Louisiana territory, Florida, Texas, and other tracts which have been secured from time to time enlarged the republic and the Constitution followed the flag into the new territory. It is now proposed to seize upon distant territory already more densely populated than our own country and to force upon the people a government for which there is no warrant in our Constitution or our laws. . . .

If we have an imperial policy we must have a great standing army as its natural and necessary complement. The spirit which will justify the forcible annexation of the Philippine Islands will justify the seizure of other islands and the domination of other people, and with wars of conquest we can expect a certain if not rapid, growth of our military establishment.

That a large permanent increase in our regular army is intended by Republican leaders is not a matter of conjecture, but a matter of fact. In his message of December 5,1898, the president asked for authority to increase the standing army to one hundred thousand. In 1896 the army contained about twenty-five thousand. Within two years the president asked for four times that many, and a Republican house of representatives complied with the request after the Spanish treaty had been signed, and when no country was at war with the United States.

If such an army is demanded when an imperial policy is contemplated, but not openly avowed, what may be expected if the people encourage the Republican Party by endorsing its policy at the polls?

A large standing army is not only a pecuniary burden to the people and, if accompanied by compulsory service, a constant source of irritation, but it is ever a menace to a republican form of government.

The army is the personification of force, and militarism will inevitably change the ideals of the people and turn the thoughts of our young men from the arts of peace to the science of war. The government which relies for its defense upon its citizens is more likely to be just than one which has at call a large body of professional soldiers.

A small standing army and a well-equipped and well-disciplined state militia are sufficient at ordinary times, and in an emergency the nation should in the future as in the past place its dependence upon the volunteers who come from all occupations at their country's call and return to productive labor when their services are no longer required—men who fight when the country needs fighters and work when the country needs workers. The Republican platform assumes that the Philippine Islands will be retained under American sovereignty, and we have a right to demand of the Republican leaders a discussion of the future status of the Filipino. Is he to be a citizen or a subject? Are we to bring into the body politic eight or ten million Asiatics so different from us in race and history that amalgamation is impossible? Are they to share with us in making the laws and shaping the destiny of this nation? No Republican of prominence has been bold enough to advocate such a proposition.

The McEnery resolution, adopted by the Senate immediately after the ratification of the treaty, expressly negatives this idea. The Democratic platform describes the situation when it says that the Filipinos cannot be citizens without endangering our civilization. Who will dispute it? And what is the alternative? If the Filipino is not to be a citizen, shall we make him a subject? On that question, the Democratic platform speaks with equal emphasis. It declares that the Filipino cannot be a subject without endangering our form of government. A republic can have no subjects. A subject is possible only in a government resting upon force; he is unknown in a government derived without consent and taxation without representation.

The Republican platform says that "the largest measure of self-government consistent with their welfare and our duties shall be secured to them [the Filipinos] by law." This is a strange doctrine for a government which owes its very existence to the men who offered

their lives as a protest against government without consent and taxation without representation. In what respect does the position of the
Republican Party differ from the position taken by the English government in 1776? Did not the English government promise a good government to the colonists? What king ever promised a bad government
to his people? Did not the English government promise that the
colonists should have the largest measure of self-government consistent
with their welfare and English duties? Did not the Spanish government promise to give to the Cubans the largest measure of self-government consistent with their welfare and Spanish duties? The whole
difference between a monarchy and a republic may be summed up in
one sentence. In a monarchy the king gives to the people what he
believes to be a good government; in a republic the people secure for
themselves what they believe to be a good government. . . .

A missionary recently told me that the stars and stripes once saved
his life because his assailant recognized our flag as a flag that had no
blood upon it. Let it be known that our missionaries are seeking souls
instead of sovereignty; let it be known that instead of being the
advance guard of conquering armies, they are going forth to help and
uplift, having their loins girt about with truth and their feet shod with
the preparation of the gospel of peace, wearing the breastplate of
righteousness and carrying the sword of the spirit; let it be known that
they are citizens of a nation which respects the rights of the citizens
of other nations as carefully as it protects the rights of its own citizens,
and the welcome given to our missionaries will be more cordial than
the welcome extended to the missionaries of any other nation . . .

—WILLIAM JENNINGS BRYAN, *speech in which he accepted*
the nomination of the Democratic Party to stand as its presidential
candidate, August 8, 1900.

∽

We recognize imperialism as only a symptom of the disease which
has been for years undermining the health of our body politic. The
disease has assumed a violent form in that direction and we intend to
fight it so far as we are able, and to fight it to the end; but we believe

the fight can be made under the flag of a new party, far better than under Mr. Bryan's tarnished banner.

—THOMAS MOSS OSBORNE, *speech to the founding convention of the National Party, which argued that Bryan was not a pure enough anti-imperialist, September 5, 1900. The third party, which pledged "to procure the renunciation of all imperial or colonial pretensions with regard to foreign countries claimed to have been acquired through or in consequence of naval or military operations of the last two years," drew initial interest from prominent anti-imperialists. Ultimately, however, most chose to back Bryan.*

The undersigned citizens of the United States regard with profound apprehension the course of the present administration in Puerto Rico and the Philippines. Our prior acquisitions were of adjacent territory for the extension of the area of constitutional government and the creation of new states of the union. We made their few inhabitants citizens; our people settled them; we there established the institutions of freedom. For the first time in our history, it is now proposed that the president and Congress shall rule vast territories and millions of men outside our constitutional system. Officials sworn to support the Constitution and deriving all their power therefrom have acquired colonies and assumed arbitrary authority to govern their inhabitants without consent and to tax them without representation. This policy offers to the people of Puerto Rico and the Philippines no hope of independence, no respect of American citizenship, no representation in the congress which taxes them. This is the government of men by arbitrary power; this is imperialism.

We believe that it is the first duty of the American people to stamp with their disapproval doctrines so hostile to liberty and dangerous to constitutional government. If they are to remain free and their government is to continue representative, their servants must not have or exercise any but constitutional powers. Between the claim of freedom that all men are entitled to equal political rights and the dogma of tyranny that might makes right there is no middle ground.

We have not prior to this year supported the candidacy of Mr.

Bryan. We do not now concur in certain of his views on minor issues. Yet his position on the supreme issue of the present campaign is so sound and his advocacy of it has been so able and courageous that we now favor his election as the most effective way of showing disapproval of Mr. McKinley's course. Without claiming any special political influence, we unite, for what our example may be worth to our fellow citizens, in this statement of proposed action in the presence of "a greater danger than we have encountered since the pilgrims landed at Plymouth—the danger that we are to be transformed from a republic, founded on the Declaration of Independence, guided by the counsels of Washington, into a vulgar, commonplace empire, founded on physical force." We invite the cooperation of all independent voters to avert this great and impending danger.

> —AMERICAN ANTI-IMPERIALIST LEAGUE STATEMENT,
> *signed by former Secretary of the Treasury George S. Boutwell,*
> *former Attorney General Judson Harmon, former American Bar*
> *Association President Moorfield Storey, journalist Edwin L. Godkin,*
> *educator John Dewey, social reformer William Lloyd Garrison,*
> *and dozens of other prominent American critics of the U.S.*
> *occupation of the Philippines, October 22, 1900.*

∽

But it was of no real avail. The country had gone too far. Too much had happened to deaden the feelings of the people. The Democratic Convention of 1900 was inspiring to the highest degree, and Mr. Bryan's speech of acceptance placed him on a higher plane as an orator than anything he had ever done. But after their echoes had died away the political atmosphere tingled with a suspicious silence. One hundred years after Thomas Jefferson routed the hosts of centralism and special privilege, imperialism in full armor stepped into power in America, easily brushing aside a man who, in some particulars, is equal to Jefferson himself.

> —EDGAR LEE MASTERS, *"Mr. Bryan's Campaigns,"* The New
> Star Chamber and Other Essays *(Hammersmark Publishing*
> *Company, 1904). Masters, the biographer and poet who authored*
> Spoon River Anthology, *expressed the disappointment of anti-*

imperialists at Bryan's defeat by McKinley. Bryan carried the South and much of the interior West, but failed to win the vote-rich states of the Middle West and New England. Bryan's anti-imperialism, while appealing, was not a sufficient lure for voters of regions that had been Republican since the party's founding. The defeat dealt a serious blow to the anti-imperialist movement.

☙

To the American People:

The Anti-Imperialist Leagues of the United States have been silent since the presidential election, but not because they have less faith in their cause or believe the battle lost. They had hoped that those who voted for Mr. McKinley, while disapproving his policy in the West Indies and the Philippines, would see that their votes were mis-interpreted, and would make their disapproval known and felt. They had hoped that Congress would claim its place in our government, and would insist that the principles of freedom must be recognized and applied wherever our country holds sway. They had hoped that the Supreme Court would with no uncertain voice declare that no human being under our control could be without the rights secured by our Constitution, and that neither president nor Congress, nor both together, could exercise absolute power over men entitled to the protection of our flag.

These hopes have not been realized. Where Benjamin Harrison nobly led, too few have followed. The war in the Philippines has been prosecuted with unrelenting cruelty until the resistance of the unhappy islanders seems to have been crushed. Many thousands of their bravest men have been killed, or have died of disease during the con-test; and today the president exercises a power as despotic as the czar's over the whole Filipino nation. Congress has abdicated its function, has given these people into the president's hands, and has adjourned without attempting to deal with the questions presented by the islands. Already it has learned that free government is hard and absolutism easy—a dangerous lesson in a republic. Liberty and abso-lutism cannot exist together.

Three years ago, Congress, by joint resolution, declared "that the people of the island of Cuba are and of right ought to be free and independent"—that they were then independent, and were justly entitled to be independent. This country intervened to establish their independence, and by the same resolution promised not to exercise "sovereignty, jurisdiction, or control over said island, except for the pacification thereof." Today, the president is the absolute ruler of Cuba. He spends the revenues of the island as he pleases. No constitution, no law, fetters his power. At his instance, Congress has violated the nation's pledge. The "independent" Cuban people have been told that they will not be allowed to establish any government in their own land, unless they surrender in part the control of their finances and foreign affairs; unless they give to this country the possession of strategic points on their territory; and unless, in addition, they give to it the right to intervene in their domestic affairs whenever in the judgment of our authorities the occasion shall demand such intervention. They are offered no option to refuse these demands, which are backed by the presence of American troops on their soil. Thus, to the whole world, our course has become an example of national perfidy. The enforced submission of the Cubans to these unjust requirements has made the stain on our national record indelible. . . .

"Let it be remembered," said the constitutional Congress, "that it has ever been the pride and boast of America that the rights for which she contended were the rights of human nature." When this country denies to millions of men the rights which we have ever claimed, not only for ourselves but for all men, its policy is suicidal. As Lincoln said, "Those who deny liberty to others deserve it not themselves, and under a just God cannot long retain it." Indifference to liberty anywhere breeds indifference to liberty everywhere. No man can defend despotic methods abroad and long retain his loyalty to democracy at home . . .

—AMERICAN ANTI-IMPERIALIST LEAGUE, *July 4, 1901,*
press release. A copy of the original document can be found in the
William Augustus Coffut Papers, located in the Library of Congress.

THE PESKY ANTI-IMPERIALIST

It is most provoking, we know, for anti-imperialists to pretend that they are still alive. They have been killed so often. After 1899, we were to hear no more of them. In 1900, they were again pronounced dead, although, like the obstinate Irishman, they continued to protest that, if they were dead, they were not conscious of it. Last year the slain were slaughtered once more, and that time buried as well, with all due ceremony. Yet the impudent creatures have resumed activity during the past few months just as if their epitaphs had not been composed again and again.

And the worst of it is that they seem to have acquired a strange power over the public and our government. What the lonely and ridiculous anti-imperialist was whispering in the closet, a year ago, thousands are now shouting from the housetops. The impossible measures which the absurd fellow was demanding have been adopted by the president of the United States, and have even compelled the approval of Congress. When General [Frederick] Funston, for example, began his blethering, it was the foolish anti-imperialists who said that the president ought to reprimand and silence him and how the jeers arose! That was just like the silly old impracticables—attacking a popular hero. But presently the said hero had a gag forcibly inserted between his teeth by executive order, just as if the anti-imperialists had been right about it from the beginning. It is not necessary to recall the triumphs of the mistaken beings in the whole matter of the Philippine investigation and of court-martial for the implicated officers. Enough to say that, in the entire affair, the administration and Congress have acted on the demand and as if by the advice of that handful of out-of-date and laughable persons, the anti-imperialists.

The phenomenon occasions much scratching of the imperialist head. How to account for it? Imperialist editors and statesmen are puzzled. Their despised and helpless opponents are actually swaying the policy of the government! It is absurd, of course, really quite preposterous, but there stands the fact. It is all very fine, and it's lots of fun, to make merry at the expense of wrong-headed people who get in the way of national progress, and hope to turn back the hands of the dial of evolution, but how if they succeed? Prodigiously unreasonable, it goes without saying, and truly disgusting to the well-ordered mind of the imperialist; but what is the explanation?

Very simple, cocksure brothers of the empire, we assure you. All you have to do is to remember that anti-imperialism is only another name for old-fashioned Americanism, and all will be clear to you. An American who has a settled body of convictions, as to which he is ready to speak out at a moment's notice, and which he is ready to apply promptly and sharply to every fresh set of circumstances that turns up; who with his inherited ideas has an inherited courage, an inherited love of equality and justice; who has also a sense of humor which cannot be imposed upon by Uncle Sam masquerading in Louis Quatorze garments—why, he is a natural born anti-imperialist, and it is simply his Americanism that makes him think and act as he does. . . .

This, in a word, is what makes the anti-imperialist so pesky—he is American to the core. He has fed on his country's tradition. With him, as with Governor Andrew and with Lincoln, justice does not depend upon the color of a man's skin. He cannot distinguish between the flag and the principles which first set the flag flying. With John Quincy Adams he believes that the Declaration of Independence is the very Alcoran of American political doctrine. And he does not in the least mind being in a minority. He remembers that the history of success is the history of minorities. Sneers and jeers are alike indifferent to him, and when the Red Slayer thinks to have made an end of him, he turns and passes and comes again. He is content to bide his time, knowing that the road of popular persuasion is a long one, though sure in the end, and that republics cannot march to their goal with "the decisiveness and consistency of despotism."

—NEW YORK EVENING POST, *May 3, 1902. The reference to "the whole matter of the Philippine investigation" serves as a reminder of the abuses carried out by U.S. forces, which caused a national outcry not unlike the firestorm that arose in 2004 over prison abuses in Iraq.*

SIX

America Is Not Threatened

A Century of Misdeeds in Latin

America and the Caribbean

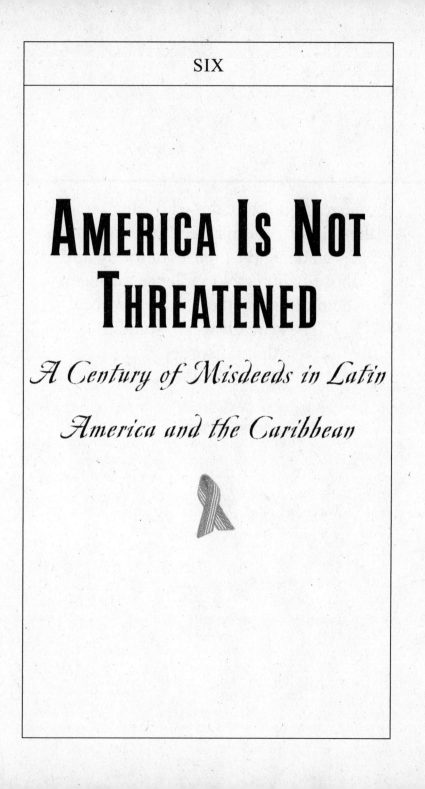

"America is not threatened by any nation in the Western Hemisphere. No assault has been made against our country by any of those nations. No violence has been committed by them upon America. They are all weak, some of them disordered.

—U.S. SENATOR JOHN BLAINE

While some of the colonies that the United States acquired in the settlement of the Spanish-American War would eventually free themselves from the grip of the American Empire, successive American presidents would remain enthralled with the imperialist enterprise. The object of the ambition, more frequently than not, was found close to home. Teddy Roosevelt, who was always up to mischief, corrupted the Monroe Doctrine by adding a corollary that committed the United States to serve as a well-armed debt collector for foreigners—i.e., U.S. corporations—that had outstanding complaints against countries in the Western Hemisphere. The era of "Dollar Diplomacy" had begun.

Suddenly, talk of democracy and justice became window dressing as, in Frederick Howe's words, "Our State Department was thinking in terms of oil in Mesopotamia, of oil in Mexico, of gold and railroads in Haiti and Santo Domingo." And if there was not a corporate whim to be satisfied, there would be an ideological urge—as U.S. troops decamped to countries throughout the Caribbean and Latin America in search of socialist, then communist, and, finally, terrorist monsters to destroy. "The dirty business," as newspaper columnist Murray Kempton described U.S. meddling in the affairs of the supposedly sovereign nations of the Western Hemisphere, would define America's engagement with her neighbors through the twentieth century. It is a measure of the singlemindedness of the American imperialists that countries that were in the sites of the expansionists at the start of the century—Cuba, Haiti, and El Salvador—would remain there at its close.

Yet, there was, always, the cry of objection from those who noted, as did Wisconsin Senator John Blaine in the 1920s, that, "America is not threatened by any nation in the Western Hemisphere." When American presidents intrigued against Mexico in the 1910s and 1920s, they were restrained by congressional oversight and popular campaigns such as

Crystal Eastman's American Union Against Militarism. After the Union succeeded in preventing a full-scale U.S. invasion of revolutionary Mexico in 1916, Eastman claimed a win for the anti-imperialists, declaring that, "We must make it known to everybody that the people acting directly—not through their governments or diplomats or armies, stopped that war and can stop all wars if enough of them will act together and act quickly." The gospel Eastman preached was a good one. Anti-imperialists did need to act quickly if they hoped to keep up with the militarists, the corporatists, and the adventurists who had occupied the federal departments of state and defense.

When they were slow to react initially, as had been the case after U.S. Marines were dispatched to occupy Haiti in 1915 and the Dominican Republic in 1916, Americans would soon find that the ugliest and most indefensible of colonialist abuses were being committed in their name. African-American activists, such as W. E. B. Du Bois and Moorfield Storey, the first president of the National Association for the Advancement of Colored People, were the first to sound the alarm, aided by the journalist Ernest Gruening, the zelig of American anti-imperialism who would turn up again and again on the right side of lonely struggles against empire. Gruening's articles, exposing the brutality of the U.S. occupation of Haiti, would inspire political progressives, such as Senate Foreign Relations Committee Chair William Borah and Wisconsin Senator Robert M. La Follette to take up the cause of the islanders. In 1924, when La Follette mounted a radical campaign for the presidency, his Progressive Party platform read, "We denounce the mercenary system of foreign policy under recent administrations in the interests of financial imperialists, oil monopolists, and international bankers, which has at times degraded our State Department from its high service as a strong and kindly intermediary of defenseless governments to a trading outpost for those interests and concession-seekers engaged in the exploitations of weaker nations, as contrary to the will of the American people, destructive of domestic development and provocative of war. We favor an active foreign policy to bring about a revision of the Treaty of Versailles in accordance with the terms of the armistice, and to promote firm treaty agreements with all nations to outlaw wars, abolish conscription, drastically reduce land, air, and naval armaments, and guarantee public referendum on peace and war."

La Follette's protégé, Blaine, would come to the Senate in 1926, align with Borah and prod the U.S. to step back from a career of empire and adopt a Good Neighbor Policy that, while still guided by mercantile impulses, would, for a time, ease the grip of empire and in some instances actually place the United States on the side of democracy. But the period of light dimmed with the coming of the Cold War. The United States made itself, in the words of muckraking journalist I. F. Stone, "a global gendarme." But the ugly record of invasions, occupations, corruptions, and assassinations—and their frequent association with new manifestations of the old "Dollar Diplomacy"—made the postwar era, in the words of 1970s Senate Foreign Relations Committee Chair Frank Church, "a period in which the moral content of government decision-making was subordinated to all the pragmatic attitudes of the time." After the U.S. Central Intelligence Agency and its network of thugs engineered a coup in Chile, Church described the agency as a "rogue elephant rampaging out of control." Church, whose hero was fellow Idahoan Borah, used his powerful committee chairmanship to impose a measure of control on U.S. intelligence agencies. Evidence of the extent of CIA lawlessness was such that a Republican president, Gerald Ford, felt compelled to issue a 1976 executive order that made it official policy that, "No employee of the United States government shall engage in, or conspire to engage in, political assassination."

Within five years, however, the administration of a new, Cold War-obsessed president, Ronald Reagan, would make a mockery of the attempts by Church and others to force American foreign policy "to conform once more to our historic ideals." As U.S. Representative Ron Dellums would note, "The tide of United States intervention and interference in the domestic politics of Caribbean and Latin American nations had risen and fallen, but with the advent of the Reagan administration in the early 1980s, it reached new heights." Reagan steered billions of U.S. dollars, via legal and illegal routes, into initiatives designed to undermine social-justice movements, land reforms, and democracy in Central America. Without a declaration of war, Reagan sent U.S. Marines to occupy the Caribbean island nation of Grenada and, in direct contravention of the laws of the land, his aides initiated and sustained the Contra War against the government of Nicaragua. Reagan and his vice president, George Bush, would avoid accountability, though key aides would be indicted for high crimes and misdemeanors.

With the end of the Cold War, the military interventions continued in countries such as Colombia. So, too, did the meddling, particularly in the affairs of Cuba and Venezuela. A new form of "Dollar Diplomacy" was introduced, in the form of free trade agreements, such as NAFTA and the proposed FTAA. And, of course, Puerto Rico, taken from Spain after the war of 1898, continued as an American colony, remaining, in the aptly chosen words of poet Martín Espada, "a political anachronism, a throwback to the age of gunboat diplomacy and the handlebar mustache." In reality, however, only the handlebar mustaches have disappeared.

⊸∞⊶

The United States has had a long and unfortunate history of supporting anti-democratic, pro-military governments in the region. Often these interventions were to support American business interests. The phrase "banana republic" comes from the invasion of Honduras by U.S. troops in 1903 to protect the interests of American banana growers.

—REAR ADMIRAL EUGENE CARROLL, JR. (USN-RETIRED), *October, 9, 1994, during the show* School of the Americas: At War With Democracy. *Carroll served for many years as the director of the Center for Defense Information.*

∽

Make it plain to Mexico and to all mankind that we will not, under any circumstances, exercise any measure of sovereignty, jurisdiction, or control over Mexico or any portion of her territory.

—U.S. SENATOR ROBERT LA FOLLETTE, *1916, from a Senate speech referenced in "La Follette's Foreign Policy: From Imperialism to Anti-Imperialism,"* Wisconsin Magazine of History, *46 (Summer 1963). La Follette urged the U.S. to withdraw troops from Veracruz in Mexico "at the earliest possible moment," 1916. The pressure on President Woodrow Wilson to curtail U.S. military adventurism in Mexico came from within Congress and from a broad cross section of American political, labor, and religious leaders— many of them associated with the American Union Against Militarism.*

We must make it known to everybody that the people acting directly—not through their governments or diplomats or armies, stopped that war and can stop all wars if enough of them will act together and act quickly.

> —CRYSTAL EASTMAN, *1916, quoted in Alan Dawley's* Changing the World: American Progressives in War and Revolution *(Princeton University Press, 2003), hailing the success of the American Union Against Militarism's campaign to prevent a full-scale invasion of Mexico after a "Punitive Expedition," led by General "Black Jack" Pershing, crossed the border in pursuit of Pancho Villa.*

∽

When we say "that every people should be left free to determine its own policy, its own way of development, unhindered, unthreatened, unafraid," do we mean the Philippine Islands, Haiti, San Domingo, Nicaragua, Mexico? If not, why not? Can we preach our doctrine at the peace table while the Philippines hang like a millstone around our necks? There is—there can be—only one answer to that question, and the president as our representative must make it, or we stand convicted of insincerity.

We cannot control other nations, or force upon them our political ideas. Our very principles forbid it, for each nation has a right to its own. But we can control our own conduct, and we can set an example to the world of sincere devotion to our principles, which will exert a far more powerful influence for good than thousands of beautifully phrased speeches proclaiming principles which in practice we reject.

> —MOORFIELD STOREY, *speech in which he argued that Wilson's preaching about "making the world safe for democracy" rang hollow when the U.S. was meddling in countries such as Haiti and Mexico, 1919. The first president of the National Association for the Advancement of Colored People, Storey was, as well, president of the Anti-Imperialist League and chair of the Haiti-Santo Domingo Independence Society.*

∽

I believe that war is murder. I believe that armies and navies are at bottom the tinsel and braggadocio of oppression and wrong, and I believe that the wicked conquest of weaker and darker nations by nations whiter and stronger, but foreshadows the death of that strength . . .

> —W. E. B. DU BOIS, Darkwater: Voices from within the Veil
> *(Harcourt, Brace and Howe, 1920). During the 1920s, Du Bois
> became an increasingly vocal critic of U.S. military meddling in
> Haiti and other countries in the Western Hemisphere. Du Bois
> argued that, "The world today consists, not of races, but of the
> imperial commercial group of master capitalists, international and
> predominantly white: the national classes of the several nations,
> white, yellow, and brown, with strong blood bonds, common
> languages, and common history; the international laboring class of
> all colors: the backward, oppressed groups of nature-folk,
> predominantly yellow, black, and brown."*

⚬⚬

In July 1915, one of the recurring revolutions broke out in Haiti. The United States forcibly intervened, and U.S. Marines were landed "for the purpose of preventing further rioting and for the protection of foreign life and property." The American forces, the secretary of the Navy reported, "were welcomed by the masses of the Haitian people." Political and financial control followed. Admiral Caperton, and not the Haitian Congress, decided when it was time to elect a Haitian president; and when that time came a Haitian agreeable to the United States was chosen because he realized "that Haiti must agree to any terms demanded by the United States and he professes to believe that any terms laid down by us will be for Haitian benefit." A treaty was duly ratified by which the United States established a customs receivership, financial control, and a native gendarmerie, officered by Americans. Thereupon, in December 1915, Secretary Daniels expressed the hope that "Haiti will soon be established on a firm basis, and that at an early date a large proportion of American forces can be withdrawn." Except for the transfer of some of the marines to quell disturbances in Santo Domingo, this hope was not fulfilled. A year later the State

Department advised the Navy Department "that the time has not yet arrived for the withdrawal of the naval forces now in that country and the termination of martial law. Until such time as the gendarmerie has proven itself loyal and efficient in all emergencies and the internal peace of Haiti is thereby definitely assured it is the desire of this department that the present status be continued." And the "present status" still continues. In the meantime the Navy Department glows in recounting, from year to year, the high achievements of intervention. In his report for 1918, Secretary Daniels tells us that Haiti, under the direction and guidance of naval administration, has, in peace and quiet, and just laws well-administered, enjoyed development, prosperity, and tranquility. The marines have not only preserved order, but have aided in the system of internal improvement.

In both Santo Domingo and Haiti the people have learned that the United States has no policy except one of unselfish friendship and neighborliness, and is using its good offices to secure stable conditions that will redound to the welfare of the people of these two countries, long disturbed by revolution and intrigue.

In his last annual report of December 1919, Secretary Daniels gave to the country this happy summary:

> Called to restore order and administer the finances of these governments [Haiti and Santo Domingo] close to us in geography and interest, it is gratifying to report that there has been freedom from all suggestion of selfish aims on the part of the occupying civilian and military agencies. The development of the country, the education and welfare of the people, improvement in agriculture, the firm and kind administration of justice have borne their fruit in the most prosperous era in the history of these neighbor governments.

This official contentment with our rule in Haiti began to be challenged first by murmurs and later by louder voices of criticism. Ugly charges became articulate—that there was financial exploitation, enforced through brutality against the natives. But the country at large, indifferent to our Caribbean ventures, was not aroused 'till it read that the major-general commandant of the crack marine corps "was shocked beyond expression by the behavior of the marines in Haiti." The behavior which aroused the burning protest of General Barnett involved nothing less than the use of the corvée system (a form of peonage) and "practically indiscriminate killing of natives." On top of this disclosure came the declaration of Admiral Knapp that the United States would have to remain in Haiti for a generation. Thus, so quickly and completely had Secretary Daniels's hope of early withdrawal vanished, at least in officialdom. To be sure the State Department, in an inspired statement, softened the gloomy outlook of Admiral Knapp by indicating that the Haitians would be granted "home rule" step by step—home rule to be accorded to a country that functioned as a republic for a hundred years before our intervention and even now is a charter member of the league.

These facts tempt generalization: It is the same old story of temporary intervention to restore order, ripening by steady stages into effectual annexation; it is the same old story of economic imperialism, the story of Great Britain, France, Italy, Belgium, and Portugal in Africa, of American enterprise in Panama, Santo Domingo, Nicaragua, and Haiti; exploitation of and brutality toward the "inferior race" and degradation of the "superior race," consequences inevitably attending any violation of the principle of non-intervention. Thus runs the argument of the doctrinaire liberal. . . .

Both President Wilson and President-elect Harding talk much about America's "leadership of the world." Only through candor and disinterestedness may she exercise it. If America truly acted upon the principle of trusteeship in the rule of alien peoples the practice would receive a powerful impetus, and we would acquire enhanced authority in asserting this principle against other nations.

—FELIX FRANKFURTER, *"Haiti and Intervention,"* The New
Republic, *December 15, 1920. Frankfurter would later
serve on the U.S. Supreme Court.*

HAITI UNDER OCCUPATION

For six years American armed forces have controlled the two small republics that share the Caribbean island that Columbus called Hispaniola, but which is now known by the original Indian name of Haiti, the "land of mountains." For the last two years, report and rumor, filtering northward, have hinted that all was not well along the Artibonite and the Ozama, respective Potomacs of the republics of Haiti and Santo Domingo. There followed in due course one of those harmless political diversions in which we take delight, a congressional investigation. . . .

It was on the steamer Haiti-bound that I gained a first-hand realization of the gulf that separates the Haitians from the Americans, who graciously assert that they are there to "big-brother" the Haitians. While chatting on the deck, several officers' wives learned that it was my first visit.

"You must come and see us," said one, with the friendly cordiality of Americans in remote corners of the globe. "We have great times there. Do you know any one in Haiti?"

I gave a name in reply. The name was nondescript.

"Is he a Frenchman?" they asked.

"No; he is a Haitian."

An almost imperceptible raising of eyebrows, and the conversation lapsed. I gathered that it was unusual, not to say queer, to go to Haiti and know Haitians.

In Haiti, I found the social line between Haitians and Americans rigidly drawn. When the military occupation took place in 1915, the Haitians, regardless of their feeling about the larger aspects of the invasion, extended to individual Americans a truly Haitian hospitality, inviting our naval officers into their homes and their clubs. Several months later, however, when the officers' wives arrived, these social relations ceased abruptly. The officers who had been generously feted never again entered the homes they had visited, nor did their wives, who instead rebuffed the kindly advances of the Haitian women. Several other episodes caused American officers to be barred from the Haitian clubs, and, conversely, the newly created American club admitted no Haitians. During my stay in Haiti, an

American newspaper representative was requested by the manage-
ment of the Hotel Montagne not to receive Haitians except on the
back porch. Complaints had been made by American officers who
were guests in the hotel. Jim Crow had arrived in Haiti! . . .

Today Haiti is peaceful, commercially stagnant, and poignantly
unhappy. After one hundred and twelve years of freedom, its people
suddenly found their country invaded and conquered. For six years,
the rigors of martial law have held this little island in its grip. Martial
law is martial law. It cannot be camouflaged into a tea party or a benefit performance.

The black man in Haiti was not very successful in his experiment
in self-government, but we Anglo-Saxons have always insisted that
even imperfect self-government is preferable to more efficient
imposed government. Then, too, Haiti was the experimental labora-
tory, the living workshop of the black race. Wasn't the experiment
worth safeguarding?

—ERNEST GRUENING, *"Haiti Under Occupation,"* The Century,
    April 1922. A Nation *magazine editor, Gruening was an active*
    supporter of Robert M. La Follette's 1924 presidential campaign on
    the Progressive Party ticket. Like Gruening, La Follette called for
    the end to U.S. military occupation of Caribbean countries.

∽

We denounce the mercenary system of foreign policy under recent
administrations in the interests of financial imperialists, oil monopolists, and international bankers, which has, at times, degraded our
State Department from its high service as a strong and kindly intermediary of defenseless governments to a trading outpost for those
interests and concession-seekers engaged in the exploitations of
weaker nations, as contrary to the will of the American people,
destructive of domestic development, and provocative of war. We
favor an active foreign policy to bring about a revision of the
Versailles Treaty in accordance with the terms of the armistice, and
to promote firm treaty agreements with all nations to outlaw wars,

abolish conscription, drastically reduce land, air and naval armaments, and guarantee public referendum on peace and war.

> —PROGRESSIVE PARTY, *platform statement on foreign policy,*
> *1924. Running the ticket of Robert La Follette and Burton K.*
> *Wheeler, the independent Progressive Party argued that it was not*
> *the job of the U.S. government, and especially not the job of the U.S.*
> *military, to protect the interests of U.S.-based corporations operating*
> *in other countries. La Follette argued that such entanglements*
> *invariably drew the United States into unnecessary wars. La Follette*
> *won one-sixth of the national vote, carried his native state of*
> *Wisconsin, and ran second in eleven additional states.*

∽

[It is] a war waged privately by President Coolidge in defiance of the
Constitution, without the consent of Congress or the approval of the
American people.

> —U.S. SENATOR BURTON K. WHEELER, *referring to the*
> *U.S. invasion of Nicaragua, 1926. Wheeler, a Montana Democrat,*
> *was a fierce critic of what came to be known as "dollar diplomacy."*
> *As Wheeler argued, "A dramatic example of the policy was Calvin*
> *Coolidge's decision to send the United States Marines into*
> *Nicaragua in late 1926. The leathernecks landed to protect the*
> *forcible overthrow of the U.S. backed Nicaraguan government—and,*
> *thus, retain control for some New York bankers of that little country's*
> *national bank and railroad." Years later, in his autobiography,*
> Yankee from the West, *the Montanan would argue that "taking sides*
> *in internal controversies is war by whatever name you call it."*

∽

[The United States must not] assume the role of censor for Central American revolutions.

> —U.S. SENATOR WILLIAM BORAH, *statement on*
> *U.S interventions in Nicaragua, December 24, 1916. Borah,*
> *the powerful chair of the Senate Foreign Relations Committee,*
> *objected to the "fetish of force in America" when it came to dealing*
> *with other countries. He said that unless the U.S. was threatened*
> *by another country, military interventions were "unnecessary*
> *and therefore immoral."*

∽

The truth is that effort is being made to get this country into a shameless, cowardly, little war with Mexico.

> —U.S. SENATOR WILLIAM BORAH, *statement condemning*
> *efforts by business interests to draw the U.S. into war with Mexico,*
> *December 24, 1926. American oil companies were upset that the*
> *government of Mexican President Plutarco Elias Calles was*
> *attempting to tax and regulate them. The oil companies cried for U.S.*
> *intervention to block Mexican "bolshevism" and their appeal gained*
> *support within the Coolidge administration. But Borah's fierce*
> *opposition to U.S. military intervention in Mexico led to a 79–0 vote*
> *by the Senate calling for arbitration rather than war. Borah's action*
> *was hailed by former Chilean President Arturo Alessandri as a*
> *"brilliant defense in favor of sovereignty of all the nations of the*
> *earth, equal before the law." When Borah was "accused of" taking*
> *the side of Mexican leaders over that of U.S. officials, he declared,*
> *"God has made us neighbors, let justice make us friends."*

∽

I have failed to find a single case, I have failed to find a single piece of legislation that justifies the conduct of the administration in the affairs of Nicaragua.

> —U.S. SENATOR JOHN BLAINE, *1928, quoted in "Senator*
> *John I. Blaine: An Independent Progressive During 'Normandy.'"*
> Wisconsin Magazine of History, *60 (Autumn 1976). Blaine, a*
> *progressive Republican from Wisconsin, came to the Senate in 1927*

and began to agitate immediately for the end of all U.S. occupations
and interventions in the affairs of Latin American and Caribbean
nations. While President Coolidge said the marines had been
dispatched to protect U.S. business interests in Nicauagua, Blaine
argued that the United States had no responsibility, or right, to
intervene in other countries on behalf of U.S. business interests.
Even when some pressed for the United States to intervene on the
side of supposedly noble forces in civil wars, Blaine said he was
"against every commitment that in any way bound us in the slightest
degree to the wars and quarrels of foreign governments." When U.S.
troops were forced to enter a country to protect the property of
American corporations, Blaine argued that they did so not under the
American flag but under "the black flag, the flag of piracy." Said
Blaine, "The imperialism of the dollar [is] as deadly, as stifling, as
the imperialism of a government acting through force of arms, and
sometimes more effective."

∽

We have turned the Monroe Doctrine into an agency of mischief for
America, not for her protection or the protection of weaker nations
and peoples (but as an instrument that made American intervention),
the wet nurse for alien governments, money lenders, adventurers,
and concession-grabbers in their career of expansion, extension, and
exploitation.

—U.S. SENATOR JOHN BLAINE, *arguing in Congress against*
claims by the Coolidge administration that the Monroe Doctrine
justified U.S. intervention in the affairs of Latin American and
Caribbean lands, 1928. Blaine argued that "all the nations of the
Western Hemisphere have an equality, and that the strong have no
right to ride down the weaker nations; and (that U.S. interventions
abroad should be seen as) an act of aggression against the small
and defenseless nations." Blaine proposed an amendment to the
Constitution that made clear that the president had no authority to
send troops beyond the borders of the U.S. without full
congressional approval. Said Blaine, "If a president then attempted
to usurp this power he would not only be liable for impeachment but
also for prosecution and imprisonment."

∽

One meets the complaint in Haiti that the Americans are training not police, but soldiers, and one cannot help wondering what the effect of such a force would be after American withdrawal.

—EMILY GREENE BALCH, Occupied Haiti, *1927.*
A Women's International League for Peace and Freedom Committee was appointed to investigate conditions in Haiti, where U.S. Marines controlled the country. Their report concluded that "there has been for some time a drift towards imperialism (in which) our actions in Haiti are perhaps most flagrant."

∽

Until 1898 we didn't own a bit of territory outside the mainland of North America. At that time our national debt was a little more than one billion dollars. Then we became "internationally minded." We forgot, or shunted aside, the advice of the father of our country. We forgot George Washington's warning about "entangling alliances." We went to war. We acquired outside territory. At the end of the World War period, as a direct result of our fiddling in international affairs, our national debt had jumped to over twenty-five billion dollars. Our total favorable trade balance during the twenty-five-year period was about twenty-four billion dollars. Therefore, on a purely bookkeeping basis, we ran a little behind year for year, and that foreign trade might well have been ours without the wars.

It would have been far cheaper (not to say safer) for the average American who pays the bills to stay out of foreign entanglements. For a very few, this racket, like bootlegging and other underworld rackets, brings fancy profits, but the cost of operations is always transferred to the people—who do not profit.

—MAJOR GENERAL SMEDLEY DARLINGTON BUTLER,
United States Marine Corps (Retired), War Is a Racket *(1935). Twice awarded the Congressional Medal of Honor, Butler was, during the first three decades of the twentieth century, a commander of major invasions by U.S. troops of countries throughout Latin America and the Caribbean. By the mid-1930s, however, the retired general was one of the country's most*

determined critics of what he had come to see as "Dollar Diplomacy"—the imperialistic use of the U.S. military to protect and extend the interests of American corporations.

⁊

Our determination to stop communist revolution in the hemisphere must not be construed as opposition to popular uprisings against injustice and oppression just because the targets of such popular uprisings say they are communist-inspired or communist-led, or even because known communists take part in them.

—U.S. SENATOR ROBERT F. KENNEDY, *Senate speech in which he expressed his opposition to intervention by the United States in the Dominican Republic, May 1965.*

⁊

U.S. POLICY IN THE DOMINICAN CRISIS

I am frankly puzzled as to the current attitude of the U.S. government toward reformist movements in Latin America. On the one hand, President Johnson's deep personal commitment to the philosophy and alms of the Alliance for Progress is clear; it was convincingly expressed, for example, in his speech to the Latin American ambassadors on the fourth anniversary of the Alliance for Progress—a statement in which the president compared the Alliance for Progress with his own enlightened program for a Great Society at home. On the other hand, one notes a general tendency on the part of our policy makers not to look beyond a Latin American politician's anti-Communism. . . .

We cannot successfully advance the cause of popular democracy and at the same time align ourselves with corrupt and reactionary oligarchies; yet that is what we seem to be trying to do. The direction of the Alliance for Progress is toward social revolution in Latin America; the direction of our Dominican intervention is toward the suppression of revolutionary movements which are supported by Communists or suspected of being influenced by Communists. The prospect of an election in nine months which may conceivably produce a strong democratic government is certainly reassuring on this score, but the fact remains that the reaction of the United States at the time of acute crisis was to intervene forcibly and illegally against a revolution which, had we sought to influence it instead of suppressing it, might have produced a strong popular government without foreign military intervention. Since just about every revolutionary movement is likely to attract Communist support, at least in the beginning, the approach followed in the Dominican Republic, if consistently pursued, must inevitably make us the enemy of all revolutions and therefore the ally of all the unpopular and corrupt oligarchies of the hemisphere. . . .

It is not surprising that we Americans are not drawn toward the uncouth revolutionaries of the non-Communist left. We are not, as we like to claim in Fourth of July speeches, the most truly revolutionary nation on earth; we are, on the contrary, much closer to being the most unrevolutionary nation on earth. We are sober and satisfied and comfortable and rich; our institutions are stable and old and even venerable; and our Revolution of 1776, for that matter, was not much of an upheaval compared to the French and Russian revolutions and to current and impending revolutions in Latin America, Asia, and Africa. . . .

In the eyes of educated, energetic and patriotic young Latin Americans—which is to say the generation that will make or break the Alliance for Progress—the United States committed a worse offense in the Dominican Republic than just intervention; it intervened against social revolution and in support, at least temporarily, of a corrupt, reactionary military oligarchy.

It is not possible at present to assess the depth and extent of disillusion with the United States on the part of democrats and reformers in Latin America. I myself think that it is deep and widespread. . . .

The tragedy of Santo Domingo is that a policy that purported to defeat Communism in the short run is more likely to have the effect of promoting it in the long run. Intervention in the Dominican Republic has alienated—temporarily or permanently, depending on our future policies—our real friends in Latin America. These, broadly, are the people of the democratic left. . . .

By our intervention on the side of a corrupt military oligarchy in the Dominican Republic, we have embarrassed before their own people the democratic reformers who have counseled trust and partnership with the United States. We have lent credence to the idea that the United States is the enemy of social revolution in Latin America and that the only choice Latin Americans have is between communism and revolution.

—SENATE FOREIGN RELATIONS COMMITTEE CHAIR J. WILLIAM FULBRIGHT, *speech to Congress, September 15, 1965. Several months after President Lyndon Johnson ordered a U.S. invasion of the Dominican Republican, supposedly to protect American citizens and to prevent the spread of communism, Fulbright denounced the invasion, arguing that the administration had inflated claims about threats to Americans and the influence of Communists. If anything, Fulbright argued, the invasion encouraged people to commit to communism as an alternative to exploitation and imperialism. This speech represented a major breaking point in the already strained relations between the powerful Democratic senator and the Democrat in the White House.*

∽

THE MARINES HAVE LANDED ON THE SHORES OF SANTO DOMINGO

The streets are still, there's silence in the hills, the town is sleeping
And the farmers yawn in the grey silver dawn, the fields they're keeping
As the first troops land and step into the sand, the flags are weaving.
The marines have landed on the shores of Santo Domingo.

The unsmiling sun is shining down upon the singing soldiers
In the cloud dust whirl they whistle at the girls, they're getting bolder

The old women sigh, think of memories gone by, they shrug their
    shoulders.
The marines have landed on the shores of Santo Domingo.

Ready for the tricks, their bayonets are fixed, now they are rolling
And the tanks make tracks past the trembling shacks where fear is
    unfolding

> —PHIL OCHS, *"The Marines Have Landed on the Shores of
> Santo Domingo," from* Phil Ochs in Concert *(1966). Among the
> many popular folk singers of the early-to-mid 1960s, Ochs was the
> most meticulous about chronicling and condemning American
> military adventurism. His critique did as much as that of any
> senator to shape the broadly held belief, especially among young
> Americans, that the U.S. was meddling where it did not belong and
> for purposes that had nothing to do
> with patriotism or the common good.*

∽

THE CHILEAN TRAGEDY

To the Editors:

We have begun to circulate the following statement on Chile. Our hope
is to get the broadest possible support, not simply from those who sympathized with the Allende government, but from all Americans who are
shocked and outraged by the destruction of democracy in Chile. Those
who want to sign the statement, help circulate it, or aid in any way
should write to Congressman Donald Fraser, Room 704, 1424
Sixteenth Street NW, Washington, D.C. 20036.

    The fall of a democracy is always a deeply distressing event. This
is particularly the case when it affects a nation with a noble tradition
of freedom, such as the nation of Chile. At the present time, the exact
extent, if any, of active U.S. complicity is unknown; but this nation's
policy of economic strangulation and its unprecedented diplomatic
rudeness must be viewed as major contributors to the staggering economic difficulties of the government of President Salvador Allende,

difficulties which, in turn, helped bring about his deposition by a violent military coup and his tragic death.

While the long process of repairing the grievous damage that has been done to the constitutional fabric of Chile has yet to be begun, we urge that the U.S. maintain only minimal diplomatic relations with the military junta and provide only humanitarian assistance to the people of Chile until the following conditions are fulfilled: the Chilean Congress must be reopened; and political parties must be allowed to function; military law must be ended and the legal system restored; and there must be a forthright return to full constitutional rights.

We are particularly troubled by reports coming from Chile that the civil rights of the upward of ten thousand political exiles in Chile have been jeopardized, and that the military junta has resorted to the cynical practice of sending some of them back to their countries of origin, at a threat to their lives. We are also alarmed by information that books are being burned, that newspapers have been suppressed, and that former members of the Allende government and many of its supporters are being brutally persecuted for their past political allegiances. We urge that the people of the world join in pressing upon the military junta of Chile the realization that they must abide by the norms of civilized practices and human decency.

—NEW YORK REVIEW OF BOOKS, *"The Chilean Tragedy,"*
October 18, 1973. This letter was signed by U.S. Representative
Donald Fraser, a key member of the House Foreign Relations
Committee; Laurence Birns, of the New School for Social Research;
and Michael Harrington, of the Democratic Socialist Organizing
Committee. A detailed picture of the extent of the role played by the
Nixon administration and the U.S. Central Intelligence Agency in the
destabilization of Chile and coup that led to the death of the elected
president of that country, Salvador Allende, began to emerge when
U.S. Representative Michael J. Harrington (D-Massachusetts),
leaked a memorandum regarding U.S. schemes to undermine and
remove Allende. In 2000, the administration of President Bill Clinton
declassified hundreds of documents that further confirmed the
involvement of U.S. intelligence agencies in the undermining of
Chilean democracy.

PENNSYLVANIA EGG FARMER

Bethine and I keep a little cabin up in the hills not far from Gettysburg in Pennsylvania, up in that beautiful Pennsylvania-Dutch countryside. We go there on weekends to escape Washington. We've done it for years. We love that beautifully kept country, the honesty of the people—too many Republicans, actually; rather like Idaho in that respect. One of them is the egg farmer we get our eggs from. Of course, it's that arrangement where you go to the back porch, the eggs are there, you put in whatever money into a little slot and take the eggs you want to take. And in all the years that I had been there the farmer had never come to see me, which was one of the reasons I suspected he was Republican.

But on this particular day, I got out of the car, and I know that he had asked his wife to watch for us because she evidently had seen us approaching through the kitchen window and she'd picked up the telephone and called him at the hen house. By the time I came back to my car with the eggs he was there in front of me. And he was a big man, and he was in overalls, and I didn't know quite what to expect. So I held the eggs up between us. . . . And he said, "Senator, I want to ask you a question." And I said, "What is it?" And he said, "I want to know whether or not it's true that my government has been mixing with the mafia for the purpose of murdering people?" And I said, "Yes, I must tell you that that is true." And I could've hit him with my hand, such was the visible effect of those words on his face, his expression. He stepped back and with his boot he kicked the dirt a few times and didn't know quite what to say. And then he looked at me and he said, "Senator, how are we going to teach our children to grow up honest if their government is in bed with the mafia?"

That's how far we came. And we paid a terrible penalty for that period in which the moral content of government decision making was subordinated to all the pragmatic attitudes of the time.

—U.S. SENATOR FRANK CHURCH, *speech discussing his charge that the CIA had attempted to arrange the assassination of Cuban President Fidel Castro during the administrations of three U.S. presidents, January 23, 1977. Like his hero, former U.S. Senator William Borah, Church chaired the Senate Foreign Relations*

Committee. Before he took that post, he served as chair of the Select Committee to Study Governmental Operations with Respect to Intelligence Activities. Organized to investigate abuses of power by the Central Intelligence Agency and the Federal Bureau of Investigation. In pressing for congressional action to prevent the United States from assassinating foreign leaders and destabilizing foreign governments, Church said, "We must remain a people who confront our mistakes and resolve not to repeat them. If we do not, we will decline. But if we do, our future will be worthy of the best of our past." Church always described anti-imperialism as a patriotic impulse, arguing that, "American foreign policy must be made to conform once more to our historic ideals, the same fundamental belief in freedom and popular government that once made us a beacon of hope for the downtrodden and oppressed throughout the world."

∽

[A] rogue elephant rampaging out of control.

—U.S. SENATOR FRANK CHURCH, *describing the role played by the CIA in plots to assassinate foreign leaders, 1975. Attempts were made on Cuba's Fidel Castro, the Dominican Republic's Rafael Trujillo, and Zaire's Patrice Lumumba, as in orchestrating the turmoil that led to the 1973 Chilean coup in which President Salvador Allende was killed. The 1976 report produced by Church's Select Committee to Study Governmental Operations with Respect to Intelligence Activities declared that in U.S. dealings with the world, "Means are as important as ends. Crisis makes it tempting to ignore the wise restraints that make men free. But each time we do so, each time the means we use are wrong, our inner strength, the strength which makes us free, is lessened."*

∽

No employee of the United States government shall engage in, or conspire to engage in, political assassination.

—PRESIDENT GERALD FORD, *executive order issued in response to the Church committee's revelations about the role the U.S. government had played in orchestrating the assassinations of leaders of other countries, February 18, 1976. President Jimmy Carter extended the order to include not just political slayings but all assassinations. President Ronald Reagan incorporated Carter's language into Executive Order 12333, which subsequent presidents have maintained.*

❦

Asia was not the only region that invited presidential overreaching. The tide of United States intervention and interference in the domestic politics of Caribbean and Latin American nations had risen and fallen, but with the advent of the Reagan administration in the early 1980s, it reached new heights.

—FORMER U.S. REPRESENTATIVE RON DELLUMS (D-CALIFORNIA), *2000. A leading congressional critic of U.S. intervention in Vietnam, Cambodia, and Laos, Dellums would, during the 1980s and 1990s, be among the most outspoken foes of U.S. interventions in Latin America and the Caribbean.*

❦

Nothing being done in Grenada constitutes a threat to the United States or her allies.

—U.S. REPRESENTATIVE RON DELLUMS, *from a report by Dellums to Congress following the California Democrat's visit to the Caribbean island nation of Grenada to examine construction projects being developed by the leftist government of Maurice Bishop and the New Jewel Movement, April 1982. A senior member of the House Armed Services Committee, Dellums would eventually chair that committee in the 1990s.*

[This is] nothing less than a crime against humanity, planned and executed by people who deserve to be condemned as war criminals.

—U.S. REPRESENTATIVE RON DELLUMS, *condemning the U.S. invasion of Grenada, which had been ordered by President Ronald Reagan during a period of unrest on the island, October, 1983. Reagan claimed that Grenada posed a threat to the United States, largely because the New Jewel Movement maintained friendly relations with Fidel Castro's Cuba.*

∽

Our foreign policy must be characterized by mutual respect, not by gunboat diplomacy, big-stick diplomacy, and threats. Our nation at its best feeds the hungry. Our nation at its worst, will mine the harbors of Nicaragua; at its worst, will try to overthrow their government; at its worst, will cut aid to American education and increase the aid to El Salvador; at its worst, our nation will have partnership with South Africa. That is a moral disgrace. It is a moral disgrace. It is a moral disgrace.

We look at Africa. We cannot just focus on Apartheid in Southern Africa. We must fight for trade with Africa, and not just aid to Africa. We cannot stand idly by and say we will not relate to Nicaragua unless they have elections there, and then embrace military regimes in Africa overthrowing democratic governments in Nigeria and Liberia and Ghana. We must fight for democracy all around the world, and play the game by one set of rules.

—REVEREND JESSE JACKSON, *address to the Democratic National Convention, July 18, 1984. Jackson's 1984 and 1988 presidential campaigns attracted broad support from activists seeking to end U.S. support for military dictatorships and death squads in Central America.*

∽

As opponents of the Cold War East and West we protest the Reagan administration's escalating war on Nicaragua. The nature of the Nicaraguan regime is not the issue. We defend the democratic right of every nation to self-determination in complete freedom from superpower control, whether that domination is justified by the Brezhnev Doctrine in Eastern Europe and Afghanistan, or by Reagan's claims of U.S. special interests in Central America and the Caribbean. The application of force against weaker nations blocks democratic social and political change, tightens the superpower's grip on their respective blocs and spheres of influence, and fuels the arms race with catastrophic consequences for all of us.

To escape from the current global impasse we must find a third way in which democratic activists and movements from around the world make common cause to build an alternative to both blocs. We are raising our voices in unison against this ominous heightening of the Cold War, and demand an immediate end to the United States' growing intervention in Nicaragua. We challenge the U.S. to set an example of non-interventionism, and we ask the Soviet Union to do the same in Eastern Europe and Afghanistan.

> —NEW YORK REVIEW OF BOOKS, *letter signed by activists, academics, entertainers, labor leaders, and political leaders from around the world, February 13, 1986. The letter's U.S. signers included Edward Asner, Steven M. Becker, Angie Berryman, Rabbi Balfour Brickner, Frank Brodhead, David R. Brower, Noam Chomsky, Dr. Charlie Clements, Gail Daneker, Richard Deats, Representative Ronald V. Dellums, Tom DeLuca, Adrian DeWind, Daniel Ellsberg, Richard Falk, W. H. and Carol Ferry, Allen Ginsberg, Todd Gitlin, Victor Gotbaum, Stephen Jay Gould, Lee Grant, A. Winton Jackson, Charlie King, Charles Komanoff, Jeri Laber, Joanne Landy, Penny Lernoux, Grace Paley, Paul Robeson Jr., Bernard Sanders, George Soros, Rose Styron, Kurt Vonnegut, Jr., and James Weinstein.*

∽

The United States government should act more like a champion of growth and less like a collection agency for the overextended banks. If we help expand Latin American economies rather than squeeze them,

we can increase U.S. exports as we strengthen southern democracies—
and our mutual security. . . . The banks should know that full repayment
of these loans is no longer tenable as a primary goal of U.S. policy.

    —U.S. SENATOR GARY HART, *speaking in Sao Paulo, Brazil,*
March 17, 1987. Hart was the leading contender for the Democratic
presidential nomination at the time he delivered this address. In the
years that followed, the cause of debt cancellation came to
increasing prominence in the U.S. and abroad.

                    ✎

We have no real Latin American policy. We have always been the big
brother telling little brother what to do.

    —U.S. REPRESENTATIVE ALBERT BUSTAMANTE, *April 10,*
1986. A Texas Democrat, Bustamante suggested that President Ronald
Reagan's claim that Latin American leftists posed a threat to the U.S.
was ridiculous, saying, "The president got people wound up with an
emotional pitch that the Commies are two days away from Texas . . .
It's an insult to my intelligence to come in with simple slogans."

                    ✎

Revolutions, like romance, rarely work when they're arranged by
outsiders.

    —U.S. SENATOR DALE BUMPERS, *arguing against providing*
U.S. aid to the Contra rebel forces that were seeking to overthrow
the Sandinista government in Nicaragua, March 27, 1986.

                    ✎

None of the funds provided in this Act may be used by the Central
Intelligence Agency or the Department of Defense to furnish military
equipment, military training or advice, or other support for military
activities, to any group or individual . . . for the purpose of overthrowing the government of Nicaragua.

    —BOLAND AMENDMENT, *December 21, 1982.*
Written by U.S. Representative Edward Boland (D-Massachusetts),

*a close ally of House Speaker Tip O'Neill, this amendment was
designed to prevent the Reagan administration from using secret
allocations of U.S. money to promote the overthrow of the Sandinista
leadership of Nicaragua. Boland, the chairman of the House
Intelligence Committee made a simple argument for his amendment
to a defense appropriations bill, saying, "I don't think our
government ought to be involved in the process of overthrowing
or destabilizing governments." It passed the House 411–0,
and Reagan signed it. But members of his administration moved
almost immediately to violate it by supporting the Contra
forces seeking to overthrow the Sandinistas.*

∽

In Watergate, the impeachment process carried forward so impressively by the House Judiciary Committee viewed the president's responsibility in constitutional terms. Each of the three articles of impeachment approved by the committee found, in different particulars, that President Nixon has violated the duty put on presidents by the Constitution to "take care that the laws be faithfully executed." The abuses of power now known to have taken place in the Reagan administration are more serious, more fundamental, than those involved in Watergate.

—ANTHONY LEWIS, *from his "Abroad at Home" column, the*
New York Times, *February 24, 1987. Here he writes about the Iran-
Contra scandal. U.S. Representative Henry B. Gonzalez (D-Texas),
brought a motion for impeachment, saying, "This is the major
constitutional crisis since the Civil War. You have a president who is
unaccountable and says that it's his interpretation of what laws he'll
select to obey. When you have that, you have a constitutional crisis."
But as* Washington Post *columnist Mary McGrory noted, "because
the president has thrown two rascals out [John Poindexter and
Oliver North] and replaced them with rational men, Congress is
ready to, like a battered wife, take back the abusive husband. . . .
Divorce, like impeachment, can be so messy."*

∽

A careful review of the voluminous investigative record of the Iran-Contra scandal clearly demonstrates that there were only eight individuals, out of the hundreds involved, who were actually "in the loop" of detailed information about both the arms-for-hostages deal with Iran and funding for the Nicaraguan Contras. One William Casey of the CIA is dead. Five of the others: Robert McFarlane, John Poindexter, Oliver North, Richard Secord, and Albert Hakim have pleaded guilty, or been indicted for their involvement in the loop. One (Ronald Reagan) is leaving office on January 20, 1989. And the last, George Bush, hopes to take office on that day.

—SCOTT ARMSTRONG AND JEFF NASON, *"Company Man,"*
Mother Jones, *November 1988. This article examined the career of*
then Vice President George Bush. The Iran-Contra scandal exposed
the illegal U.S. support of the Contras, who sought to overthrow the
elected government of Nicaragua.

∽

IN SOLIDARITY WITH THE SLAIN JESUITS OF EL SALVADOR

The occasion for our liturgy is the tragedy of last Thursday, November 16, when six Jesuits and two of their household family at the Central American University in San Salvador were brutally murdered and mutilated in the early morning hours. We mourn not only for them, but for all the victims of this wasteful war that for more than ten years has bled a tiny, tortured country. We mourn for the seventy thousand people of El Salvador who have died in this war and the hundreds of thousands who have been displaced by the fighting. We remember the martyrs that preceded last Thursday's victims, Rutillo Grande, a Jesuit assassinated in 1977, the same year that a right-wing paramilitary group ordered all Jesuits to leave the country or face a sentence of death. We remember Archbishop Oscar Romero, struck down by an assassin's bullet in 1980 while celebrating Mass. We remember also the four American women missionaries who were kidnapped, assaulted, and murdered by military forces in December of 1980.

Our celebration today, then, is marked by a deep sense of sorrow at the loss of human life and the cruelty of ten years of fruitless fighting. But our sorrow is based on a strong sense of solidarity with the people and the church of El Salvador. It is a solidarity based on a common faith in a God of justice, on a common mission that all Jesuits share, with the Jesuits of El Salvador, and on the common identity that unites a Catholic university in El Salvador with all Catholic universities throughout the world. Our sense of solidarity, however, also arises from the more troubling fact that the national policies of our two countries have been, for good or ill, inextricably linked. And, finally, our solidarity with the people of El Salvador is based on fundamental Christian hope, which declares that no matter how dark the signs of death, in the end the radiance of life will prove victorious. . . .

This liturgy is not the time for political analysis or political advocacy. At the same time, we would not be faithful to the truth of this moment if we did not recognize than another more troubling source of our solidarity with the people of El Salvador is the history of the last ten years, in which the government of the United States has worked closely with the government of El Salvador. The policy of the United States toward El Salvador, in theory at least, has had respectable objectives: to control extremist forces on left and right, to encourage an environment in which the people of El Salvador can choose through democratic process the government they wish. But our government has also insisted that massive military assistance to the government of El Salvador is necessary to achieve these goals.

Before his assassination in 1980, Archbishop Romero had written to President Jimmy Carter asking him to curtail American military aid to the government because, in Archbishop Romero's opinion, such aid only escalated the level of violence in that country and prevented the achievement of a negotiated political settlement. Now, nearly ten years later, can anyone doubt the accuracy of Archbishop Romero's warning? Does anyone believe that the national security of the United States can possibly be endangered by the results of the civil war now raging in El Salvador? At a time when our government leaders and our corporate executives hasten to socialize with the leaders of the Communist giants elsewhere in the world, why must we assemble our military might to deal with revolutionary movements in tiny Central American nations? Are our national interests really at stake? Or are we obsessed with the myth of the national security state, a myth that is discredited each day by events elsewhere in the world? After ten years of evasions and equivocations, a tissue of ambiguities, the assassinations of November 16 pose, with brutal clarity, the question that continues to haunt the policy of the United States toward El Salvador: Can we hand weapons to butchers and remain unstained by the blood of their innocent victims?

—JOSEPH A. O'HARE, S.J., *November 22, 1989. A former editor of the magazine* America *and the president of Fordham University, O'Hare delivered this homily at a memorial Mass at St. Ignatius Church in New York City for the six slain Jesuit priests of El Salvador. The slaying of the priests shocked American sensibilities from parish churches to the White House and hastened a shift in U.S. policy regarding Central America. That did not, however, prevent top officials from attempting to cover up the story of U.S. links to the slayings.*

∽

MOAKLEY SPOKE UP FOR CENTRAL AMERICA'S POOR

Here's a story about how a good Congressman got the best of a bad system. Back in 1990, when Dick Cheney was serving as secretary of defense under Bush the elder, U.S. Representative Joe Moakley (D-Massachusetts) was investigating the 1989 murders of six Jesuit priests, their cook, and her daughter in San Salvador. Moakley, a wily Irish pol who lived by his friend Tip O'Neill's "all politics is local" dictum, had known two of the priests. That made the Salvadoran capital local enough for Moakley.

Long a critic of U.S. intervention in Latin America, he refused to accept Bush administration arguments that the incident was merely a Salvadoran matter. Such claims, the blunt Bostonian said, constituted "awful bullshit."

Moakley learned that military aides in the U.S. Embassy in San Salvador were in possession of an affidavit that implicated the Salvadoran military in the slayings—and, by extension, the U.S. military attachés who provided the Salvadoran thugs with training, money, and official cover. In his capacity as head of a special commission appointed by House Speaker Thomas Foley to investigate the murders, Moakley asked Cheney for a copy of the affidavit. Cheney refused.

Moakley then flew to San Salvador and arranged a meeting with the chief Salvadoran investigator of the crime. Moakley's former aide Jim McGovern—himself now a Democratic Congressman from Massachusetts—picks up the story from there: "He said to the investigator, 'There was something in that affidavit that I have a question about. Darn, I left it in my hotel room. Do you have an extra copy here?' The investigator gives him a copy, Moakley says he doesn't remember the question, and leaves (with the document). Then he goes back to the embassy and tells the ambassador, 'Tell your friends at the Department of Defense they can go fuck themselves, because I got a copy.'"

There's no record of Cheney's response. But there's a record of what Moakley did with the information. He tracked the killers down—personally. When the congressman learned that several of the murderers were attending Mass in a church at a government police compound, Moakley—a devout Catholic—suddenly felt an urge to take Communion. "He said we should ambush them," McGovern recalls. Armed with a photograph of the triggermen, Moakley and McGovern headed for the church. They spotted two of the murderers. Moakley, as he walked back from the Communion altar, leaned down toward one of the men and said, "I'd like to see you and your family together after the Mass."

In a nearby room, Moakley and McGovern questioned the men and got confirmation that they had acted under orders from senior Salvadoran military officers with ties to the U.S. military.

Moakley eventually succeeded in getting Congress to slash military aid to the Salvadoran regime, and he led the fight to shut down the Army's notorious School of the Americas, where generations of military thugs from El Salvador and other Latin American countries received their training in torture, er, "counterinsurgency" techniques.

Before Moakley died May 28 at age seventy-four, after a battle with leukemia, the great Salvadoran scholar Rodolfo Cardenal said,

"He is very well-known and considered very, very important by the Salvadoran people in terms of human rights, peace, and justice. We know from declassified documents that the armed forces and [the Salvadoran] government fear him."

Not a bad epitaph for an "all politics is local" pol, who joined the search for the priests' killers because, he said, "It is never a crime to speak up for the poor, the helpless or the ill; it is never a crime to tell the truth; it is never a crime to demand justice; it is never a crime to teach people their rights; it is never a crime to struggle for a just peace. It is never a crime. It is always a duty."

—JOHN NICHOLS, *"Moakley Spoke Up for Central America's Poor,"* Capital Times *(Madison, Wisconsin), May 31, 2001.*

∽

How quickly we abandon countries once peace is achieved. The U.S. invested six billion dollars in economic and military aid in the Salvadoran war. Today, we can barely muster thirty million dollars for development projects. Each year, thousands of Salvadorans emigrate to the United States legally and illegally because we have failed over the past five years to invest in El Salvador's rural and economic development.

Over a decade ago, the Salvadoran Jesuits taught me that a life committed to social justice, to protecting human rights, to seeking the truth is a life filled with meaning and purpose. I hope my life will be such a life. And if it is, it will be due to my long association with the people of El Salvador.

—U.S. REPRESENTATIVE JAMES MCGOVERN, *1999, from "Lessons Learned in El Salvador," an essay accompanying the release of the documentary* Enemies of War.
An aide to U.S. Representative Joe Moakley during the 1980s and early 1990s, McGovern worked closely with the congressman to investigate the slaying of the six Jesuit priests in El Salvador.

∽

A BICENTENNIAL WITHOUT A PUERTO RICAN COLONY

When the founders of the United States affirmed the inalienable right of nations to be free, they hardly had Puerto Rico on their minds. Yet, what was held to be philosophically pure for the thirteen colonies of 1776, is true today for the colony of Puerto Rico.

The United States revolution of 1776 loses validity in light of Puerto Rico's colonial situation under the stars and stripes. The plight of the Puerto Rican people is similar to that of the Euro-American settlers under the thumbscrew of British imperialism.

In 1776, England was responsible for draining the natural resources and manufacturing products from the colonies, without concern for the well-being of its colonial subjects. . . . In 1776, the colonists raised the demand of "no taxation without representation," which, as a battle cry of resistance, became the slogan for revolution. Today in 1976, Puerto Ricans who live on the island cannot vote for president, nor does the representative in Congress have the vote. . . .

The yoke of King George was not destroyed in 1776; it merely changed hands. That yoke was captured by those who usurped the revolution of 1776, and it was then used to slaughter Native Americans and Mexicans under the hideous pretext of "Manifest Destiny." In 1898 that yoke was fastened around the collective neck of the Puerto Rican nation. . . .

The roots of Borinquen [the original Indian name for the island] were trampled from the beginning of the European presence, where it was colonially renamed Puerto Rico, "rich port" by some lost sea captain who called himself Christopher Columbus. The worst mistake the Caribe Indians made was in discovering that lost and confused person who had, no doubt, gotten his directions from Leif Erikson. Columbus and the conquistadores who followed him knew only how to plunder. Their modern counterparts, the business interests and armies of the United States, are still raping the earth and have now set their sights on the universe. . . .

Since . . . 1898, the United States has looked upon Puerto Rico as belonging to the United States, but hardly a part of it. Puerto Rico has always had an immense strategic value for the United States. The island lies over fifteen hundred miles southeast of New York, almost five hundred miles east of Cuba, and about a thousand miles from Miami.

Thus, during Congressional hearings on the Jones Act, the 1917 law which forced citizenship on all Puerto Ricans, Congressman Cooper of Wisconsin declared, "We are never to give up Puerto Rico for, now that we have completed the Panama Canal, the retention of the island becomes very important to the safety of the Canal, and in that way to the safety of the nation itself. It helps to make the Gulf of Mexico an American lake. . . ."

The United States began a systematic drive to get Puerto Ricans to come to the United States as a cheap labor force, thus making more room for the colonial representatives to occupy the island, and to work to crush the ideals of independence.

In its plan of forced migration, the United States replaced the gun and whip with the weapons of economic pressure. The people of Puerto Rico, as part of this grand plan, have been forced to separate from their homeland. Economic pressure forces them to leave Puerto Rico and come to the United States. The resultant break up and separation of the family structure in Puerto Rico is due entirely to capitalist exploitation.

Puerto Ricans have no say in the control of their natural resources. As of this very moment, outside U.S. interests are negotiating to begin strip-mining our copper. The foreign oil industries of the U.S. are attempting to build a superport, proposing to turn Puerto Rico into a giant gasoline station, which will open a veritable Pandora's box of pollution and environmental destruction. One-third of the women of child-bearing age have been sterilized as an answer to unemployment and national resistance. Where agriculture once thrived, it is now dead, the arable land occupied by large military bases, petrochemical plants, and rich tourist hotels.

To my way of thinking, the Constitution and the Bill of Rights were only meant for the ruling class. Proof of this is the woe that has befallen Native Americans and other non-whites, as well as poor whites. The very originators of this "democracy" came from European countries with a long history of building empires on the homes of other peoples whose only desire was to live in peace in their own land. For Puerto Ricans, being citizens of the United States has only meant that they were meant to be cannon fodders for the huge war machine. . . .

How can the U.S. look with pride and satisfaction to the Bicentennial, which celebrates the fight against exploitation by England? How can the U.S. celebrate its historic cry of "no taxation without representation," while it denies the cry of the Puerto Rican patriots? Humans cannot mouth the words of freedom while holding others in bondage.

—PIRI THOMAS, *"A Bicentennial without a Puerto Rican colony," published in* The Crisis, *December 1975. As the United States prepared to celebrate the Bicentennial of the American revolution of 1776, anti-imperialists sought to call the nation back to its anti-colonial roots. A focus of many activists was the continuing U.S. control of the Caribbean island of Puerto Rico, which the U.S. had occupied since 1898.*

∽

ON THE ONE HUNDRETH ANNIVERSARY OF THE U.S. INVASION, PUERTO RICO STILL DESERVES INDEPENDENCE

One nation should never be the property of another. Yet, Puerto Rico is a colony of the United States. July 25 marks the centennial of U.S. occupation; in 1898, U.S. troops landed in Puerto Rico and seized the island as a prize of the Spanish-American War. The colonial relationship between the United States and Puerto Rico has not fundamentally changed since that time. The island remains a political anachronism, a throwback to the age of gunboat diplomacy and the handlebar mustache.

The invasion of Puerto Rico was directed by General Nelson Miles, who once hunted down Sitting Bull and Crazy Horse. He promised Puerto Ricans the "blessings" of an "enlightened civilization." That civilization imposed a series of North American governors, prohibiting Puerto Rico from electing its own governor until after World War II; greedily exploited the labor and natural resources of the island; established a menacing, strategic military presence; forced English on the public schools and the court system; and repressed the independence movement. . . .

Puerto Rico is the oldest colony in the world: four centuries under Spain and a century under the United States. In five hundred years, Puerto Ricans have not determined their own destiny for five minutes.

—MARTÍN ESPADA, *"On the One-Hundredth Anniversary of the U.S. Invasion, Puerto Rico Still Deserves Independence," from* The Progressive, *July 20, 1998.*

℘

In Colombia . . . the U.S. is becoming involved in a counterinsurgency war just like in Vietnam, or El Salvador or Nicaragua or Guatemala.

—CECELIA ZARATE-LAUN, *from an interview with Detroit's* Metro Times *newspaper, September 9, 1998. The founder of the Colombia Support Network, Zarate-Laun was one of the first U.S. activists to alert members of Congress and others to the growing U.S. military presence in Colombia, and to the fact the U.S. was not merely fighting the "drug war" but meddling in the internal political struggles of that country. "Because it's presented as a war on drugs and all of us are against drugs," Zarate-Laun explained, "people assume that this is a good thing." But, Zarate-Laun argued, by aiding the military, which has maintained close ties to paramilitary "death squads" (paras), the U.S. was taking the side of those who opposed a fair distribution of land and the country's wealth. "The paras receive support from trade organizations and powerful businesses, such as export agriculture, cattlemen, oil companies, and drug traffickers. They get political support from leaders of the traditional parties. The judicial system protects them by absolving the responsible parties and discontinuing the criminal proceedings. . . . There are around three thousand political killings a year. This year it will be at least four thousand. Remember, during the seventeen years of Pinochet in Chile, there were three thousand political killings in seventeen years. In Colombia, it's*

every year," Zarate-Laun said. "Those who have been killed include
journalists, university professors, priests, nuns, labor leaders,
indigenous leaders, cooperative members, women leaders,
peasant leaders—anybody who thinks."

∽

Mr. Chairman, we are about to go to war in Colombia. We are about to allocate $1.7 billion for sixty-three helicopters and the United States military advisers to help the military in Colombia to fight a civil war. We are about to go to war in the jungles of Colombia.

We are about to take on an insurgency that controls 40 percent of the land mass of Colombia that has been at war with the government of Colombia for twenty years. We are about to relocate farmers off the land where they are growing coca leaf and put them into what can only be called strategic hamlets and protect them, of course, from attack during this time while we teach them to grow something other than coca leaf.

The time will come when these military advisers are fired upon, I fear. And when they are, what will the United States' response be? I suggest its response will be as it was in Vietnam, to increase the number of advisers, to protect those previously sent, to protect the air bases where the helicopters are, to protect the strategic hamlets where we have relocated the villagers to try to teach them to grow something other than coca leaf.

What we are voting on today is the last moment that we have, really, given the way that the war powers have been exercised by this president and previous presidents, the last moment we have to say no. Because once this starts, the next step will be to put more troops in to defend the investment that we have already made.

Can anyone doubt that this will be the case given what has happened in Bosnia, given what has happened in Kosovo? We originally were supposed to be in Bosnia for six months. It has now been five years. Kosovo we thought would be short term, now our troops will be there for as long as we can see.

We are today voting at the last moment we will have before being asked to observe another war. We are being asked to go to war in

Colombia. I think that my good friend and colleague, the gentleman from Minnesota (Mr. Ramstad), expressed the point very ably, we will always have a problem of drugs while we have a demand for drugs.

Already chemicals, synthetic substitutes are available that do almost as much harm, in fact, in some cases more. The problem is one of demand. Today we vote to go to war.

I urge my colleagues to vote no.

—U.S. REPRESENTATIVE TOM CAMPBELL (R-CALIFORNIA), *speech in Congress opposing Plan Colombia, a Clinton administration scheme to dramatically increase aid to the Colombian military and to place U.S. military advisers on the ground in that country, March 29, 2000. A California Republican, Campbell argued that, by essentially hiring the Colombian military to become an arm of the U.S. war on drugs, the Clinton administration was entangling Americans in a distant conflict in a manner that would serve neither the interests of the U.S. nor Colombia. Despite Campbell's protests, Congress authorized Plan Columbia, and the U.S. entered into a formal partnership with the Columbian military.*

∽

THE SCHOOL OF THE ASSASSINS

Ten years ago this week, a Salvadoran death squad burst into the Jesuit University in San Salvador, dragged six Jesuit priests and two school employees from their beds, murdered them and mutilated their bodies.

As Leo J. O'Donovan, S.J., the president of Georgetown University, notes in an article that appears in today's editions of the *Capital Times*, several of the assassins were trained by the United States Army.

Indeed, it is not at all irresponsible to suggest that the United States government was directly responsible for the murders.

How can that be?

How could the United States possibly have been responsible for the brutal murders of Catholic priests? How can the United States bear the blame for the acts of shadowy death squads bent on silencing religion's advocacy on behalf of the poor?

No mystery. Ronald Reagan and George Bush supported the

Salvadoran government and its military—the spawning ground for those death squads. That support extended to the training of Salvadoran officers who eventually murdered those who dared to question the Salvadoran government's corrupt and murderous practices.

That training took place at the U.S. School of the Americas in Fort Benning, Georgia. For decades that "school" has served as a primary place of preparation for murderers, assassins, rapists, and thugs who have terrorized much of the Western Hemisphere. Today, the school trains the butchers who are killing progressive political activists in Colombia—including elected officials in Dane County's sister community of Apartado. The School of the Americas is the single darkest blot on the soil of the United States. It is a bloody stain on this country's landscape, and the stain grows with each day that it is allowed to carry out its mission of training the forces that oppress and kill the people of Latin America.

This weekend, thousands of political activists will converge on Fort Benning to demand the closing of what has commonly come to be known as "The School of the Assassins." Many of those present will be Wisconsinites, including Democratic State Representative Mark Pocan of Madison, Cecilia Zarate-Laun of the Madison-based Colombia Support Network, and a contingent from Edgewood College.

Pocan's presence at Fort Benning this weekend will be particularly significant. There are not many elected officials who are willing to travel cross-country on a bus to challenge the wrongdoing of the federal government. There are even fewer who are willing, as Pocan has been, to travel to El Salvador, Colombia, and other regions where he has directly witnessed the damage done by the sixty-thousand "graduates" of the School of the Assassins.

"Every day the School of the Americas remains open, it brings shame to the United States and terror to Colombia," Pocan has said. "There is no justification for keeping this training ground for terrorists operating with U.S. taxpayer dollars."

Pocan is right. And in making the trip to Fort Benning, along with other Madison-area activists, he is representing Wisconsin well. Indeed, he is bringing to his electoral service the genuine moral commitment that too few officials exhibit.

The same goes for Cecilia Zarate-Laun, whose long and sometimes lonely battle to shift U.S. policy towards Colombia will be a
prime focus of the activism at Fort Benning this weekend. For years,
Zarate-Laun has warned that Colombia could be the next Vietnam.
Now, as U.S. military advisors on the ground in Colombia work with
School of the Americas-trained forces, and as the Congress authorizes
hundreds of millions of dollars in military aid to that troubled country, the dark machinations of the Pentagon and the State Department
are becoming all too clear.

One protest in Georgia will not cleanse the U.S. foreign policy
establishment of its cynicism, its preposterous assumptions, and its
dangerous tendency to meddle where it doesn't belong. But the voices raised at Fort Benning could well force Congress and the American
people to wake up to the fact that the School of the Americas produces
nothing less than genocide.

—CAPITAL TIMES, *editorial condemning the School of the*
Americas, November 18, 1999. This "school," a U.S.-funded center
at Fort Benning, Georgia, has trained Latin American military forces
that have been linked to acts of rape, torture, and murder in a
number of countries. Though renamed, the school remains in
operation and continues to be a symbol of one of the darkest aspects
of U.S. meddling in South and Central America and the Caribbean.

SEVEN

We Are About to Do the Bidding of Wealth's Terrible Mandate

World War I, the League to

Perpetuate War, and the Dream

of a Great Force, Disentangled

"I feel we are about to put the dollar sign upon the American flag.

—GEORGE NORRIS

If the 1900s were "the American century," they were as well the century of horrific world wars that would draw the United States into broader and more distant conflicts than it had ever known. The prospect of U.S. involvement in both the First and Second World Wars provoked fierce internal debates over where the line was to be drawn between military adventurism and moral duty to countries and peoples that were in peril. Anti-imperialists argued as each war swelled in Europe that America must avoid being drawn into the foreign entanglements against which Washington and Jefferson had warned. And evidence of war-time repression within the U.S. confirmed the fears of those who had argued across history that a republic could not long survive the pressure of war making. After the United States was drawn into World War I, Richard F. Pettigrew, the former South Dakota senator who had battled the imperialists verbally and at times physically on the floor of the Senate during the Spanish-American War, argued, "We are no longer a republic or democracy or any semblance of either one. The entrance of the United States into the great war extinguished all possibilities in that direction. We are a feudal aristocracy with artificial persons for our feudal lords, the most cruel form of society it is possible to imagine. The old feudal aristocracy was composed of natural persons with some human sympathy; but our feudal lords have none of these attributes."

Pettigrew's bitter denunciation of President Woodrow Wilson's decision to involve the United States in a war between European kings and kaisers reflected one of the most powerful arguments against allowing the U.S. to join the fight. Along with that of pacifists, such as Helen Keller and Jeannette Rankin—the only woman serving in Congress at the time of the 1917 declaration of war—socialists, such as Eugene Victor Debs, and anarchists, such as Emma Goldman, the most intense opposition to the war came from rural populists who argued that it was not the right or responsibility of an American president to sacrifice the sons of farmhands and factory workers on the killing fields of Europe. "Shall we hind up our future with foreign powers and hazard the peace of this nation for all time by linking the destiny of American democracy with the ever-menacing antagonisms of foreign monarchies?" demanded Senator Robert M. La Follette, the Wisconsin progressive. "[Europe is] cursed with a contagious, deadly plague, whose spread threatens to devastate the civilized world." La Follette and the small band of war foes he led in the Senate argued, with some credibility it would turn out, that much of the agitation for U.S. involvement in World War I was coming from a burgeoning military-industrial complex that would profit handsomely from the sale of munitions. "Their object in having war and in preparing for war is to make money," Nebraska Senator George Norris said of the arms merchants, "Human suffering and the sacrifice of human life are necessary, but Wall Street considers only the dollars and the cents. The men who do the fighting, the people who make the sacrifices are the ones who will not be counted in the measure of this great prosperity that he depicts. The stockbrokers would not, of course, go to war because the very object they have in bringing on the war is profit, and, therefore, they must remain in their Wall Street offices in order to share in that great prosperity which they say war will bring. The volunteer officer, even the drafting officer, will not find them. They will be concealed in their palatial offices on Wall Street, sitting behind mahogany desks, covered up with clipped coupons—coupons soiled with the sweat of honest toil, coupons stained with mothers' tears, coupons dyed in the lifeblood of their fellow men."

The fastest way to end the war, argued Wisconsin Congressman Victor Berger, was to "tax the profiteers!"

Once the war began, La Follette and Berger saw, in the suppression of freedom of speech and the censorship of the press, evidence that James Madison had been right when he warned, "Of all the enemies of true liberty, war is, perhaps, the most to be dreaded, because it comprises and develops the germ of every other. War is the parent of armies; from these proceed debts and taxes; and armies, and debts, and taxes are the known instruments for bringing the many under the domination of the few." Said Berger, "Our plutocracy and its government in Washington is now establishing an absolute autocracy in our country with the slogan: 'War necessitates autocracy.'"

When World War I was done, its most ardent foes objected to the Treaty of Versailles that Wilson brought before the Senate. They were, in particular, opposed to the entanglement of the United States in Wilson's pet project, the League of Nations. Berger referred to the proposed League as "an alliance of more or less plutocratic governments," while La Follette noted that the Treaty of Versailles and, by extension, the League of Nations, had been proposed by old colonial powers that talked of remaking the world but did nothing to loose "the chains on the subject peoples of Ireland, Egypt, and India." Idaho Senator William Borah, who called the proposed organization of nations "the League to Perpetuate War," complained that it empowered wealthy and white nations while keeping the exploited countries of the world "under the heel of Western businessmen."

Said Borah, "The advocates of the League of Nations claim for it that it will end war. 'If we do not adopt it,' says Mr. Wilson, 'we will break the heart of the world.' If we do adopt it, we shall help to bleed the Western world white in the series of frightful international struggles that will follow upon any attempt to enforce the Treaty and the League Covenant as they are written."

Dismissing the proposed Treaty of Versailles as "the same old game of grab and gouge," California Senator Hiram Johnson described the League proposal as a tool to force American soldiers to help European imperialists "set up the kind of governments we wish in the world, and eliminate, where necessary, the kind of government the various people wish for themselves." With La Follette and Borah, Johnson would lead radical opposition to joining the League. In coalition with conservative critics of Wilson's ambitious internationalism, they would succeed in blocking U.S. participation in the League. Some historians would eventually claim that, by denying a U.S. presence in its deliberations, the League's foes hindered its ability to prevent World War II. But Johnson and his allies would dismiss the charge, arguing that the purpose of those who drew up the League was to perpetuate their own power, not to ease the tensions that would lead to future wars.

The decision to keep the U.S. out of the League proved to be popular with the American people, who reelected the League's most passionate critics by wide margins. So empowered, the anti-imperialists explored proposals to "outlaw war." More practically, they sought to take the profit out of war. Victor Berger, never at a loss for words, declared in 1928, "Thinking people the world over now agree that the war was a capitalistic war and an imperialistic war." That view took hold in the Senate, where a young progressive from North Dakota, Gerald Nye, said, "It would not be fair to say that the House of Morgan took us to war to save their investment in the Allies, but the record of facts makes it altogether fair to say that these bankers were in the heart and center of a system that made our going to war inevitable. We started in 1914 with a neutrality policy which permitted the sale of arms and munitions to belligerents, but which forbad loans to belligerents. Then, in the name of our own business welfare, President Wilson permitted the policy to be stretched to the extent of permitting the house of Morgan to supply the credit needs of the Allies. After this error of neutrality, the road to war was paved and greased for us." Through much of the 1930s, Nye was a pivotal player on the Senate's Munitions Investigating Committee, which produced a 1936 report that argued, in Nye's words, that "economic interests do lie at the bottom of modern war."

The evidence of war profiteering uncovered by the Munitions Investigating Committee inspired a public outcry so great that Congress responded by approving the Neutrality Act of 1935. As the 1930s wore on, the desire to avoid being drawn into another European war led to the development of a broad anti-intervention movement. It included sincere pacifists, such as Jeannette Rankin, the World War I foe who was reelected to the House in 1940. But there were also apologists for European fascists, as well as old-fashioned isolationists who argued for an unrealistic level of disengagement from the world. Many of them were associated with the America First movement.

The media focus on the crackpot elements among the American Firsters tended to obscure the sincere challenges by veteran critics of imperialism and war profiteering to President Franklin Roosevelt's preparedness initiatives. After the December 7, 1941, Japanese attack on Pearl Harbor, the vast majority of anti-intervention campaigners signed on for the duration. World War II earned far more universal support than World War I because America had been attacked, and because the fascist threat was more serious than the comic characatures of the kaiser. Indeed, some of the old anti-interventionists made the case that Hitler and Mussolini were the ultimate imperialists. Yet, even as the war was waged, they argued for taking steps to, in Nye's words, discourage "imperialistic and world-domination ambitions" by denying to the victors—including the United States—"the acquisition of any territory without the consent of the people of the proposed newly acquired territory."

War is a terrible destructive force, even beyond the limits of the battlefront and the war zone. Its influence involves the whole community. It warps men's judgment, distorts the true standards of patriotism, breeds distrust and suspicion among neighbors, inflames passions, encourages violence, develops abuse of power, tyrannizes over men and women even in the purely social relations of life and terrifies whole communities into the abject surrender of every right which is the heritage of free government.

—ROBERT M. LA FOLLETTE, *1917.*

The cause of war is the preparation for war.

—W. E. B. DU BOIS, *"Of the Children of Peace,"* The Crisis, 1914. *The years between the beginning of World War I in Europe and the entry of the United States into that war in 1917 saw a passionate debate in the U.S. between those who favored preparation for war and those who believed that preparation would ultimately lead to engagement in a distant war that was Europe's concern, not America's.*

I DIDN'T RAISE MY BOY TO BE A SOLDIER

Ten million soldiers to the war have gone,
Who may never return again.
Ten million mothers' hearts must break,
For the ones who died in vain.
Head bowed down in sorrow in her lonely years,
I heard a mother murmur thro' her tears:

Chorus:
I didn't raise my boy to be a soldier,
I brought him up to be my pride and joy,
Who dares to put a musket on his shoulder,
To shoot some other mother's darling boy?
Let nations arbitrate their future troubles,
It's time to lay the sword and gun away,
There'd be no war today,
If mothers all would say,
I didn't raise my boy to be a soldier.

(Chorus)

What victory can cheer a mother's heart,
When she looks at her blighted home?
What victory can bring her back,
All she cared to call her own?
Let each mother answer in the year to be,
Remember that my boy belongs to me!

—ALFRED BRYAN, *"I Didn't Raise My Boy to be a Soldier,"*
1915. The song was denounced publicly by former president
Theodore Roosevelt, a militant interventionist, who said the place
for women who opposed entry into World War I was "in China—or,
by preference, in a harem—and not in the United States."

Militarism consumes the strongest and most productive elements of each nation. Militarism swallows the largest part of the national revenue. Almost nothing is spent on education, art, literature and science . . .

—EMMA GOLDMAN, *article first published in* Mother Earth, *December 1915. When President Woodrow Wilson launched a military preparedness program, it drew loud protests not just from Goldman and other radicals, but from more conservative Americans who believed that militarization would necessarily lead to U.S. entry into what was broadly seen as a European war.*

∽

[When] war murders the husbands and sons of women, destroys their homes, desolates their country and makes them refugees and paupers, it becomes the undeniable business of women.

—CARRIE CHAPMAN CATT, *from an article on why women opposed U.S. entry into World War I, 1915. Catt and many other leading figures in the National American Woman Suffrage Association were outspoken critics of militarism and U.S. expansionism.*

∽

Everywhere, we hear fear advanced as argument for armament. It reminds me of a fable I read. A certain man found a horseshoe. His neighbor began to weep and wail because, as he justly pointed out, the man who found the horseshoe might someday find a horse. Having found the shoe, he might shoe him. The neighbor's child might some day go so near the horse's heels as to be kicked, and die. Undoubtedly, the two families would quarrel and fight, and several valuable lives would be lost through the finding of the horseshoe. You know the last war we had we quite accidentally picked up some islands in the Pacific Ocean which may some day be the cause of a quarrel between ourselves and Japan. I'd rather drop those islands right now and forget about them than go to war to keep them. Wouldn't you?

>—HELEN KELLER, *speech to the Women's Peace Party forum at Carnegie Hall, January 5, 1916. Keller was a militant foe of preparedness initiatives, which sought to ready the United States for entry into a war she felt was unnecessary. She traveled the country arguing against moves that would entangle the United States in Europe's wars.*

∽

If I had the right to vote, I would vote for you, Mr. Hillquist, because a vote for you would be a blow at the militarism that is one of the chief bulwarks of capitalism, and the day that militarism is undermined, capitalism will fall.

>—HELEN KELLER, *letter to New York City Socialist Party mayoral candidate Morris Hillquist, November 5, 1917. Foes of World War I poured their energy into electoral activity before, during, and after the war, believing that they could convince Americans that the country had been drawn into war by British and American profiteers. Keller references the fact that women were not allowed to vote. War foes believed that giving women the vote would create an electoral majority opposed to military adventurism abroad.*

∽

Let the people rule. Nowhere is their rule more needed than in deciding upon war policies—nowhere would their influence be more salutary.

>—WILLIAM JENNINGS BRYAN, *declaration in his magazine* The Commoner, *February 1916. The three-time Democratic presidential candidate stepped down as Woodrow Wilson's secretary of state rather than support moves that he thought were preparing the U.S. entry into World War I. Bryan proposed an amendment to the Constitution that would allow the American people to vote on whether to launch an overseas war, arguing that, "I so believe in the right of the people to have what they want that I admit the right of the people to go to war if*

they really want it. There should be a referendum vote about it, however, and those who voted for war should enlist first, together with the jingo newspaper editors." Bryan said, "the real safety of our nation lies in the people themselves, and not in their representatives." But he actually had a number of close allies in the Congress, including Oklahoma populist Thomas P. Gore and Pennsylvania Democrat Warren Worth Bailey, who fought every piece of preparedness legislation and supported the war referendum amendment.

∽

I will never rob the cradle to gorge the dogs of war.

—U.S. SENATOR T. P. GORE, *1917, from campaign leaflets distributed by the senator in his home state of Oklahoma. Gore's grandson, the author Gore Vidal, recalls the phrase as a classic in his grandfather's oratorical arsenal. Even after the war began, Gore continued to advocate for measures that would "democratize war" as "the best way to prevent and minimize war." In August 1917, as the war raged, he proposed a constitutional amendment that would have allowed the structuring of treaties with other nations so that each could agree not to "declare or levy war against the other until the question of declaring or levying war shall have been submitted to the qualified electors of the country proposing the same and shall have been approved by a majority thereof." Along with U.S. Senator Robert M. La Follette, Gore argued that placing the responsibility for declaring wars in the hands of the people would make peace inevitable. Gore's antiwar stances did not serve him well politically. As his grandson, Gore Vidal, recalled, "(The) first Gore to become well-known in the country was my grandfather, who was thirty years a senator and very much against the First World War. Wilson was maneuvering us into it, and around 1916 my grandfather got a telegram from the Chamber of Commerce of Oklahoma City saying if he didn't vote for war, he would be defeated in the next election. He sent them a telegram saying, 'How many members of the Chamber of Commerce are of draft age?' They defeated him in 1920, but he came back." When he campaigned for the Senate, T. P. Gore would distribute literature that declared: "Senator Gore says today as he said in 1917: I will never rob the cradle to gorge the dogs of war." "Courage," his grandson observed, "was Gore's most notable trait."*

Shall we hind up our future with foreign powers and hazard the peace of this nation for all time by linking the destiny of American democracy with the ever-menacing antagonisms of foreign monarchies? [Europe is] cursed with a contagious, deadly plague, whose spread threatens to devastate the civilized world.

> —U.S. SENATOR ROBERT M. LA FOLLETTE,
> *1917, arguing against U.S. entry into World War I. La Follette, a*
> *progressive Republican from Wisconsin, led the antiwar bloc in the*
> *Senate. Six senators voted against Woodrow Wilson's declaration of*
> *war, while fifty members of the House—including the only woman,*
> *Jeannette Rankin, of Montana—were opposed. The congressional*
> *opposition provided a sense of the deep divisions in the country*
> *over whether the U.S. should enter a European war.*

∞

I have no quarrel to find with the man who does not desire our country to remain neutral. While many such people are moved by selfish motives and hopes of gain, I have no doubt but that in a great many instances, through what I believe to be a misunderstanding of the real condition, there are many honest, patriotic citizens who think we ought to engage in this war and who are behind the president in his demand that we should declare war against Germany. I think such people err in judgment and to a great extent have been misled as to the real history and the true facts by the almost unanimous demand of the great combination of wealth that has a direct financial interest in our participation in the war.

We have loaned many hundreds of millions of dollars to the Allies in this controversy. While such action was legal and countenanced by international law, there is no doubt in my mind but the enormous amount of money loaned to the Allies in this country has been instrumental in bringing about a public sentiment in favor of our country taking a course that would make every bond worth a hundred cents on the dollar and making the payment of every debt certain and sure. Through this instrumentality and also through the instrumentality of others who have not only made millions out of the war in the manufacture of munitions, etc., and who would expect to make millions more if our country can be drawn into the catastrophe, a large number of the great newspapers and news agencies of the country have been controlled and enlisted in the greatest propaganda that the world has ever known to manufacture sentiment in favor of war.

It is now demanded that the American citizens shall be used as insurance policies to guarantee the safe delivery of munitions of war to belligerent nations. The enormous profits of munition manufacturers, stockbrokers, and bond dealers must be still further increased by our entrance into the war. This has brought us to the present moment, when Congress, urged by the president and backed by the artificial sentiment, is about to declare war and engulf our country in the greatest holocaust that the world has ever known.

In showing the position of the bondholder and the stockbroker, I desire to read an extract from a letter written by a member of the New York Stock Exchange to his customers. This writer says:

"Regarding the war as inevitable, Wall Street believes that it would be preferable to this uncertainty about the actual date of its commencement. Canada and Japan are at war and are more prosperous than ever before. The popular view is that stocks would have a quick, clear, sharp reaction immediately upon outbreak of hostilities, and that then they would enjoy an old-fashioned bull market such as followed the outbreak of war with Spain in 1898. The advent of peace would force a readjustment of commodity prices and would probably mean a postponement of new enterprises. As peace negotiations would be long drawn out, the period of waiting and uncertainty for business would be long. If the United States does not go to war, it is nevertheless good opinion that the preparedness program will compensate in good measure for the loss of the stimulus of actual war."

Here we have the Wall Street view. Here we have the man representing the class of people who will be made prosperous should we become entangled in the present war, who have already made millions of dollars, and who will make many hundreds of millions more if we get into the war. Here we have the cold-blooded proposition that war brings prosperity to that class of people who are within the viewpoint of this writer.

He expresses the view, undoubtedly, of Wall Street, and of thousands of men elsewhere who see only dollars coming to them through the handling of stocks and bonds that will be necessary in case of war. "Canada and Japan," he says, "are at war, and are more prosperous than ever before."

To whom does war bring prosperity? Not to the soldier who, for the munificent compensation of sixteen dollars per month, shoulders his musket and goes into the trench, there to shed his blood and to die if necessary; not to the brokenhearted widow who waits for the return of the mangled body of her husband; not to the mother who weeps at the death of her brave boy; not to the little children who shiver with cold; not to the babe who suffers from hunger; nor to the millions of mothers and daughters who carry broken hearts to their graves. War brings no prosperity to the great mass of common and patriotic citizens. It increases the cost of living of those who toil and those who already must strain every effort to keep soul and body together. War brings prosperity to the stock gambler on Wall Street—to those who are already in possession of more wealth than can be realized or enjoyed.

Again this writer says that if we cannot get war, "it is nevertheless good opinion that the preparedness program will compensate in good measure for the loss of the stimulus of actual war." That is, if we cannot get war, let us go as far in that direction as possible. If we cannot get war, let us cry for additional ships, additional guns, additional munitions, and everything else that will have a tendency to bring us as near as possible to the verge of war. And if war comes, do such men as these shoulder the musket and go into the trenches?

Their object in having war and in preparing for war is to make money. Human suffering and the sacrifice of human life are necessary, but Wall Street considers only the dollars and the cents. The men who do the fighting, the people who make the sacrifices are the ones who will not be counted in the measure of this great prosperity that he depicts. The stockbrokers would not, of course, go to war because the very object they have in bringing on the war is profit, and, therefore, they must remain in their Wall Street offices in order to share in that great prosperity which they say war will bring. The volunteer officer, even the drafting officer, will not find them. They will be concealed in their palatial offices on Wall Street, sitting behind mahogany desks, covered up with clipped coupons—coupons soiled with the sweat of honest toil, coupons stained with mothers' tears, coupons dyed in the lifeblood of their fellowmen.

We are taking a step today that is fraught with untold danger. We are going into war upon the command of gold. We are going to run the risk of sacrificing millions of our countrymen's lives in order that other countrymen may coin their lifeblood into money. And even if we do not cross the Atlantic and go into the trenches, we are going to pile up a debt that the tolling masses that shall come many generations after us will have to pay. Unborn millions will bend their backs in toil in order to pay for the terrible step we are now about to take.

We are about to do the bidding of wealth's terrible mandate. By our act, we will make millions of our countrymen suffer, and the consequences of it may well be that millions of our brethren must shed their lifeblood, millions of brokenhearted women must weep, millions of children must suffer with cold, and millions of babes must die from hunger, and all because we want to preserve the commercial right of American citizens to deliver munitions of war to belligerent nations.

—U.S. SENATOR GEORGE W. NORRIS, *speech to the Senate opposing U.S. entry into World War I, April 4, 1917. A progressive Republican from Nebraska, Norris faced reelection in 1918 while the war was being fought. He campaigned across Nebraska, telling voters, "I have come home to tell you the truth." Norris won the election overwhelmingly, as did a number of other war foes.*

∽

In the political landscape today, there is no Senator George Norris.

—JOE AUCIELLO, *"Democrats Follow Bush on the Road to War,"* Labor Standard, *Fall 2002. The article bemoaned the lack of congressional opposition to George W. Bush's request for authorization to use military force against Iraq.*

∽

I want to stand by my country, but I cannot vote for war. I vote, "No."

> —U.S. REPRESENTATIVE JEANNETTE RANKIN, *explaining her vote against entry into World War I, April 1917. A Montana suffragist who was elected to the House in 1916 as a progressive Republican, Rankin was the first woman to serve in Congress. She was one of fifty members of the House to oppose the war. Rankin later explained, "I knew that we were asked to vote for a commercial war, that none of the idealistic hopes would be carried out, and I was aware of the falseness of much of the propaganda. It was easy to stand against the pressure of the militarists, but very difficult to go against the friends and dear ones who felt that I was making a needless sacrifice by voting against the war, since my vote would not be a decisive one . . . I said I would listen to those who wanted war and would not vote until the last opportunity and if I could see any reason for going to war I would change it." The fears of her friends and loved ones were confirmed. In 1918, she was defeated in a Republican primary campaign for a U.S. Senate seat. She became a prominent campaigner against militarism and said in 1929, "There can be no compromise with war; it cannot be reformed or controlled; cannot be disciplined into decency or codified into common sense; for war is the slaughter of human beings, temporarily regarded as enemies, on as large a scale as possible."*

∽

To President Wilson:

Lynching, Jim Crow, segregation, discrimination in the armed forces and out, disenfranchisement of millions of black souls in the South— all these things make your cry of making the world safe for democracy a sham, a mockery, a rape on decency, and a travesty on common justice.

> —A. PHILIP RANDOLPH, *editorial in* The Messenger, *November, 1917. This magazine billed itself as the "only radical Negro magazine in America." Randolph edited it with Chandler Owen, a fellow socialist. Randolph would go on to organize and lead the Brotherhood of Sleeping Car Porters union. In 1963, he issued the call for the March on Washington for jobs and freedom.*

The editors of The Messenger *argued that Wilson's hypocrisy when it came to democracy abroad and at home made it unreasonable to ask African-American men to serve in the military. Until racist discrimination was ended in America,* The Messenger *declared, "This world . . . is not safe for any democracy."*

❧

Wisconsin! For a Speedy, General and Lasting Peace—Tax the Profiteers.

—VICTOR BERGER, *1918, campaign slogan in the campaign by the former congressman from Milwaukee for a U.S. Senate seat. He won more than 100,000 votes and, later that year, was elected to the U.S. House. Even after the war had ended, he was refused his seat because of his militant opposition to the war. The House leadership deemed him insufficiently patriotic to serve, but the voters of Milwaukee thought differently. Berger was repeatedly reelected until he was finally seated in 1923.*

❧

They ought to be in the penitentiary, wearing stripes.

—U.S. SENATOR ROBERT M. LA FOLLETTE, *May 16, 1920, from a Senate speech regarding the munitions merchants of World War I.*

❧

The first casualty, when war comes, is truth.

—U.S. SENATOR HIRAM JOHNSON, 1917. *Johnson, a progressive Republican, was an outspoken critic of U.S. entanglements abroad during a Senate career that lasted from 1917 to 1945.*

❧

Our plutocracy and its government in Washington is now establishing an absolute autocracy in our country with the slogan: "War necessitates autocracy."

> —VICTOR BERGER, *"Why We Are in This War,"*
> Milwaukee Leader, *June 20, 1917. Berger, a Socialist, condemned*
> *the "capitalist press—the kept prostitute of the capitalist system"*
> *for publishing the Wilson administration's "lies" about the*
> *necessity of war. The postmaster general revoked the* Leader's
> *second-class mailing privileges.*

∽

We declare freedom of speech to be the bulwark of human liberty, and we decry all attempts to muzzle the public press, upon any pretext whatsoever. A declaration of war does not repeal the Constitution of the United States, and the unwarranted interference of military and other authorities with the rights of individuals must cease.

> —NORTH DAKOTA NONPARTISAN LEAGUE RESOLUTION,
> MAY 1917. *This resolution was passed at group meetings across*
> *North Dakota in the late spring of 1917. The radical North Dakota*
> *Nonpartisan League became the dominant political force in that state*
> *during the war era. Like many Midwestern populist groups, the*
> *league was skeptical of the war and fearful that it would be used as*
> *an excuse by reactionaries to suppress freedom at home.*

∽

We want to get a lot of good flags, talk a good deal about the Constitution and what our forefathers wanted to make of this country, and to show that we are the folks that really stand for the spirit of our institutions.

> —ROGER BALDWIN, *letter to Louis Lochner, August 21, 1917.*
> *Baldwin helped form the National Civil Liberties Bureau of the*
> *American Union Against Militarism to defend the constitutional*

*rights of wartime dissenters. The Civil Liberties Bureau evolved into
the American Civil Liberties Union, which Baldwin headed for its
first three decades.*

⁓

To maintain something over here that will be worth coming back to
when the weary war is over.

—CRYSTAL EASTMAN, *describing the purpose of the National
Civil Liberties Bureau's struggle to defend First Amendment
protections during World War I, 1917. Like many war foes, Eastman
had argued that entry into the war would threaten American
democracy. Widespread assaults by authorities on freedom of speech
and expression after the war's beginning confirmed those concerns.
Eastman, a lawyer, served as chief counsel for the bureau. Along
with Roger Baldwin and Norman Thomas, she signed the statement
announcing that the defense of civil liberties would become a prime
focus of the American Union Against Militarism during the course of
the war. That statement declared that, "It is the tendency even of the
most 'democratic' of governments embarked upon the most
'idealistic of wars' to sacrifice everything for complete military
efficiency. To combat this tendency where it threatens free speech,
free press, freedom of assembly, and freedom of conscience—the
essentials of liberty and the heritage of all past wars worth
fighting—that is the first function of the AUAM today."*

⁓

FREE SPEECH IN WARTIME

Six members of the Senate and fifty members of the House voted
against the declaration of war. Immediately there was let loose upon
those senators and representatives a flood of invective and abuse
from newspapers and individuals who had been clamoring for war,
unequalled, I believe, in the history of civilized society.

Prior to the declaration of war every man who had venture to
oppose our entrance into it had been condemned as a coward or

worse, and even the president had by no means been immune from these attacks.

Since the declaration of war, the triumphant war press has pursued those senators and representatives who voted against war with malicious falsehood and recklessly libelous attacks, going to the extreme limit of charging them with treason against their country.

This campaign of libel and character assassination directed against the members of Congress who opposed our entrance into the war has been continued down to the present hour, and I have upon my desk newspaper clippings, some of them libels upon me alone, some directed as well against other senators who voted in opposition to the declaration of war. One of these newspaper reports most widely circulated represents a federal judge in the state of Texas as saying, in a charge of a grand jury—I read the article as it appeared in the newspaper and the headline with which it is introduced:

"District Judge Would Like to Take Shot at Traditions in Congress (by Associated Press lease wire), Houston, Texas, October 1, 1917. Judge Waller T. Burns, of the United States district court, in charging a federal grand jury at the beginning of the October term today, after calling by name Senators Stone of Missouri, Hardwick of Georgia, Vardaman of Mississippi, Gronna of North Dakota, Gore of Oklahoma, and La Follette of Wisconsin, said: "If I had a wish, I would wish that you men had jurisdiction to return bills of indictment against these men. They ought to be tried promptly and fairly, and I believe this court could administer the law fairly; but I have a conviction, as strong as life, that this country should stand them up against an adobe wall tomorrow and give them what they deserve. If any man deserves death, it is a traitor. I wish that I could pay for the ammunition. I would like to attend the execution, and if I were in the firing squad I would not want to be the marksman who had the blank shell. . . ."

If this newspaper clipping were a single or exceptional instance of lawless defamation, I should not trouble the Senate with a reference to it. But, Mr. President, it is not. . . .

I am aware, Mr. President, that in pursuance of this campaign of vilification and attempted intimidation, requests from various individuals and certain organizations have been submitted to the Senate for my expulsion from this body, and that such requests have been referred to and considered by one of the committees of the Senate.

If I alone had been made the victim of these attacks, I should not take one moment of the Senate's time for their consideration, and I believe that other senators who have been unjustly and unfairly assailed, as I have been, hold the same attitude upon this that I do. Neither the clamor of the mob nor the voice of power will ever turn me by the breadth of a hair from the course I mark out for myself, guided by such knowledge as I can obtain and controlled and directed by a solemn conviction of right and duty.

But, Sir, it is not alone members of Congress that the war party in this country has sought to intimidate. The mandate seems to have gone forth to the sovereign people of this country that they must be silent while those things are being done by their government which most vitally concern their well-being, their happiness, and their lives. Today, and for weeks past, honest and law-abiding citizens of this country are being terrorized and outraged in their rights by those sworn to uphold the laws and protect the rights of the people. I have, in my possession, numerous affidavits establishing the fact that people are being unlawfully arrested, thrown into jail, held incommunicado for days, only to be eventually discharged without ever having been taken into court, because they have committed no crime. Private residences are being invaded, loyal citizens of undoubted integrity and probity arrested, cross-examined, and the most sacred constitutional rights guaranteed to every American citizen are being violated.

It appears to be the purpose of those conducting this campaign to throw the country into a state of terror, to coerce public opinion, to stifle criticism, and suppress discussion of the great issues involved in this war.

—U.S. SENATOR ROBERT M. LA FOLLETTE, *speech to the Senate, October 6, 1917. La Follette faced several resolutions of expulsion for a public statement condemning America's participation in the war, but he refused to back away from his stand. Despite a* New York Sun *article that headlined "New Proof of La Follette's Sedition Filed," which appeared on the day a Senate committee considered the resolution, La Follette survived the attempt to remove*

him. After the war's end, the expulsion resolutions were dropped
and the Senate paid the Wisconsinite's legal expenses. In 1959,
La Follette was named by special committee of the Senate one of
the five greatest senators in the chamber's history.

∽

To the *Star*:

I see that it is, after all, necessary to send a statement for publication over my own signature, and I trust that you will give it space in your columns.

A headline in the evening's issue of the *Star* reads: "Mrs. Stokes for Government and Against War at the Same Time." I am not for the government. In the interview that follows I am quoted as having said, "I believe the government of the United States should have the unqualified support of every citizen in its war aims."

I made no such statement, and I believe no such thing. No government which is for the profiteers can also be for the people, while the government is for the profiteers.

I expect my working-class point of view to receive no sympathy from your paper, but I do expect that the traditional courtesy of publication by the newspapers of a signed statement of correction, which even our most Bourbon papers grant, will be extended to this statement by yours.

Yours truly,
Rose Pastor Stokes

　—ROSE PASTOR STOKES, *letter to the editor of the* Kansas City
　Star, *March 20, 1918. A woman of considerable wealth, Stokes was*
　also a prominent Socialist. She campaigned across the country in
　opposition to the war and the war profiteers. This attempt to clarify
　an interview she had given to the paper caught the attention of the
　federal authorities. She was prosecuted for violating the Espionage
　Act of 1917 and sentenced to ten years in a federal penitentiary.
　After Stokes's conviction, Eugene V. Debs asked, "What did Rose
　Pastor Stokes say? Why, she said that a government could not at the

*same time serve both the profiteers and the victims of the profiteers.
Is it not true? Certainly it is and no one can successfully dispute it.
Think of it! Ten years! What atrocious crime had she committed?
What frightful things had she said? Let me answer candidly. She
said nothing more than I have said here this afternoon. I want to
admit—I want to admit without reservation that if Rose Pastor
Stokes is guilty of crime, so am I. If she is guilty for the brave part
she has taken in this testing time of human souls, I would not be
cowardly enough to plead my innocence. And if she ought to be sent
to the penitentiary for ten years, so ought I without a doubt."*

∞

[The] gentry who are today wrapped up in the American flag, who
shout their claim from the housetops that they are the only patriots,
and who have their magnifying glasses in hand, [are] scanning the
country for evidence of disloyalty, eager to apply the brand of treason to the men who dare to even whisper their opposition to Junker
rule in the United States.

No wonder Sam Johnson declared that "patriotism is the last refuge
of the scoundrel." He must have had this Wall Street gentry in mind,
or at least their prototypes—for in every age it has been the tyrant, the
oppressor, and the exploiter who has wrapped himself in the cloak of
patriotism or religion or both, to deceive and overawe the people . . .

—EUGENE VICTOR DEBS, *from a speech at a Socialist Party
convention in Canton, Ohio, June 16, 1918. For voicing the view
that World War I was being fought for "conquest and plunder," as
opposed to saving democracy, Debs was charged under the Sedition
Act with the crime of interfering with military recruitment. Debs
received a ten-year sentence and was incarcerated at the Atlanta
Federal Penitentiary, from which he sought the presidency in 1920
as "Convict No. 9653." He won 919,000 votes and was pardoned by
the man who defeated him, President Warren Harding. Said former
U.S. Senator Richard F. Pettigrew, "The Great War is over. Peace has
been restored. Sanity is supposed to have replaced the hysteria of
war frenzy. Yet Harding, spokesman of plutocratic imperialism, is in
the White House, while Debs, the champion of economic
emancipation, is in the Atlanta penitentiary."*

The little group of men who sat in secret conclave for months at Versailles were not peacemakers. They were war makers. They cut and slashed the map of the Old World in violation of the terms of the Armistice. They patched up a new map of the Old World in consummation of the terms of the secret treaties the existence of which they had denied because they feared to expose the sordid aims and purposes for which men were sent to death by the tens of thousands.

They betrayed China. They locked the chains on the subject peoples of Ireland, Egypt, and India. They partitioned territory and traded off peoples in mockery of the sanctified formula of Fourteen Points, and made it our nation's shame.

> —U.S. SENATOR ROBERT M. LA FOLLETTE, *denouncing the Treaty of Versailles and the proposed League of Nations, 1919. The treaty was seen by La Follette and other progressives as a tool to involve the United States in the defense of the British Empire and the suppression of movements for independence by colonies of European lands. It was, as well, seen as a threat to the national sovereignty of the United States and a structure that, ultimately, would involve the United States in more European wars. La Follette and his allies saw President Woodrow Wilson's endorsement of the treaty as an abandonment of the principles for promoting peace and democracy laid out by Wilson in his Fourteen Points statement.*

∽

An alliance of more or less plutocratic governments.

> —U.S. REPRESENTATIVE VICTOR BERGER, *describing the proposed League of Nations, 1919. Berger warned that the United States must do everything in its power to avoid becoming "a world constable."*

∽

The same old game of grab and gouge.

> —U.S. SENATOR HIRAM JOHNSON, *describing the Treaty*
> *of Versailles and the attempt to create a League of Nations, May 31,*
> *1919. Johnson, a California Republican who had been Teddy*
> *Roosevelt's running mate for vice president in 1912, complained that*
> *the League would quickly become a tool to force American soldiers*
> *to help "set up the kind of governments we wish in the world, and*
> *eliminate, where necessary, the kind of government the various*
> *people wish for themselves." With La Follette and William Borah,*
> *an Idaho Republican who would go on to chair the Senate Foreign*
> *Relations Committee, Johnson would lead radical opposition to*
> *joining the League.*

∽

THE LEAGUE TO PERPETUATE WAR

The war has just begun. I said that when the Armistice terms were published and when I read the Treaty and the League Covenant I felt more than ever convinced of the justice of my conclusion. The Treaty of Versailles is merely an armistice—a suspension of hostilities, while the combatants get their wind. There is a war in every chapter of the Treaty and in every section of the League Covenant; war all over the world; war without end so long as the conditions endure which produce these documents. The League of Nations is a League to perpetuate war. I do not charge that its sponsors intended this, though I have sufficient respect for the intellectual ability of men like Balfour and Lloyd George, Makino and Orlando to believe that they knew quite well what they were about. But whether by intention or accident, the "Big Five" presented the world with two documents, the attempted enforcement of which is destined to bathe the earth in blood and wipe out what remains of "Western civilization."

The advocates of the League of Nations claim for it that it will end war. "If we do not adopt it," says Mr. Wilson, "we will break the heart of the world." If we do adopt it, we shall help to bleed the Western world white in the series of frightful international struggles that will follow upon any attempt to enforce the Treaty and the League Covenant as they are written.

Let me state, briefly, my reasons for believing that the League of Nations is a war league rather than a peace league.

1. The League of Nations is not a league of all nations. On the contrary, three kinds of nations are deliberately excluded from it—the Socialist nations like Russia; the enemy nations, like Germany; and the "undeveloped nations," like Mexico. The "Big Five" who wrote the Armistice Terms, the Peace Treaty, and the League Covenant were Great Britain, France, Italy, Japan, and the United States. These are the five great capitalist empires of the world. They are also the five leaders among the Allied Nations. The League is therefore a Holy Alliance of capitalist empires against socialist states; a League of the Allies against the Central Powers; a League of the five great exploiting nations of the world against those whom they propose to rob. This situation creates a series of alignments any one of which may lead to an outbreak at almost any moment.

2. On the one hand, there is the alignment against Russia. Ever since the Revolution of 1917, the Allies have done everything in their power to destroy the government of Russia. They have sent their armies against her at Vladivostock and at Archangel; they have attacked her with their fleets on the Black Sea and in the Baltic; they have financed and equipped those like Yudenich, Kolchak, Denikine, and Wrangel who were in rebellion against the established government of Russia; they have financed and equipped the Ukranians, the Finns, and the Poles, on condition that they should make war on Russia; they have established a "sanitary cordon" of border states in an effort to cut Russia off from the rest of Europe; they have maintained a blockade which has resulted in the death, by starvation and by disease, of Russian men, women, and children. During three long years, the Allies have carried on these activities without succeeding in forcing a declaration of war from Russia.

   The Russian people are very patient. They had need of patience under the czars, but there is a limit to everything. There are a hundred and fifty million of Russians. These people feel bitter against the capitalist governments that have attacked and blockaded them. They have an army—the largest now in Europe, if report speaks true. Some day that army will come into action against the armies of the Allies—come with the fervor and ardor of revolution, and when it comes, Europe will witness another terrible massacre and another fearful destruction of wealth.

3. Then, there are the enemy countries—defeated in the great war, stripped of their navies and of their merchant ships; of their colonies; of their investments in foreign countries; of their coal and iron; dismembered, saddled with heavy indemnities in addition to their onerous taxes. These enemy countries are suffering under the smart of a terrible military defeat. But more than that, after revolting and driving out their despotic rulers they have been subjected to an economic punishment more frightful than any that has ever been administered in modern times. The governing classes feel this; the people feel it, and they are all ready, at the first opportunity, to rush to arms in vindication of their international position and of their national rights, which they believe were grossly violated by the Treaty of Versailles. No opportunity was lost; no effort was spared to humiliate the defeated and to visit upon them a drastic economic punishment. The vanquished and humiliated are preparing to come back, and the Allied Nations know it.

4. There are the exploited countries; the "undeveloped" portions of the earth; the promising investment field; the good markets—Mexico, India, Korea, Egypt, Persia, China, and the others. Africa has been under the heel of Western businessmen for generations. The same thing is true of India and other portions of Western and Southern Asia. These peoples, numbering hundreds of millions, have been kept in ignorance and held in bondage, while the British, German, French, Belgian and other traders and investors made free with their property and their lives. In the Belgian Congo, the black men were treated with indescribable cruelty; the people of India, after a century and a half of British rule, are almost wholly illiterate, while their industries have been deliberately curtailed in order that the Indian market might be open for British manufacturers.

Mexico has been victimized again and again by the United States. Haiti, Santo Domingo, and Nicaragua have felt the weight of America's imperial fist. Under the Treaty, with its "mandates" and its guarantees of territorial integrity, these peoples, comprising the bulk of the world's populations, are to be continued in "tutelage" while Allied capitalists plunder and Allied governments tax and kill.

The Baku Conference of the Eastern People [September 1920] is the beginning of an organized protest that challenges the right of the West to continue its exploitation of the East. India is aflame with revolt, and the smaller Eastern countries are awaiting the signal to begin a holy war, a religious crusade, against the domination of Western civilization. Whether the proposed expulsion of the sultan from Europe will start the conflagration, or whether some other spark will set it off remains to be seen. But the spirit of liberation is abroad in the earth, and any group of nations that seeks, with or without a covenant, to continue a system of virtual slavery, is heading for bitter and terrible conflicts.

5. Finally, there is an item of immense significance. The "Big Five" are five capitalist empires, each one of which is struggling for markets and for investment opportunities. Britain and Germany fought the recent war because Germany challenged Britain's economic supremacy. Today, each of the Big Five is busy with just such an economic battle as that which preceded the war of 1914. British and American oil interests are in open conflict; Japan is seeking to exclude Western bankers from the Chinese field; France and Italy are bitter rivals for the control of the Mediterranean; Britain and France are contending for the resources of Central Europe and of the near East. Besides that, it must not be forgotten that naval and military appropriations are larger among the Big Five than they were before the world war.

I have another reason for insisting that the League will make for war rather than for peace—a reason growing out of the League's own record. During its brief existence, the League has witnessed more than a score of wars in Europe, Africa, and in Asia. These wars have been participated in by Great Britain, France, Italy, and Japan—the leading exponents of the League. France has sent men and money to back Poland and to uphold General Wrangel's insurrection against the Russian government, while her armies are busy conquering and subjugating Syria. Great Britain is fighting in Ireland and in Mesopotamia. Spain, France, and Italy all are fighting in North Africa, and Thrace is being ravaged by contending armies.

Since the League came into being, Europe has blazed with war. The League is not a war preventor, but a war maker.

So much for the character and history of the League. Now as to its purposes. These are three in number:

1. To crush out Socialism.
2. To safeguard the British Empire.
3. To unite the exploiters against the exploited.

The relation of the League and of its principal members toward Soviet Russia is a sufficient guarantee of the first point. The position of the British Empire, combined with the working of Article X of the League Covenant establishes the second.

British statesmen insisted that they desired nothing as a result of the war. As things turned out, however, they received over two million square miles, including important possessions in East Africa, Mesopotamia, the lands bordering the Red Sea and the Persian Gulf, Persia, Tibet, and the German possessions in the South Pacific. This gives the British Empire control over something like a third of the earth, including a continuous stretch of territory from the Cape of Good Hope to Cairo and from Cairo to Bengal. These things are guaranteed under the Treaty, and Article X of the Covenant provides that: "The members of the League undertake to respect and preserve against external aggression, the territorial integrity and existing political independence of all members of the League." This clause commits all members of the League to back the British Empire in its efforts to hold hundreds of millions of human beings in subjection.

The original Holy Alliance organized in 1815 between Austria, Russia, Prussia, and France, carried a mutual guarantee to protect from internal disturbances like the French Revolution, the members of the Alliance. This new Alliance guarantees its members against the possible loss of their colonies and possessions by any form of external oppression. They bind each other to help hold what they have stolen in this and previous wars. According to the original plan, the United States was to furnish the men and the money necessary to carry this League Covenant into effect.

The League is intended to organize and unite the exploiter nations. Under League Covenant provisions, the exploited nations have no rights that the exploiters are bound to respect. Japanese troops will remain in Korea; British rule stays in India and American Marines hold their ground in Haiti. The robbers will unite and plunder their victims in severalty.

Thus, the League is intended, not to secure freedom and self-determination, but to perpetuate autocracy and the rule of force of which the leading members of the League are the chief exponents.

The Treaty and the League Covenant intensify every cause that led up to the World War. International capitalism, with its economic rivalries and commercial struggles is perpetuated and consecrated; the exploitation of the weak by the rich and the strong is provided for; out of such a situation there can come nothing less than revolution and a struggle for independence on the one hand and the bitterest conflicts between the members of the League on the other. The League will perpetuate, will compel war. It makes peace unthinkable; impossible. It condemns the world to generations of bloodletting and destruction. The League is a logical product of the forces that made the last war and will prove an instrument of immense value in bringing about the next one.

—FORMER U.S. SENATOR RICHARD F. PETTIGREW, *1922,*
Imperial Washington. *A two-term Democratic senator from South
Dakota, Pettigrew was a militant critic of U.S. imperialism abroad
and corporate monopolies at home.*

⌒

What if we become obligated to protect the territorial integrity and independence of nations who join the League? That obligation immediately destroys the principles of Washington and Jefferson.

—U.S. SENATOR WILLIAM BORAH, *speaking in opposition to the treaty that would have made the United States part of the League of Nations, November 19, 1919. Borah referred to the proposed alliance as "a league to guarantee the integrity of the British Empire."*

ॐ

This League and Treaty is nothing but the old, old scheme, modified a little to fit the times—of an alliance among the victorious governments, following a great war, by which their conquered enemies may be kept in subjugation and exploited to the uttermost.

—LA FOLLETTE'S MAGAZINE, *September 19, 1919. Editorial. A widely circulated journal of the Progressive Movement,* La Follette's Magazine *is published today as* The Progressive.

ॐ

What is the result of all this [the U.S.'s joining the League of Nations]? We are in the midst of all of the affairs of Europe. We have entangled ourselves with all European concerns. We have joined in alliance with all the European nations which have thus far joined the League, and all nations which may be admitted to the League. We are sitting there dabbling in their affairs and intermeddling in their concerns. In other words, Mr. President—and this comes to the question which is fundamental with me—we have forfeited and surrendered, once and for all, the great policy of "no entangling alliances" upon which the strength of this Republic has been founded for one hundred fifty years. . . .

No, your treaty means injustice. It means slavery. It means war. And to all this you ask this Republic to become a party. You ask it to abandon the creed under which it has grown to power and accept the creed of autocracy, the creed of repression and force.

> —U.S. SENATOR WILLIAM BORAH, *speech to the Senate opposing U.S. entry into the League of Nations, November 19, 1919. President Woodrow Wilson campaigned across the United States for the League, but Borah, a Progressive Republican from Idaho, and California's Hiram Johnson, toured the country in opposition. Borah, Johnson, Robert M. La Follette, and their allies in the Senate were called the "Irreconcilables" because of their militant opposition to a treaty agreement they believed would forever entangle the U.S. in the battles of distant lands.*

∽

If you think the American people do want to join the League, then let's give them an opportunity to vote upon it. This is their government and their country. *If* they want to do this, *if* they want to change the Constitution, then let them. But let us have their wisdom and judgment before we usurp their authority and say we are going to take this action.

> —U.S. SENATOR WILLIAM BORAH, *1919. Borah did not succeed in getting his national referendum. But he and the Irreconcilables, voting in coalition with more conservative foes of the League, succeeded in blocking Wilson's proposal. The United States never joined the League.*

∽

Take away the gun
From ev-ry mother's son.
We're taught by God above
To forgive, forget and love,

The weary world is waiting for,
Peace, forevermore,

So take away the gun
From ev-ry mother's son,

And put an end to war.

> —AL JOLSON, *from a letter to newly elected President Warren Harding, December 2, 1920. The singer proposed to "start the song of peace thinly coated with ragtime, a-echoing through the land."*

∽

I would not trade my war record for any living man.

> —U.S. SENATOR ROBERT M. LA FOLLETTE, *announcing his candidacy for reelection, March 25, 1921. Though critics said he would be swept from office because of his militant opposition to World War I and his continuing criticism of war profiteers, he was instead reelected by the widest margin of his career.*

∽

A great moral force, disentangled.

> —U.S. SENATOR WILLIAM BORAH, *letter describing his vision of the role of the United States in the post-World War I era, November 5, 1922. After Borah became chairman of the Senate Foreign Relations Committee in 1924, he argued continually against "any political associations with Europe based on military force" and said of the United States, "We have a great service to perform, but we must perform it independently." In 1923, Borah proposed Senate Resolution 441 to outlaw war and create a "judicial substitute for war." That bill did not become law but, in 1928, Borah used his position to win Senate approval, by a vote of 85–1, for the Pact of Paris Treaty (popularly known as the Kellogg-Briand Peace Pact) that outlawed war as an instrument of national policy. The essentially symbolic agreement between the United States, France, Great Britain, Japan, and Germany committed each nation "to condemn war as an instrument of national policy" in their relations with each other.*

∽

Section 1: Except in the event of attack or invasion, the authority of Congress to declare war shall not become effective until confirmed by the majority of all votes cast therein in a nationwide referendum.

Section 2: Whenever war is declared, the president shall immediately conscript and take for use by the government all the public and private properties, yards, factories, and supplies, together with employees necessary for their operation, fixing the compensation (to previous owners) for private properties temporarily employed for the war period at a rate not in excess of 4 percent based on tax values assessed in the year preceding the war.

—CONSTITUTIONAL AMENDMENT, *proposed by U.S. Representative Louis Ludlow, an Indiana Democrat who had been a friend and associate of William Jennings Bryan, 1935. As Bryan had before World War I, Ludlow argued that, except in cases of direct attacks on the U.S., citizens should be permitted to vote on whether to enter a foreign war. Influenced by congressional investigations of World War I profiteering, Ludlow said his amendment was written "to save civilization from the munitions manufacturers." He asked President Franklin Delano Roosevelt to support the amendment as a "fitting capsheaf to your great program of social benefits." Roosevelt opposed Ludlow's campaign "to complete the democratic processes by democratizing the war power," but a campaign in favor of the resolution by the Fellowship for Reconciliation and the Women's International League for Peace and Freedom drew broad support. By October 1937, an American Institute for Public Opinion survey found that 73 percent of Americans supported the war referendum resolution.*

It may be true that Mussolini, Hitler, and Stalin sneer at the very idea of permitting the American people to vote on the question of foreign wars. If, however, we set such an example, the people of Italy, Germany, and Soviet Russia would eventually clamor for the same privilege, because they have far more to fear from the horrors of war than we.

>   —U.S. REPRESENTATIVE HAMILTON FISH, *comment said
>   during the debate on Ludlow's war referendum resolution, January
>   10, 1938. A conservative Republican from New York, Fish called the
>   bill "the greatest peace proposal" Congress had addressed in two
>   decades. Under the amendment, only in the case of an actual attack
>   on the U.S. could the president and Congress engage the military.
>   When the plan came to a vote in the House, it received 188 votes,
>   despite intense opposition from the Roosevelt administration and the
>   leadership of the chamber.*

∽

Modern war cannot be fought under democratic control. It requires dictatorship for total war.

>   —U.S. SENATOR ROBERT M. LA FOLLETTE, JR.,
>   *November 2, 1940. Like his father, La Follette campaigned in
>   opposition to U.S. intervention in a European War he felt was being
>   foisted upon America by big business interests and profiteers. "I feel
>   as though I had walked into a movie only to discover that I had seen
>   it years ago, under a somewhat different name and with a different
>   cast," said La Follette, Jr., who explained that he believed the United
>   States was "going down the same road we took in 1916–17." A
>   Wisconsin Progressive, La Follette argued, "We have seen
>   democracies fall, not so much because they failed in a military sense
>   but because they failed to make democracy work."*

∽

Americans today are faced with making the most fundamental and far-reaching decision in the history of our country—war or peace. . . . At this point let me say that there is no moral, economic, or social justification for our entry into the war in Europe. It is an imperialistic war. While there may be a difference between the contending powers, that difference is one of degree and the degree is not big enough to warrant the loss of one American life. . . . If this were a war of ideologies, if it were truly a war on which the outcome of our American way of living depended. . . . I would unhesitatingly advocate our immediate entry into it. . . . I am not a pacifist, I am willing to fight for the defense of my country, and in any war in which the interests of our American people are involved. The present war is no such war."

—U.S. REPRESENTATIVE VITO MARCANTONIO, *radio address to the nation, 1940. Perhaps the most radical member of Congress in the 1930s and 1940s, Marcantonio was a member of the left-wing American Labor Party, though he also ran on the Republican Party line. Running for reelection in 1940, Marcantonio recalled the devastation of World War I and said of his opposition to preparations for a new war, "My record is clear and my stand is well-known. I voted against repeating 1917 all over again." That fall, Marcantonio was reelected by the widest margin than he had received in his three previous congressional contests.*

∽

In the [1940] election, I voted for Norman Thomas, the Socialist candidate, for president because I thought he was the ablest candidate running and was genuinely interested in keeping us out of war.

—U.S. SENATOR BURTON K. WHEELER (DEMOCRAT OF MONTANA), Yankee from the West *(Doubleday, 1962). Wheeler refused to campaign for President Franklin Roosevelt, a fellow Democrat, because he felt the incumbent was positioning the country to enter the war in Europe. Concerned by the criticism of Wheeler and other war foes, Roosevelt sought to assure the American people by delivering a campaign speech in which he told the mothers of America, "I have said this before, but I shall say it again and again and again: Your boys are not going to be sent into any foreign wars." Roosevelt was reelected by a wide margin, as was Wheeler.*

∽

KILL BILL 1776, NOT OUR BOYS

—SLOGAN OF OPPONENTS OF PRESIDENT FRANKLIN
ROOSEVELT'S LEND-LEASE BILL, 1941. *The legislation
gave Roosevelt the power to lend, exchange, transfer, or sell
equipment to any country that he determined was defending itself
against German, Italian, or Japanese aggression. Of the fifty billion
dollars appropriated to pay for the initiative, thirty-one billion
dollars went to Britain.*

∾

It is impossible to listen to Mr. Roosevelt's recent speeches, to study
the Lease-Lend Bill, and to read the testimony of Cabinet officers
upon it without coming to the conclusion that the president now
requires us to underwrite a British victory, and apparently a Chinese
and a Greek victory, too. We are going to try to produce the victory
by supplying our friends with the materials of war. But what if this is
not enough? We have abandoned all pretense of neutrality. We are to
turn our ports into British naval bases. But what if this is not enough?
Then we must send the navy, the air force, and, if Mr. Churchill wants
it, the army. We must guarantee the victory.

If we stay out of war, we may perhaps some day understand and
practice freedom of speech, freedom of worship, freedom from want,
and freedom from fear. We may even be able to comprehend and support justice, democracy, the moral order, and the supremacy of human
rights. Today we have barely begun to grasp the meaning of the words.

Those beginnings are important. They place us ahead of where we
were at the end of the last century. They raise us, in accomplishment
as well as in ideals, far above the accomplishment and ideals of total-
itarian powers. They leave us, however, a good deal short of that level
of excellence which entitles us to convert the world by force of arms.

Have we freedom of speech and freedom of worship in this country?
We do have freedom to say what everybody else is saying and freedom
of worship if we do not take our religion too seriously. But teachers who
do not conform to the established canons of social thought lose their
jobs. People who are called "radicals" have mysterious difficulties in

renting halls. Labor organizers sometimes get beaten up and ridden out of town on a rail. Norman Thomas had some troubles in Jersey City. And the Daughters of the American Revolution refused to let Marian Anderson sing in the national capital in a building called Constitution Hall . . .

—ROBERT M. HUTCHINS, *speech opposing President Roosevelt's Lend-Lease proposal, January 23, 1941. The president of the University of Chicago, Hutchins was a leading progressive proponent of the old American view that the U.S. should serve as an example of democracy in action—rather than as democracy's battering ram.*

∽

Approval of this legislation means war, open and complete warfare.

—U.S. SENATOR BURTON K. WHEELER, *radio address opposing Lend-Lease legislation, January 12, 1941. Wheeler argued that, if the U.S. began by lending materials for war, it would soon be lending soldiers to fight. Then, the senator said, "Our boys will be returned—returned in caskets, maybe; returned with bodies maimed; returned with minds warped and twisted by sights of horrors and the scream and shriek of high-powered shells." Strongly supported by the Roosevelt administration, the Lend-Lease legislation passed both the House and Senate.*

∽

The word "isolationist" also has very sinister overtones. In the late '30s and early '40s, many Americans—and I was one—were isolationists. We thought that, as we had gained nothing from the First World War—except an erosion of our civil liberties and the prohibition of alcohol—why should we again help England and France against Germany? There is now a myth that the isolationists were pro-Hitler and anti-Semitic. This is nonsense. Practically every Socialist in the country, starting with Norman Thomas, was an isolationist, while agrarian populists, like Senators Wheeler and Nye, tended to be wary of foreign wars and entanglements. Also, the only foreign power that we were hostile to—and feared—was Hitler's enemy, the Soviet Union, the exporter of godless and atheistic Communism. America Firsters ranged from the historian Charles Beard to the young Kingman Brewster, not to mention a brilliant young football coach at Yale, Gerald R. Ford. The pro-German anti-Semites were at home in the German-American Bund, not in the America First Committee. Hitler's infamous final solution was not known as of 1940 and did not figure into the debate. As it turned out, no American majority ever favored American intervention in the European war. Had the Japanese not been inspired—or, perhaps, incited—to attack us, we might never have gone to war at all.

> —GORE VIDAL, *"America First? America Last? America At Last?" Lowell lecture, April 20, 1992. The grandson of Oklahoma populist T. P. Gore, Vidal has, for more than sixty years, been an outspoken critic of American Empire.*

⁓

Our frontier is no longer England nor, in any sense, is it European. Our frontier is our own shores.

> —FRANK LLOYD WRIGHT, *"Of What Use Is a Great Navy with No Place to Hide?" A Taliesin Square—Paper, 2, May, 1941. The nephew of Jenkin Lloyd Jones, an outspoken critic of American imperialism and entanglement in the wars of Europe, Wright was a passionate foe of U.S. entry into World War II.*

⁓

If going to war is now your way, you have never settled anything for yourself nor ever will for anyone else. Yours is the mind that would throw the dead cat back and forth across the backyard fence. . . . You prate of culture, Lewis. Organic character is the basis of true greatness in that or in any individual or in any nation. War is the negation of all these potentialities now as ever and forever. You know that. And yet you wrote to me that you had been busy getting the United States ready to fight and having accomplished that to your satisfaction you were ready to go back and write another book.

Christ! Lewis, is it possible that you are unable to see your own hypocrisy? Why do you hide behind what you call mine?

No honest believer in truth or beauty in his right mind could do what you say you have done. Time will discover you a deserter. A traitor on a battlefield that did you honor only to discover in you a vengeful, conceited writer. Another writer out of ideas. The Chinese say it well, "He who runs out of ideas first strikes the first blow."

You standing with the frightened crowd for the time-cursed expedient! What a disappointment . . . you, too, are yellow with this strange but ancient sickness: The malady that has thrown down civilization after civilization by meeting force with force. Is meeting force with force the only way you see now? Then I am sorry for you—you amateur essayist on culture. It is not the only way I see. I—a builder—see that there is still a chance for democracy in this world and one on this continent just because the leaders of our culture are not all like Lewis Mumford, as he shows his teeth now.

> —FRANK LLOYD WRIGHT, *letter to author and social commentator Lewis Mumford, June 3, 1941. Mumford, an admirer and friend of Wright, the nation's most prominent architect, had criticized his stance against entering the war.*

∽

For the same reason that I despise eclecticism and reaction, I despise your attitude toward war and empire. There is no good empire . . .

> —FRANK LLOYD WRIGHT, *letter to Mumford, June 3, 1941.*

∽

As a woman, I can't go to war, and I refuse to send anyone else.

> —U.S. REPRESENTATIVE JEANNETTE RANKIN, *explaining
> her vote against the declaration of war that brought the U.S. into
> World War II, December 8, 1941. Reelected to Congress in 1940 on
> an antiwar platform, she cast the only vote against declaration. That
> vote made her the only member of Congress to vote against entry into
> both of the twentieth century's world wars. Referring to Rankin some
> years later, John Fitzgerald Kennedy said, "Few members of
> Congress have ever stood more alone while being true to a higher
> honor and loyalty." After the war began, Rankin proposed resolutions
> that would have required members of Congress to live as soldiers
> did: on a wage of thirty dollars a month, drinking from tin cups and
> obtaining food only with a bread ration card. She did not return to
> Congress after the 1942 election. The Japanese attack on Pearl
> Harbor ended most anti-intervention activism instantly.*

∽

Our principles were right. Had they been followed, war could have
been avoided. No good purpose can now be served by considering
what might have been, had our objectives been attained.

> —THE AMERICA FIRST COMMITTEE, *letter announcing that
> the group would disband following the commencement of war,
> December 11, 1941. The committee's letter expressed hope U.S.
> involvement in the war would not interfere with "the fundamental
> rights of American citizens." It also declared that "secret treaties
> committing America to imperialistic aims or vast burden in other
> parts of the world shall be scrupulously avoided."*

∽

It will be necessary for the American people to decide in their wisdom what shall be done with those islands in the oceans, and with
those sections of continental areas which have been reclaimed from
Axis militarism by American soldiers. The United States, in this new
world of a "war of movement," will need bases far from the soil of

continental United States. It should not permanently undertake to retain vast amounts of territory. It should not embark upon imperialism. Never in its entire history has America coveted the lands and the wealth of other peoples, and nothing in the present struggle suggests a departure from its fixed tradition of goodwill toward all the other peoples and races of the world. Quite to the contrary, the expressed aims of the American people renounce all thought of territorial enrichment as a result of this war, and its frightful financial burden. In the maintenance of law and order, the reestablishment of governments, and the rehabilitation of regions destroyed or damaged by war, the American people should interfere as little as possible with the life of the peoples of those regions.

If out of this war, the world wins emancipation from conflict, the United States should see to it that such territory as has been occupied for military purposes should be returned to the rightful owners, together with all natural resources.

—U.S. SENATOR GEORGE W. NORRIS, Fighting Liberal: The Autobiography of George Norris *(AMS Press, 1945). A foe of entry into World War I, Norris had been more supportive of World War II. Yet, he retained the faith that the United States must not be allowed to follow the imperialist path of the European empires he condemned as a young senator.*

EIGHT

COME HOME AMERICA

Korea, Vietnam, and a Return to

the War-Bred Tyranny of Kings

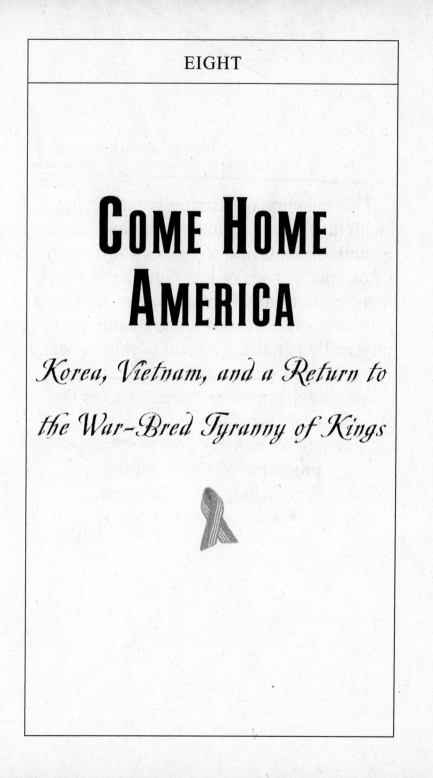

"This business of burning human beings with napalm, of filling our nation's homes with orphans and widows, of injecting poisonous drugs of hate into the veins of peoples normally humane, of sending men home from dark and bloody battlefields physically handicapped and psychologically deranged, cannot be reconciled with wisdom, justice, and love. A nation that continues year after year to spend more money on military defense than on programs of social uplift is approaching spiritual death."

—MARTIN LUTHER KING, JR.

In the closing days of World War II, Robert M. La Follette, Jr., who held the same Senate seat and the same anti-imperialist views as his father, delivered a sober warning to the Congress. Worried that adventurists within the administration of the new president, Harry Truman, were already preparing to extend the global reach of the United States in the postwar years, La Follette observed, "Unless we change our direction soon, we shall find that our fantastic expenditure of men, money, and materials has brought us only a short and uneasy truce—not the enduring peace we pray for and seek." La Follette, Hiram Johnson, and the handful of other anti-imperialists that remained in the Senate tried to raise the alarm against those who would involve America in a Cold War with the Soviet Union that would squander the promise of peace on an endless global crusade against Communism and whatever other threats might be conjured by those engaged in the career of empire.

The signs of trouble were already arriving from distant corners of the globe, particularly southeast Asia. In November of 1945, as American troops who had fought the Japanese in the South Pacific awaited the boats that would bring them home, an urgent cable was dispatched to Washington by the merchant marines who crewed the troopship *Winchester Victory*. Addressed to President Truman, the cable announced, "[We] vigorously protest the use of this and other American vessels for carrying foreign combat troops to foreign soil . . . to further the imperialist policies of foreign governments when there are American troops waiting to come home." Turned off course from their task of ferrying American soldiers homeward, the merchant marines had been assigned to carry French troops to Vietnam to put down an insurrection against the reintroduction of French colonial rule. When they arrived in Vietnam, the merchant marines learned that the French were attacking revolutionaries who had issued a Vietnamese Declaration of Independence that opened with a quote from the U.S. Declaration of Independence. The crews of four troopships used to transport French troops signed a letter condemning the U.S. government for using their ships to help the French "to subjugate the native population of Vietnam."

It was the first protest against the misguided U.S. role in that far-off land.

Through the late 1940s, America experienced a genuine, if unbalanced, debate about how it would engage with other countries in the aftermath of World War II. Former Vice President Henry Wallace campaigned for the presidency as a third-party candidate in 1948, declaring that, "I am utterly against any kind of imperialism or expansionism whether sponsored by Britain, Russia, or the United States, and I call on Russia as well as the United States to look at all our differences objectively and free from that prejudice which the hatemongers have engendered on both sides." Wallace was soundly defeated, and the years that followed saw the death of the dream he had described when he said, "We seek a peace that is more than just a breathing space between the death of an old tyranny and the birth of a new one. We will not be satisfied with a peace which will merely lead us from the concentration camps and mass murder of Fascism into an international jungle of gangster governments operated behind the scenes by power-crazed, money-mad imperialists."

Again and again, the United States would be drawn, without the approval of Congress, into the endless Asian conflicts of Korea, Taiwan and China, Vietnam, Cambodia, and Laos.

In the 1950s, when Senator Joe McCarthy and his minions created a climate where any questioning of U.S. policy was portrayed as treason, dissenting voices were few. The actor Paul Robeson would note in 1954 that, "Vast quantities of U.S. bombers, tanks, and guns have been sent against Ho Chi Minh and his freedom fighters; and now we are told that soon it may be 'advisable' to send American GIs into Indochina in order that the tin, rubber and tungsten of Southeast Asia be kept by the 'free world'—meaning white imperialism." Robeson was prescient. Unfortunately, he had already been dismissed by most of the media as a dangerous radical. No more respect was accorded the aging senator from Colorado, Edwin Johnson, who echoed Robeson when he told the Senate in the same year that, "I am against sending American GIs into the mud and muck of Indochina on a bloodletting spree to perpetuate colonialism and white man's exploitation in Asia."

Thirteen years later, Edwin Johnson, now out of the Senate and several generations older than the students he addressed, would appear at
a rally at the University of Colorado to declare the Vietnam fight "the
worst war that the United States has ever been in." By then, the United
States was definitely "in" Vietnam. Only two senators had opposed
President Lyndon Johnson's 1964 Gulf of Tonkin Resolution—
Oregon's Wayne Morse and Alaska's Ernest Gruening, both veterans of
Robert M. La Follette's anti-imperialist campaign for the presidency in
1924. But by 1967, the opposition was growing in Congress and in the
streets. It was even turning up in poetry of Adrienne Rich and Denise
Levertov, and in popular songs of the day, especially those of Phil
Ochs, whose albums "read" like pages from the anti-imperialist mani-
festos of the late nineteenth and early twentieth centuries.

The anti-Vietnam War movement was not merely an anti-imperialist
enterprise. In fact, much of the most passionate opposition was
inspired by the simple self-interest of young Americans who did not
want to be drafted into a pointless war. Among African-Americans
and Latinos there was, as well, an understanding that they were being
asked to fight and die for a government that had yet to afford them a
full measure of equality.

Yet, it is important to understand that the anti-imperialist impulse
underpinned much of the most thoughtful opposition to the Vietnam
War. The 1962 Port Huron Statement, which gave rise to the Students
for a Democratic Society (SDS), echoed the anti-imperialists of old
with its condemnations of "gunboat diplomacy" and its declaration
that, "With rare variation, American foreign policy in the fifties was
guided by a concern for foreign investment and a negative anti-
Communist political stance linked to a series of military alliances,
both undergirded by military threat." Reverend Martin Luther King,
Jr. warned in 1967 that, "We are engaged in a war that seeks to turn
the clock of history back and perpetuate white colonialism. The
greatest irony and tragedy of all is that our nation which initiated so
much of the revolutionary spirit of the modern world, is now cast in
the mold of being an arch antirevolutionary." And, as he initiated
hearings that would expose the madness of the war, Senate Foreign
Relations Committee Chair J. William Fulbright would decry "the
arrogance of power" and "the price of empire."

As had been the case at the start of the twentieth century, the anti-imperialists turned their attention to politics, recognizing that a change of administrations was the first step toward a change of policy. The antiwar presidential candidacies of Eugene McCarthy and Bobby Kennedy in 1968, and of George McGovern in 1972, would reopen the national discourse about morality and foreign policy that had been silent for too long. Kennedy, in particular, spoke of the damage done to America by a career of empire, saying, "Our country is in danger: Not just from foreign enemies; but above all from our own misguided policies," while launching his campaign. And, "This is a contest, not for the rule of America, but for the heart of America. In the next eight months, we are going to decide what this country will stand for and what kind of men we are."

After Kennedy's death, his friend and comrade, McGovern, would take up the cause. As the nominee of the Democratic Party in 1972, McGovern would run the most explicitly anti-imperialist campaign of any major-party presidential candidate since William Jennings Bryan in 1900. McGovern's slogan, "Come Home, America," was a conscious echo of the questioning of entanglement, expansion, and empire that had been a part of the American dialogue from the time of Washington and Jefferson.

McGovern would lose the 1972 election, but one of his platform's most radical promises—a pledge to "return to Congress, and to the people, a meaningful role in decisions on peace and war"—would seemingly be realized with the 1973 votes of the House and Senate for a War Powers Act that was intended to limit the ability of president's to launch undeclared wars. Senator Thomas Eagleton, a cosponsor of the act said that it was written to "institutionalize the original intent of the Founders" that he described as "a very restrictive view of the president's right to conduct war without congressional authorization."

A handful of members of Congress argued, however, that the War Powers Act would create more problems than it solved. "It won't prevent future presidents from committing us to a military folly," warned Representative Ron Dellums.

Unfortunately, Dellums would be proved right.

———— ✕ ————

Unless we change our direction soon, we shall find that our fantastic expenditure of men, money, and materials has brought us only a short and uneasy truce—not the enduring peace we pray for and seek.

—U.S. SENATOR ROBERT M. LA FOLLETTE, *speech on the floor of the Senate, May 31, 1945. La Follette worried that the United States would squander opportunities to forge a lasting peace in the aftermath of World War II and instead embark upon a career of empire that would involve the U.S. in endless and ever more costly wars.*

∽

The time has come for a new party to fight these war makers. We say that peace is mandatory and that it can be had if we only want it.

Universal military training is the first decisive step on the road toward Fascism. We shall fight it to the limit and all congressmen who vote for it.

A new party must stand for a positive youth program of abundance and security, not scarcity and war. We can prevent depression and war if we only organize for peace in the same comprehensive way we organize for war.

I personally was for the humanitarian aspects of the Marshall Plan long before it was announced. Because I saw the post-war need of helping human beings, I was accused of wanting a quart of milk for every Hottentot. I pushed for help for Greece against the opposition of the administration eight months before the Truman Doctrine was announced.

But I have fought and shall continue to fight programs which give guns to people when they want plows. I fight the Truman Doctrine and the Marshall Plan as applied because they divide Europe into two warring camps. Those whom we buy politically with our food will soon desert us. They will pay us in the basic coin of temporary gratitude and then turn to hate us because our policies are destroying their freedom.

We are restoring western Europe and Germany through United States agencies rather than United Nations agencies because we want to hem Russia in. We are acting in the same way as France and

England after the last war and the end result will be the same—confusion, digression, and war.

It just doesn't need to happen. The cost of organizing for peace, prosperity, and progress is infinitely less than the organizing for war.

—HENRY WALLACE, *speech announcing his candidacy for president in 1948, December 29, 1947. Wallace became the leading voice of opposition to the developing Cold War, which he and others feared would cause the United States to play the role of an imperialist power. He and his running mate, U.S. Senator Glen Taylor, an Idaho Democrat, ran on the Progressive Party ticket, drawing support from disenchanted Democrats, Midwestern independent Populists, and Communists. Their campaign sought to rally broad support against Cold War policies, arguing that Franklin Roosevelt's vision of international cooperation had been abandoned by Truman. "Franklin Roosevelt looked beyond the horizon and gave us a vision of peace, an economic bill of rights; the right to work, for every man willing. The right of every family to a decent home. The right to protection from the fears of old age and sickness. The right to a good education. All the rights which spell security for every man, woman, and child, from the cradle to the grave. It was the dream that all of us had, and Roosevelt put it into words, and we loved him for it," Wallace told delegates at the Progressive Party convention. "Two years later the war was over, and Franklin Roosevelt was dead. And what followed was the great betrayal. Instead of the dream, we have inherited disillusion. Instead of the promised years of harvest, the years of the locust are upon us. In Hyde Park, they buried our president and in Washington, they buried our dreams." Like many critics of the looming Cold War, Wallace was portrayed as a tool of the Soviet Union by his critics. "If I fail to cry out that I am anti-Communist, it is not because I am friendly to Communism, but because at this time of growing intolerance I refuse to join even the outer circle of that band of men who stir the steaming cauldron of hate and fear," he replied, in one of the most pointed criticisms of those who sought to silence domestic debate over foreign policy. Yet, the attacks damaged his candidacy. Wallace received only 1,157,000 votes. Most of Wallace's predictions about the costs—economic and democratic—of the Cold War came to pass.*

Think of the untold billions of dollars and the untold lives wasted on the Vietnam War. Think of the ruinous inflation it set off, which certainly would not have happened if Wallace and I had been elected. I did my best. I tried.

—FORMER U.S. SENATOR GLEN TAYLOR, *The Way It Was With Me: A Personal and Political Memoir, Told With Relish and Laced With Dire Truth, (Book Sales, 1979). Taylor was Henry Wallace's running mate.*

∾

I supported Henry Wallace for a while in '48. . . . Because he foresaw the revolutionary movements around the world, and felt as I did—that our foreign policy was becoming too militarized, too "get tough," and we were being identified with an order that was passing.

—GEORGE MCGOVERN, *interview with* Life *magazine, July 7, 1972. Fifty years after Wallace's defeat, McGovern spoke at Department of Agriculture celebration to honor Wallace's memory. "Nineteen forty-eight was the first presidential election year in which my wife Eleanor and I were able to vote. That was the year Henry Wallace ran for president on the Progressive ticket . . . I supported Mr. Wallace and we served as delegates to his convention in Philadelphia. Wallace believed that the Cold War and the global arms race between Russians and Americans were over done," said McGovern. "He believed that fundamental economic and political problems could not be resolved by military means. Twenty-four years later I won the Democratic presidential nomination on a similar platform—ending U.S. involvement in Vietnam and bringing the Cold War and the arms race under control . . . Mr. Wallace and I did not win those two elections. But I'm glad that I stood with Wallace in 1948 and with McGovern in 1972!"*

∾

If it is to be contended that if we enter into this treaty we take the power away from the Congress, and the president can send troops all over the world to fight battles anywhere, if it is to be said that that is to be the policy of this country, I say that the American people will never support any senator or any representative who advocates such a policy; and make no mistake about it.

> —U.S. SENATOR BURTON WHEELER, *comment made during the Senate debate over whether to approve the United Nations Charter, July 1945. Wheeler worried about whether, in response to a decision by the United Nations, U.S. troops could be committed to combat without congressional approval. President Harry Truman pledged to Congress that, "When any such agreement or agreements are negotiated it will be my purpose to ask the Congress for appropriate legislation to approve them." That assurance secured an 89–2 Senate vote approving the UN Charter.*

℘

When we agreed to the United Nations Charter we never agreed to supplant our Constitution with the United Nations Charter. The power to declare and make war is vested in the representatives of the people, in the Congress of the United States.

> —U.S. REPRESENTATIVE VITO MARCANTONIO, *complaining about President Truman's commitment of U.S. forces to serve in Korea without congressional approval, 1951. Four decades after Marcantonio's death, one of his supporters recalled the congressman's lonely opposition to the Korean War. "He was the only one who voted in 1950 against the Korean War, and he was right," Mark Anthony Varrichia said in 1995.*

℘

[If President Truman can intervene in Korea] without congressional approval, he can go to war in Malaya or Indonesia or Iran or South America.

—U.S. SENATOR ROBERT TAFT, *1950 from 96 Congressional Record at 9323. The Ohio Republican, a leader of conservatives in Congress, echoed the concerns of the House's most radical member, Vito Marcantonio, about the loss of congressional authority and the threat that this would lead to more U.S. military adventurism. Taft accepted that the commitment of the United States to the United Nations would require different approaches, but he added, "I do not think it justifies the president's present action without approval by Congress."*

‹

⚮

Six months ago the truce negotiations began in Korea. But today the bloodshed continues, and the American diplomats and top brass persist in carrying on the most shameful war in which our country has ever been engaged.

A hundred thousand American dead, wounded, and missing have been listed in this war . . . and more than that, we have killed, maimed, and rendered homeless a million Koreans, all in the name of preserving Western civilization. U.S. troops have acted like beasts, as do all aggressive, invading, imperialist armies. North and South of the 38th parallel, they have looked upon the Korean people with contempt, called them filthy names, raped their women, lorded it over old women and children, and shot prisoners in the back.

Is it any wonder that Reverend Adam Powell, New York congressman, returns from a lengthy tour of Britain, Europe, the Near East, and Africa to report that the United States is "the most hated nation in the world"?

Yes, our government is well hated because it has forced on the people a policy which places this nation in deadly opposition to the liberation movements of hundred of millions of people in all parts of the globe.

When the Iranians took back their rich oil fields from the British exploiters, whose side were we on? Now that the Egyptian masses are calling for John Bull to get out of Egypt, and the Suez Canal, what position do we take? With Chiang Kai-shek's mercenary troops violating the border of Burma to achieve a springboard for attack upon the Chinese mainland, do we rush to protect the sovereignty of Burmese soil or do we lend covert and open support to Chiang's marauders?

In Indochina, Indonesia, Malaya—which side are we on? The question almost answers itself. In each case, we have been on the side of the Dutch, the French, and the British colonial powers who stand arrogantly, arms akimbo, feet spread wide, blocking the road to national liberation and independence. . . . Millions in the colonial world want peace, not war. And they are joined by millions in Europe, Latin America, Canada, and the U.S. who are tired of slaughter. . . . The war means a government bent on conquest has no interest in preserving civil rights at home because civil rights imply the right to protest and war-bent rulers need conformity, not protest.

—PAUL ROBESON, *speaking in opposition to the Korean War, 1952. Robeson, one of the country's best-known actors, was an outspoken critic of U.S. military adventurism abroad and of the entanglement of the United States in the defense of the colonial possessions of European nations.*

∽

Leading this new colonial imperialism comes my own native land built by my father's toil and blood, the United States. The United States is a great nation; rich by grace of God and prosperous by the hard work of its humblest citizens. . . . Drunk with power we are leading the world to hell in a new colonialism with the same old human slavery which once ruined us; and to a third world war which will ruin the world.

—W. E. B. DU BOIS, *from his speech expressing his anger over the role the United States was playing in supporting colonial powers and undermining uprisings in the dawning Cold War era, 1949. An America obsessed with controlling Communism, DuBois warned, would soon move from supporting colonialism and imperialism to practicing colonialism and imperialism.*

So who is the real aggressor and the real threat to peace? Who is behaving like an international bandit? We have no business making these unilateral resolutions when we should be taking the entire dilemma to the United Nations.

—U.S. Senator Wayne Morse, *opposing the Formosa Resolution that authorized the president "to employ the Armed Forces of the United States as he deems necessary for the specific purpose of securing and protecting Formosa and the Pescadores against armed attack," January 28, 1955. Morse, who served in the Senate as a Republican, then as an Independent and, finally, as a Democrat representing Oregon, objected to the delegation to the executive branch of long-term discretionary authority over whether to dispatch military forces to defend Taiwan against China. He warned that, in the name of battling Communism abroad, the United States was abandoning its Constitution and embarking on a career of military adventurism abroad. Morse did not prevail. The Senate approved the resolution by an 83–2 margin, while the House voted for it 410–3. A year later, Congress passed a joint resolution authorizing President Eisenhower to order U.S. military forces into action in the "general area" of the Middle East to help nations "requesting assistance against armed aggression from any country controlled by international Communism." Morse opposed that resolution, as well, saying, "I am not going to vote to give the president any power to make war in the Middle East by a predated declaration of war." Suggesting that, rather than fighting Communism, U.S. troops were actually being dispatched in the region to defend oil interests, Morse said, "I am not in favor of spilling American blood for oil."*

We strike against death, desolation, destruction, and on behalf of life and liberty.

—WOMEN STRIKE FOR PEACE, *appeal of the group that urged American women not to work on November 1, 1961, in order to register their anger at nuclear testing and other preparations for war that they argued were endangering the safety, health, and security of Americans, September 21, 1961. Noting reports that levels of strontium-90 in milk had risen sharply since atmospheric testing of hydrogen bombs began, their "Pure Milk, Not Poison" campaign urged women to boycott milk unless it was decontaminated. They also protested against civil-defense requirements and in favor of a testing moratorium—which was eventually agreed to—and disarmament.*

New York lawyer Bella Abzug chaired the group's legislative committee. Chapters were organized across the country and eventually formed a part of the infrastructure for the anti-Vietnam War movement. The Ann Arbor, Michigan, chapter declared in 1962 that, "We present a resolute stand of women in the United States against the unprecedented threat to life from nuclear holocaust. We are women of all races, creeds, and political persuasions who are dedicated to the achievement of general and complete disarmament under effective international control. We cherish the right and respect the responsibility of the individual in a democratic society to act to influence the course of government. We join with women throughout the world to challenge the right of any nation or group of nations to hold the power of life or death over the world." The Women Strike for Peace movement provided inspiration for the nuclear freeze movement of the early 1980s and for Code Pink—Women for Peace, which opposed the U.S. attack on Iraq in the spring of 2003.

It was generally conceded that had an election been held, Ho Chi Minh would have been elected premier . . . I have never talked or corresponded with a person knowledgeable in Indochinese affairs who did not agree that had elections been held as of the time of the fighting, possibly 80 percent of the population would have voted for the Communist Ho Chi Minh as their leader.

—FORMER PRESIDENT DWIGHT D. EISENHOWER, *1963, from* Mandate for Change *(Doubleday, 1963). When the French*

withdrew their military forces from Vietnam in 1954, the United States
began to provide military aid to anti-Communist forces in the southern
part of the country. Popular sentiment in Vietnam was with the veteran
campaigner for Vietnamese independence, Ho Chi Minh. A Geneva
Conference agreement to hold free elections was not honored by the
U.S. and its minions because the party of Ho Chi Minh was all but
certain to win the election. The U.S. was assuming the role of the
French colonialists.

∽

The policy of our government to continue to support military dictatorship is costing us heavily in prestige around the world, because the policy proves us to be hypocritical. . . . So long as Diem is the head of the government of South Vietnam, we continue to support a tyrant, we continue to support a police-state dictator. . . . On the basis of the present policies that prevail there, South Vietnam is not worth the life of a single American boy.

—U.S. SENATOR WAYNE MORSE, *September 6, 1963. From*
the mid-1950s on, the Oregon Democrat grew increasingly concerned
about the expanding U.S. military presence around the world during
the Cold War. Initially troubled by the prospect of presidents waging
wars without congressional authorization, Morse came to believe
that the United States was sacrificing its post-World War II position
as a respected world leader because successive presidents were
siding with dictators against popular movements for liberation.

∽

I would look with great dismay on a situation involving the landing of large armies on the continent of Asia. Is there anything in the resolution which would authorize or recommend or approve the landing of large American armies in Vietnam or in China?

> —U.S. SENATOR DANIEL B. BREWSTER, *comment said to Senate Foreign Relations Committee chair William Fulbright during the floor debate on the Gulf of Tonkin Resolution, August 6, 1964. Fulbright replied to Brewster, "There is nothing in the resolution, as I read it, that contemplates it. I agree with the senator that that is the last thing we would want to do." But Fulbright added, "However, the language of the resolution would not prevent it. It would authorize whatever the commander in chief feels is necessary. It does not restrain the executive from doing it." The Gulf of Tonkin Resolution was rushed through the Senate by Fulbright, who later said he was mistaken to support President Lyndon Johnson's request for authorization to "take all necessary measures to repel armed attack against the forces of the United States and to prevent further aggression."*

[handwritten marginal note: drastic increase in troops during Vietnam]

[The Tonkin Gulf Resolution is] a predated declaration of war in clear violation of Article 1, Section 8 of the Constitution, which vests the power to declare war in the Congress and not in the president. . . . There is no power in the Constitution to wage a preventive war.

> —U.S. SENATOR WAYNE MORSE, *comment said during the Gulf of Tonkin Resolution debate, August 6, 1964. Morse warned that, "When we were through, we should have killed millions and won military victory after military victory, but we should have still lost the war." During a break in the debate, however, he admitted to journalist George Wilson, "Everything I'm saying is being met with a deafening silence."*

I believe that history will record that we have made a great mistake in subverting and circumventing the Constitution of the United States . . . I believe this resolution to be a historic mistake. I believe that within the next century, future generations will look with dismay and great disappointment upon a Congress which is now about to make such a historic mistake.

—U.S. SENATOR WAYNE MORSE, *statement made toward the end of the Gulf of Tonkin debate, August 7, 1964. Barely three years later, Senate Foreign Relations Committee chairman William Fulbright, who had refused to take Morse's side in opposition to the Gulf of Tonkin Resolution, would hold hearings to investigate how the resolution had led to an undeclared war in which hundreds of thousands of American troops were serving in southeast Asia. On an angrier note, Morse told fellow Democratic senators, "You have no right to call yourselves 'liberal.' There's no other bonafide liberal in the Senate except my colleague from Alaska [Gruening]. You've let yourselves become jelly-bellied puppets of the administration."*

⌇

WE SEEK NO WIDER WAR

We're teaching people freedom for which they are yearning
While were dragging them down to the path of never returning
But we'll condescend to talk while the cities are burning
But please be reassured, we seek no wider war.

And the evil is done in hopes that evil surrenders
but the deeds of the devil are burned too deep in the embers
and a world of hunger in vengeance will always remember
So please be reassured, we seek no wider war,
we seek no wider war.

—PHIL OCHS, *"We Seek No Wider War," from* Phil Ochs in Concert *(1966). The title of the song was taken from a statement by Lyndon Johnson, in which the president assured the American people and the world that he did not intend to commit large numbers of troops to Vietnam, saying, "We have no ambition there for ourselves. We seek no wider war." Arnie Albert, a New Hampshire peace activist explains, "Ochs used it to highlight the deception and self-deception of the time. The song refers to advisers, defoliants, escalation, and the French wars in Vietnam that preceded ours. As Ochs no doubt expected, the war widened and went on for another ten years." Alpert wrote an essay*

> *decades later explaining that, "Phil Ochs's songs about Vietnam*
> *reflected his understanding of past wars, against enemies foreign and*
> *domestic, real and imagined, praiseworthy, and evil." Writing as the*
> *Bush administration prepared for attacks on Afghanistan and Iraq,*
> *Alpert asked, "Could we hope for a better critique of the latest U.S.*
> *war?" Ochs was a regular at antiwar rallies, but rarely was invited to*
> *appear on television during the war years. He died in 1973.*

∽

LET US SHAPE THE FUTURE

And others will make of it that I sound mighty anti-American. To these, I say: Don't blame me for that! Blame those who mouthed my liberal values and broke my American heart.

Just who might they be, by the way? Let's take a brief factual inventory of the latter-day Cold War.

In 1953, our Central Intelligence Agency managed to overthrow Mossadegh in Iran, the complaint being his neutralism in the Cold War and his plans to nationalize the country's oil resources to improve his people's lives. Most evil aims, most evil man. In his place we put in General Zahedi, a World War II Nazi collaborator. New arrangements on Iran's oil gave twenty-five year leases on 40 percent of it to three U.S. firms, one of which was Gulf Oil. The CIA's leader for this coup was Kermit Roosevelt. In 1960, Kermit Roosevelt became a vice president of Gulf Oil.

In 1954, the democratically elected Arbenz of Guatemala wanted to nationalize a portion of United Fruit Company's plantations in his country, land he needed badly for a modest program of agrarian reform. His government was overthrown in a CIA-supported right-wing coup. The following year, General Walter Bedell Smith, director of the CIA when the Guatemala venture was being planned, joined the board of directors of the United Fruit Company.

Comes 1960 and Castro cries we are about to invade Cuba. The administration sneers, "poppycock," and we Americans believe it. Comes 1961 and the invasion. Comes with it the awful realization that the United States government had lied.

Comes 1962 and the missile crisis, and our administration stands prepared to fight global atomic war on the curious principle that another state does not have the right to its own foreign policy.

Comes 1963 and British Guiana where Cheddi Jagan wants independence from England and a labor law modeled on the Wagner Act. And Jay Lovestone, the AFL-CIO foreign policy chief, acting, as always, quite independently of labor's rank and file, arranges with our government to finance an eleven-week dock strike that brings Jagan down, ensuring that the state will remain British Guiana, and that any workingman who wants a wage better than fifty cents a day is a dupe of Communism.

Comes 1964. Two weeks after Undersecretary Thomas Mann announces that we have abandoned the Alianza's principle of no aid to tyrants, Brazil's Goulart is overthrown by the vicious right-winger, Ademar Barros, supported by a show of American gunboats at Rio de Janeiro. Within twenty-four hours, the new head of state, Mazzilli, receives a congratulatory wire from our president.

Comes 1965. The Dominican Republic. Rebellion in the streets. We scurry to the spot with twenty thousand neutral marines and our neutral peacemakers—like Ellsworth Bunker, Jr., ambassador to the organization of American States. Most of us know that our neutral marines fought openly on the side of the junta, a fact that the administration still denies. But how many also know that what was at stake was our new Caribbean sugar bowl? That this same neutral peacemaking Bunker is a board member and stock owner of the National Sugar Refining Company, a firm his father founded in the good old days, and one which has a major interest in maintaining the status quo in the Dominican Republic? Or that the president's close personal friend and advisor, our new Supreme Court Justice Abe Fortas, has sat for the past nineteen years on the board of the Sucrest Company, which imports blackstrap molasses from the Dominican Republic? Or that the rhetorician of corporate liberalism and the late President Kennedy's close friend, Adolf Berle, was chairman of that same board? Or that our roving ambassador Averill Harriman's brother Roland is on the board of National Sugar? Or that our former ambassador to the Dominican Republic, Joseph Farland, is a board member of the South Puerto Rico Sugar Co., which owns two hundred and seventy-five thousand acres of rich land in the Dominican Republic and is the largest employer on the island—at about one dollar a day?

Neutralists! God save the hungry people of the world from such neutralists!

—CARL OGLESBY, *speech by the then president of Students for a Democratic Society, 1965. SDS chapters on more than four hundred campuses had a membership estimated at one hundred thousand.*

✺

I prefer the term "maternalism" for American policy in countries like Vietnam, because it reminds me of the story of an elephant who, as she strolled benignly in the jungle, stepped on a mother partridge and killed her. When she noticed the orphaned siblings, tears filled the kind elephant's eyes. "Ah, I too have maternal instincts," she said, turning to the orphans, and sat on them.

—EQBAL AHMAD, *"How to Tell When the Rebels Have Won,"
from* The Nation, *August 30, 1965.*

✺

The editors ask for a counterpolicy. I offer it. It is to get out of Asia.

—NORMAN MAILER, *from "A Happy Solution to Vietnam,"*
Partisan Review, *1966. This article was his response to an editorial request from the editors of that journal for an alternative policy to that of the Johnson administration. Rejecting the domino theory, which suggested that the U.S. had to fight the expansion of Communism, Mailer argued, "Look to the other side. To absolute isolation. If all the world but American were Communist, American would be militarily in no poor position. We could still fight the rest of the world if we chose to. That is the paradoxical nature of nuclear war. But it is doubtful if Communism would then have the impetus to fight anything. Can anyone conceive of Communism remaining unruptured in its cast-concrete heart on a diet of English Lords, French intellectuals, Italian lovers, African drums, Zen, yoga, pot, the New Wave, Pop art, camp—the prospect invites occupation."*

✺

The mounting fury of the richest and most powerful country is today being directed against one of the smallest and poorest countries in the world. The average income of the people of Vietnam is about fifty dollars a year—what the average American earns in a single week. The war today is costing the United States three million dollars an hour. What could not the Vietnamese do for their country with what we spend in one day fighting them! It is costing the United States four hundred thousand to kill one guerrilla—enough to pay the annual income of eight thousand Vietnamese. The United States can burn and devastate; it can annihilate the Vietnamese; but it cannot conquer them.

> —FELIX GREENE, Vietnam! Vietnam! *(Palo Alto Fulton Publishing, 1966). Journalist Seymour Hersh wrote in his 1983 book,* The Price of Power *(Summit Books, 1983), that the rapid growth in antiwar activism caused President Nixon to back away from a proposal by his national security adviser, Henry A. Kissinger, to use tactical nuclear weapons against ports and supply lines in an attack on North Vietnam.*

∽

I ain't got no quarrel with the Vietcong. . . . No Vietcong ever called me "nigger."

> —MUHAMMAD ALI, *explaining why he did not intend to fight in Vietnam, 1966. In 1967, Ali would say, "No, I am not going ten thousand miles to help murder, kill, and burn other people to simply help continue the domination of white slavemasters over dark people the world over. This is the day and age when such evil injustice must come to an end." In 1967, Ali, the heavyweight boxing champion of the world, was sentenced to five years in jail for refusing to be drafted to serve in Vietnam. The World Boxing Association (WBA) stripped him of his title. After three years of court battles, the conviction was overturned by the U.S. Supreme Court, which upheld Ali's right to conscientious-objector status, and the boxing association was forced to reinstate him. Ali's stance only served to heighten his popular appeal around the world.*

∽

It is a sad fact that, because of comfort, complacency, a morbid fear of Communism, and our proneness to add just to injustice, the Western nations that initiated so much of the revolutionary spirit of the modern world have now become the arch anti-revolutionaries. This has driven many to feel that only Marxism has the revolutionary spirit. Therefore, Communism is a judgment against our failure to make democracy real and follow through on the revolutions that we initiated. Our only hope today lies in our ability to recapture the revolutionary spirit and go out into a sometimes hostile world declaring eternal hostility to poverty, racism, and militarism.

—REVEREND MARTIN LUTHER KING, JR., *"Declaration of Independence from the War in Vietnam" speech at Riverside Church in New York City, April 4, 1967.*

∽

Today we are fighting an all-out war—undeclared by Congress. We have well over three hundred thousand American servicemen fighting in that benighted and unhappy country. American planes are bombing the territory of another country, and we are committing atrocities equal to any perpetrated by the Vietcong. This is the third largest war in American history.

All of this reveals that we are in an untenable position morally and politically. We are left standing before the world glutted by our barbarity. We are engaged in a war that seeks to turn the clock of history back and perpetuate white colonialism. The greatest irony and tragedy of all is that our nation which initiated so much of the revolutionary spirit of the modern world, is not cast in the mold of being an arch anti-revolutionary.

A third casualty of the war in Vietnam is the "Great Society." This confused war has played havoc with our domestic destinies.

Despite feeble protestations to the contrary, the promises of the Great Society have been shot down on the battlefield of Vietnam. The pursuit of this widened war has narrowed domestic welfare programs, making the poor, white, and Negro, bear the heaviest burdens both at the front and at home.

While the anti-poverty program is cautiously initiated, zealously supervised and evaluated for immediate results, billions are liberally expended for this ill-considered war. The recently revealed mis-estimate of the war budget amounts to ten billions of dollars for a single year. This error alone is more than five times the amount committed to anti-poverty programs. The security we profess to seek in foreign adventures we will lose in our decaying cities. The bombs in Vietnam explode at home: They destroy the hopes and possibilities for a decent America. If we reversed investments and gave the armed forces the anti-poverty budget, the generals could be forgiven if they walked off the battlefield in disgust.

Poverty, urban problems, and social progress generally are ignored when the guns of war become a national obsession. When it is not our security that is at stake, but questionable and vague commitments to reactionary regimes, values disintegrate into foolish and adolescent slogans.

It is estimated that we spend three hundred twenty-two thousand dollars for each enemy we kill, while we spend in the so-called war on poverty in America only about fifty-three dollars for each person classified as "poor." And much of that fifty-three dollars goes for salaries of people who are not poor. We have escalated the war in Vietnam and de-escalated the skirmish against poverty. It challenges the imagination to contemplate what lives we could transform if we were to cease killing.

—Reverend Martin Luther King, Jr.,
from a speech in Los Angeles, February 25, 1967.

∽

I would submit to you this morning that what is wrong in the world today is that the nations of the world are engaged in a bitter, colossal contest for supremacy. And if something doesn't happen to stop this trend, I'm sorely afraid that we won't be here to talk about Jesus Christ and about God and about brotherhood too many more years. (Yeah.) If somebody doesn't bring an end to this suicidal thrust that we see in the world today, none of us are going to be around, because somebody's going to make the mistake through our senseless blunderings of dropping a nuclear bomb somewhere. And then another one is going to drop. And don't let anybody fool you, this can happen within a matter of seconds. (Amen.) They have twenty-megaton bombs in Russia right now that can destroy a city as big as New York in three seconds, with everybody wiped away, and every building. And we can do the same thing to Russia and China.

But this is why we are drifting. And we are drifting there because nations are caught up with the drum major instinct. "I must be first." "I must be supreme." "Our nation must rule the world." (Preach it.) And I am sad to say that the nation in which we live is the supreme culprit. And I'm going to continue to say it to America, because I love this country too much to see the drift that it has taken.

God didn't call America to do what she's doing in the world now. (Preach it, preach it.) God didn't call America to engage in a senseless, unjust war as the war in Vietnam. And we are criminals in that war. We've committed more war crimes almost than any nation in the world, and I'm going to continue to say it. And we won't stop it because of our pride and our arrogance as a nation.

But God has a way of even putting nations in their place. (Amen.) The God that I worship has a way of saying, "Don't play with me." (Yes.) He has a way of saying, as the God of the Old Testament used to say to the Hebrews, "Don't play with me, Israel. Don't play with me, Babylon. (Yes.) Be still and know that I'm God. And if you don't stop your reckless course, I'll rise up and break the backbone of your power." (Yes.) And that can happen to America. (Yes.) Every now and then I go back and read Gibbons' *Decline and Fall of the Roman Empire.* And when I come and look at America, I say to myself, the parallels are frightening. And we have perverted the drum major instinct.

—REVEREND MARTIN LUTHER KING, JR., *sermon
delivered at Ebenezer Baptist Church, February 4, 1968.*

∽

The attitude above all others which I feel sure is no longer valid is the arrogance of power, the tendency of great nations to equate power with virtue and major responsibilities with a universal mission. The dilemmas involved are preeminently American dilemmas, not because America has weaknesses that others do not have but because America is powerful as no nation has ever been before and the discrepancy between its power and the power of others appears to be increasing. . . .

We are now engaged in a war to "defend freedom" in South Vietnam. Unlike the Republic of Korea, South Vietnam has an army which [is] without notable success and a weak, dictatorial government which does not command the loyalty of the South Vietnamese people. The official war aims of the United States government, as I understand them, are to defeat what is regarded as North Vietnamese aggression, to demonstrate the futility of what the Communists call "wars of national liberation," and to create conditions under which the South Vietnamese people will be able freely to determine their own future. I have not the slightest doubt of the sincerity of the president and the vice president and the secretaries of state and defense in propounding these aims. What I do doubt—and doubt very much—is the ability of the United States to achieve these aims by the means being used. I do not question the power of our weapons and the efficiency of our logistics; I cannot say these things delight me as they seem to delight some of our officials, but they are certainly impressive. What I do question is the ability of the United States, or France, or any other Western nation, to go into a small, alien, undeveloped Asian nation and create stability where there is chaos, the will to fight where there is defeatism, democracy where there is no tradition of it, and honest government where corruption is almost a way of life. Our handicap is well expressed in the pungent Chinese proverb, "In shallow waters, dragons become the sport of shrimps."

Early last month, demonstrators in Saigon burned American jeeps, tried to assault American soldiers, and marched through the streets shouting, "Down with the American imperialists," while one of the Buddhist leaders made a speech equating the United States with the Communists as a threat to South Vietnamese independence. Most Americans are understandably shocked and angered to encounter such hostility from people who by now would be under the rule of the

Vietcong but for the sacrifice of American lives and money. Why, we may ask, are they so shockingly ungrateful? Surely they must know that their very right to parade and protest and demonstrate depends on the Americans who are defending them.

The answer, I think, is that "fatal impact" of the rich and strong on the poor and weak. Dependent on it, though the Vietnamese are, our very strength is a reproach to their weakness, our wealth a mockery of their poverty, our success a reminder of their failures. What they resent is the disruptive effect of our strong culture upon their fragile one, an effect which we can no more avoid than a man can help being bigger than a child. What they fear, I think rightly, is that traditional Vietnamese society cannot survive the American economic and cultural impact. . . .

The cause of our difficulties in southeast Asia is not a deficiency of power but an excess of the wrong kind of power which results in a feeling of impotence when it fails to achieve its desired ends. We are still acting like Boy Scouts dragging reluctant old ladies across the streets they do not want to cross. We are trying to remake Vietnamese society, a task which certainly cannot be accomplished by force and which probably cannot be accomplished by any means available to outsiders. The objective may be desirable, but it is not feasible . . .

—U.S. SENATOR J. WILLIAM FULBRIGHT, The Arrogance of Power *(Random House, 1966). Fulbright, the chairman of the Senate Foreign Relations Committee, continually expressed concern about the damage the war in Vietnam was doing to American institutions and values. Fulbright's criticism of the Johnson administration's foreign policies brought antiwar sentiment into the congressional and media mainstream. As the war wore on, Fulbright said, "If I am remembered, I suppose it will be as a dissenter." Presidents Lyndon Johnson and Richard Nixon called him much worse. In February 1966, Fulbright, as chair of the Senate Committee on Foreign Relations, convened nationally televised hearings on the U.S. role in Vietnam. Defense Secretary Robert McNamara defended the U.S. intervention. Retired General James Gavin and veteran diplomat George Kennan criticized it. These so-called "Vietnam Hearings," one of the first examples in the post-World War II era of Congress asserting itself critically into the war-making process, are still cited as a groundbreaking indication of the breadth of opposition to the American role in Vietnam. "The hearings made it possible for responsible people to oppose the war," said Curtis Gans, who was on the staff of the liberal group Americans for Democratic Action. Gans joined Allard Lowenstein and other activists in working to turn that opposition into a political force.*

∽

By using our power like a giant we are fostering a world environment which is, to put it mildly, uncongenial to our society. By our undisciplined use of physical power, we have divested ourselves of a greater power: the power of example.

—U.S. SENATOR J. WILLIAM FULBRIGHT, *1967, from his speech, "A Sick Society," which developed on themes contained in the book* The Arrogance of Power *(Random House, 1966).*

∽

Vietnam, it seems to me, has become a theater of the absurd.

—HOWARD ZINN, Vietnam: The Logic of Withdrawal *(Beacon Press, 1967). In calling for a complete withdrawal of U.S. troops, Zinn explained that, "Thus far almost all of the nationally known critics of our Vietnam policy—perceptive as they are—have been reluctant to call for the withdrawal of the United States from Vietnam. Sometimes this is for substantative reasons, which I will discuss later on. But, often, I believe, it is because critics consider total military withdrawal, while logical and right, 'too extreme' as a tactical position, and therefore unpalatable to the public and unlikely to be adopted as national policy."*

∽

A nation has prestige according to its merits. America's contribution to world civilization must be more than a continuous performance demonstration that we can police the planet.

—U.S. SENATOR EUGENE MCCARTHY, *1967,* The Limits of Power *(Holt, Rinehart and Winston, 1967). McCarthy argued in that*

book that, "Many of our problems today are the result of our unwillingness or inability in the past to anticipate what may be the shape of the world twenty years in the future. . . . There is never a totally painless way to pull back from either unwise, ill-advised, or outdated ideas or commitments. But throughout history, mighty nations have learned the limit of power. There are lessons to be learned from Athens, from Rome, from sixteenth-century Spain."
McCarthy's opposition to the war struck a chord with Allard Lowenstein and other activists, who convinced the Minnesota Democrat to challenge Lyndon Johnson for the Democratic presidential nomination in 1968.

∽

Are we like the God of the Old Testament that we can decide in Washington, D.C., what cities, what towns, what hamlets in Vietnam are to be destroyed? Is it because we think it may possibly protect the people of Thailand, the people of Malaysia, the people of Hawaii, or keep certain people out of Texas or California or Massachusetts or New York? Or do we have that authority to kill tens and tens of thousands of people because we say we have a commitment to the South Vietnamese people? But have they been consulted, in Hue, in Ben Tre, or in the other towns that have been destroyed? Do we have the authority to put hundreds of thousands of people—in fact, millions of people—into refugee camps for their protection, or should these decisions be left to them? Do we have to accept that? . . . I do not think we have to. I think we can do something about it.

—U.S. SENATOR ROBERT F. KENNEDY, *statement made on the floor of the Senate, March 7, 1968. Eleven days later, the New York Democrat would announce his candidacy for the presidency. "I run for the presidency because I want the Democratic Party and the United States of America to stand for hope instead of despair, for reconciliation of men instead of the growing risk of world war," Kennedy said in his announcement speech. "I run because it is now unmistakably clear that we can change these disastrous, divisive policies only by changing the men who are now making them. For the reality of recent events in Vietnam has been glossed over with illusions." Kennedy added, "In private talks and in public, I have tried in vain to alter our course in Vietnam before it further saps our spirit and our manpower, further raises the risks of wider war, and further destroys the country and the people it was meant to save. I cannot stand aside from the contest that will decide our nation's future and our children's future."*

෴

When we are told to forgo all dissent and division, we must ask: Who is it that is truly dividing the country? It is not those who call for change; it is those who make present policy who divide our country . . . those who have removed themselves from the American tradition, from the enduring and generous impulses that are the soul of the nation. . . .

Those who now call for an end to dissent, moreover, seem not to understand what this country is all about. For debate and dissent are the very heart of the American process. We have followed the wisdom of ancient Greece: "All things are to be examined and brought into question. There is no limit set to thought. . . . How else is error to be corrected, if not by the informed reason of dissent . . ."

—U.S. SENATOR ROBERT F. KENNEDY, *from a speech at Vanderbilt University, March 1968. Kennedy defended antiwar activists, saying, "It is not enough to allow dissent, we must demand it, for there is much to dissent from."*

෴

The sharpest criticism often goes hand in hand with the deepest idealism and love of country.

—ROBERT F. KENNEDY, *speech in Philadelphia, February 24, 1967.*

෴

A man was killed on the fifth of June last year, and our experiment in political democracy—in political action—was stopped. You can't prove that political action can succeed, because it hasn't. But you can't prove that political action can't succeed, because I think we were on the way to success when Robert Kennedy was assassinated.

—ALLARD LOWENSTEIN, *in an interview with Erwin Knoll of* The Progressive, *August 1969. Kennedy won the California primary and many believed that his antiwar candidacy was in striking distance of securing the Democratic nomination and the presidency. After delivering his victory speech, he was assassinated on June 5, 1968. Johnson's vice president, Hubert Humphrey, was nominated and in November narrowly lost to Republican Richard Nixon. Nixon said he had a "secret plan" to end the Vietnam War, but never ended it. Lowenstein was elected to Congress from a New York State district.*

∽

All that we have proven in four years of bitter, inconclusive warfare is that, even with an army of half a million Americans, we cannot win a victory for an unpopular and incompetent regime against a disciplined, well-organized indigenous nationalist insurrectionary force, and this after the expenditure of one hundred-thirty thousand American lives in dead and wounded, and one hundred billion dollars. In the harsh but accurate summation of a British conservative who was once a supporter of the war:

"Instead of the Americans impressing the world with their strength and virtue, they are making themselves hated by some for what they are doing, and despised by the remainder for not doing it more efficaciously." . . .

Now, however, a hue and cry has been raised, this is the reason for the turmoil in American today, and for that we may be grateful, because the great debate in which we are engaged can, if we wish, be corrective as well as cathartic, by laying the foundations for a new approach in our foreign relations.

The shape and content of a new foreign policy are still beyond our view. For the moment all that comes clearly into focus are the contradictions of our present approach and a few basic inferences that can be drawn from recent experience, notably: that we need not rely on military intervention to give freedom a chance of surviving in the world; that we indeed cannot do so without compromising our own freedom; and that only by being true to our traditional values and our own best concept of ourselves can we hope to play a decent and constructive role in a revolutionary age.

—U.S. SENATOR FRANK CHURCH, *speech to the Empire Club of Canada, February 6, 1969. A Democrat from Idaho, Church traced his ideological roots to U.S. Senator Borah, the Republican anti-imperialist who chaired the Senate Foreign Relations Committee in the 1920s.*

∽

Is dissent a crime? Is this a reason for killing her? Have we come to such a state in this country that a young girl has to be shot because she disagrees deeply with the actions of her government?

—ARTHUR KRAUSE, *comment by the father of Allison Krause, one of four students killed by the National Guard during protests at Ohio's Kent State University on May 4, 1970. The Kent State killings came during a national wave of protests against President Nixon's unilateral decision to send U.S. troops into Cambodia. Two students were killed at Jackson State University in Mississippi during the same period, and dozens of campuses across the country were shut down. The Krause family fought a long legal battle in which they sought to hold officials accountable for what happened at Kent State. In the end, Arthur Krause said, "Kent State, 1970 means we no longer have our daughter, but it also means something to all Americans. . . . Our court battles establish without a doubt one thing. There is no Constitution. There is no Bill of Rights."*

∽

Los Chicanos estan muriendo en proporción del 2-a-1 en Vietnam.
[Mexicans are dying at a two to one ratio in Vietnam.]

> —ROSALIO MUNOZ, *speech to the Chicano Moratorium rally in Los Angeles against the war, August 29, 1970. One of a series of increasingly large antiwar protests by Latinos, the August 29 moratorium drew an estimated twenty-five thousand marchers. Banners declared, "Our War is Not in Vietnam, It is here at Home!" (¡Nuestra Guerra es Aqui!). Police attacked the crowd, killing three people, including journalist Ruben Salazar, a* Los Angeles Times *writer who had documented growing opposition to the war among Latinos. Salazar was posthumously awarded a special Robert F. Kennedy Journalism Award, and the park where Chicano Moratorium events were held was named in his honor. Rosalio Munoz remained active in antiwar movements, often echoing the concerns he raised back in 1970. At a gathering marking the thirty-second anniversary of the Chicano moratorium, Munoz said, "Our youth need to have more opportunities than prison or the military. We will not stand by and allow war fever to overwhelm our people."*

∽

I wear the black in mourning for the lives that could have been
Each week we lose a hundred fine young men
And I wear it for the thousands who have died
Believin' that the Lord was on their side
I wear it for another hundred thousand who have died
Believin' that we all were on their side
Well there's things that never will be right I know
And things need changin' everywhere you go
But 'till we start to make a move to make a few things right
You'll never see me wear a suit of white
Oh I'd love to wear a rainbow every day and tell the world that everything's okay
But I'll try to carry off a little darkness on my back
'Till things're brighter I'm the man in black

> —JOHNNY CASH, *"Man In Black," from the album* Man in Black, *1971. Cash performed for the troops in Vietnam. Asked if that made him a hawk, he replied that, no, he was "a dove with claws."*

In our opinion and from our experience, there is nothing in South Vietnam which could happen that realistically threatens the United States of America. And to attempt to justify the loss of one American life in Vietnam, Cambodia, or Laos by linking such loss to the preservation of freedom, which those misfits supposedly abuse, is to us the height of criminal hypocrisy.

We are probably angriest about all that we were told about Vietnam and about the mystical war against Communism. We found that not only was it a civil war, an effort by people who had for years been seeking their liberation from any colonial influence whatsoever, but also we found that the Vietnamese whom we had enthusiastically molded after our own image were hard put to take up the fight against the threat we were supposedly saving them from. We found most people didn't even know the difference between Communism and democracy. They only wanted to work in rice paddies without helicopters strafing them and bombs with napalm burning their villages and tearing their country apart. They practiced the art of survival by siding with whichever military force was present at a particular time, be it Vietcong, North Vietnamese, or American. . . .

And now we are told that the men who fought there must watch quietly while American lives are lost so that we can exercise the incredible arrogance of Vietnamizing the Vietnamese. Each day to facilitate the process by which the United States washes her hands of Vietnam someone has to give up his life so that the United States doesn't have to admit something that the entire world already knows, so that we can't say that we have made a mistake. Someone has to die so that President Nixon won't be, and these are his words, "the first president to lose a war."

We are asking Americans to think about that because how do you ask a man to be the last man to die in Vietnam? How do you ask a man to be the last man to die for a mistake? But we are trying to do that, and we are doing it with thousands of rationalizations, and if you read carefully the President's last speech to the people of this country, you can see that he says, and says clearly, "but the issue, gentlemen, the issue is Communism, and the question is whether or not we will leave that country to the Communists or whether or not we will try to give it hope to be a free people." But the point is that

they are not a free people now, and we cannot fight Communism all
over the world.

—JOHN KERRY, *testimony before the Senate Foreign Relations
Committee, April 22, 1971. Kerry, a Yale University graduate,
volunteered to serve in the Navy during the Vietnam War. He received
a Silver Star, Bronze Star with Combat V, and three awards of the
Purple Heart for his service in combat. After leaving the navy, he
became a leading activist with Vietnam Veterans Against the War. After
Kerry testified, U.S. Senator Claiborne Pell, a Rhode Island
Democrat, said he hoped that Kerry "might one day be a colleague of
ours in this body." Fourteen years later, as a U.S. Senator from
Massachusetts, Kerry joined Pell on the Foreign Relations Committee.*

∽

Women have been trained to speak softly and carry a lipstick. Those
days are over.

—U.S. REPRESENTATIVE BELLA ABZUG, *June 9, 1972. A
founder and former legislative director for the national group Women
Strike for Peace—an antinuclear group that, she said, "flowed
naturally into the campaign to get U.S. troops out of Vietnam"—
Abzug was elected to Congress from New York City in 1970 as both a
feminist and a militantly antiwar candidate. A passionate critic of
U.S. interventions abroad, she argued that the United States had
plenty of issues to address at home—sexism, racism, economic
inequality—before it started telling other countries how to manage
their affairs. Writing of the anti-Vietnam War movement, columnist
Jimmy Breslin said, "Some came early, some came late, Bella was
always there." Abzug traced her attitudes about militarism to her
father's opposition to World War I. "I spend all day figuring out how
to beat the machine and knock the crap out of the power structure,"
Abzug wrote in her diary. "I'm not being facetious when I say the
real enemies in this country are the Pentagon and its pals in big
business." When House Speaker Carl Albert and Democratic Leader
Hale Boggs voted against her resolution to end the Vietnam War, she
reportedly turned to them and said, "Fuck you!"*

∽

Every senator in this chamber is partly responsible for sending fifty thousand young Americans to an early grave. This chamber reeks of blood. Every senator here is partly responsible for that human wreckage at Walter Reed and Bethesda Naval [hospitals] and all across our land—young men without legs, or arms, or genitals, or faces, or hopes. There are not very many of these blasted and broken boys who think this war is a glorious adventure. Do not talk to them about bugging out, or national honor, or courage. It does not take any courage at all for a congressman, or a senator, or a president to wrap himself in the flag and say we are staying in Vietnam, because it is not our blood that is being shed. But we are responsible for those young men and their lives and their hopes.

—U.S. SENATOR GEORGE MCGOVERN, *during a Senate debate on the McGovern-Hatfield amendment, a proposal written with the purpose of bringing a quick conclusion to U.S. involvement in the Vietnam War, September 1, 1970. The amendment was not enacted, but McGovern emerged as one of the Senate's most prominent war critics and began campaigning for the Democratic nomination as an antiwar candidate.*

∽

Come home, America!

—GEORGE MCGOVERN, *theme of his acceptance speech after winning the nomination of the Democratic Party for president, July 13, 1972. A native South Dakotan who had supported Henry Wallace's 1948 Progressive Party campaign, McGovern was not a 1960s peacenik, as the media frequently portrayed him. Rather, his politics were rooted in the Midwestern Farmer-Labor, Non-Partisan League, Progressive traditions of Robert M. La Follette and other foes of U.S. military adventurism abroad. Hampered by his own poorly run campaign, and undermined by the Nixon team's dirty tricks that would eventually come to be known as "Watergate," McGovern won only 39 percent of the vote. He carried just the District of Columbia and Massachusetts. Less than one year after the election, Nixon would begin major withdrawals of U.S. troops from Vietnam. Within two years, Nixon would be forced from office*

> *by the Watergate scandal. Two decades later, when many of McGovern's views had been vindicated, U.S. Senator Edward Kennedy would say of McGovern, "Before almost anyone else in the Senate, George McGovern spoke out against the failure of our policy. By 1965, he had seen enough. He knew that the ongoing crisis in Vietnam was the result of Vietnam's internal problems, and was no military threat to the United States. He called for an end to the widespread carpet bombings that were producing negligible military results but were having a devastating effect on the lives of millions of innocent Vietnamese civilians. The war was the issue, and it was natural that George would run for president in 1972. A watershed election became the Watergate election and in the eyes of history, George emerged as the true winner—even if he wasn't the Electoral College winner. But I still have my bumper sticker that says, 'Don't blame me—I'm from Massachusetts.'"*

✑

What remains, finally, is a warning: With so much power of decision on issues of war and peace concentrated in the hands of so few, the war-bred tyranny of kings that was banished by the war-power clauses of the Constitution returns in democratic disguise and the American Republic is in peril.

—ANTHONY AUSTIN, *from* The President's War: The Story of the Tonkin Gulf Resolution and How The Nation Was Trapped in Vietnam *(Lippincott, 1971).*

✑

The constitutional powers of the president as commander in chief to introduce United States Armed Forces into hostilities, or into situations where imminent involvement in hostilities is clearly indicated by the circumstances, are exercised only pursuant to (1) a declaration of war, (2) specific statutory authorization, or (3) a national emergency created by attack upon the United States, its territories or possessions, or its armed forces. . . .

The president in every possible instance shall consult with Congress before introducing United States Armed Forces into hostilities or into situation where imminent involvement in hostilities is clearly indicated by the circumstances, and after every such introduction shall consult regularly with the Congress until United States Armed Forces are no longer engaged in hostilities or have been removed from such situations.

—WAR POWERS ACT, *November 7, 1973. Passed by the House and Senate overwhelmingly, the act was vetoed by President Nixon. The veto was overridden and the act became law. The act spelled out a new, more formal relationship between the executive and legislative branches, with the president required to seek congressional approval within sixty days of the commitment of troops to any struggle.*

∽

Whether or not it was legitimate to consider [enactment of the War Powers Act] a symbolic victory against the Vietnam War and against presidential war making generally, I believe the resolution did dramatic harm to the constitutional balance of power.

—U.S. REPRESENTATIVE RON DELLUMS (WITH H. LEE HALTERMAN), Lying Down with the Lions *(Beacon, 2000). Dellums, a progressive Democrat from California who was a militant foe of the Vietnam War, argued that the War Powers Act, while portrayed as a limitation on presidents, actually represented a grant of new powers to the executive branch. Allowing a president to launch any sort of offensive action without congressional approval, he argued, "won't end the Vietnam War and it won't prevent future presidents from committing us to a military follow." He told colleagues, "It's not enough for me to hand Nixon a defeat." "Someday he'll be gone and we will have created a monster for some new president—to use in the future. I think we're going to come to regret this vote."*

∽

What if someone gave a war and nobody came?
Life would ring the bells of Ecstasy and Forever be Itself again.

> —ALLEN GINSBERG, *"Graffiti 12th Cubicle Men's Room*
> *Syracuse Airport,"* The Fall of America, *1973.*

∽

The biggest lesson I learned from Vietnam is not to trust our own government statements. I had no idea until then that you could not rely on them.

> —FORMER U.S. SENATOR WILLIAM FULBRIGHT,
> *interview with the* New York Times, *April 30, 1985.*

∽

I became convinced that the United States truly is an imperialist country. I had never given a thought to that accusation before. And I realized that as surely as the government represents industry on the international scene, it also represents industry on the domestic scene. I became a socialist. I used to be a very cautious person and considered very carefully anything I said. But when the federal government tried to throw me in jail and I beat them at their own game, that did a lot of good for me. I became much bolder. I don't mean that I'm terribly bold, but I'm a lot bolder than I used to be. At one point, one of my sisters, who hadn't seen me for a couple years, said to another of my sisters, "Say what's come over Ben?"

> —DR. BENJAMIN SPOCK, *1989, quoted in* It Did Happen Here
> *by Bud and Ruth Schultz (University of California Press, 1989).*
> *Spock was reflecting on the experience of his trial for counseling*
> *young people to resist the draft during the Vietnam War. The world-*
> *reknowned pediatrician had campaigned for Lyndon Johnson in*
> *1964, but by 1972 he sought the presidency himself as a militant*
> *antiwar candidate running on the People's Party ticket. Radicalized*
> *by the Vietnam War, he would spend the remainder of his life*
> *campaigning against U.S. military adventurism abroad.*

Spock, the author of books on raising children that were bestsellers during the 1950s and 1960s, said, "I was proud of the youths who opposed the war in Vietnam because they were my babies."

∽

In fact, since 1945, nothing has gone right for us. The war in Korea was a draw. The war in Vietnam was a defeat. Our constant meddling in the affairs of countries has made us not only widely hated but, rather more serious, despised.

—GORE VIDAL, AUGUST,
"The State of the Union Revisited," Esquire, *1980.*

NINE

And in the Process, They Made America a Lesser and a Less Respected Land

Arguing Against Preemptive War, Guarding Against Blowback, and Imagining the Republic Restored

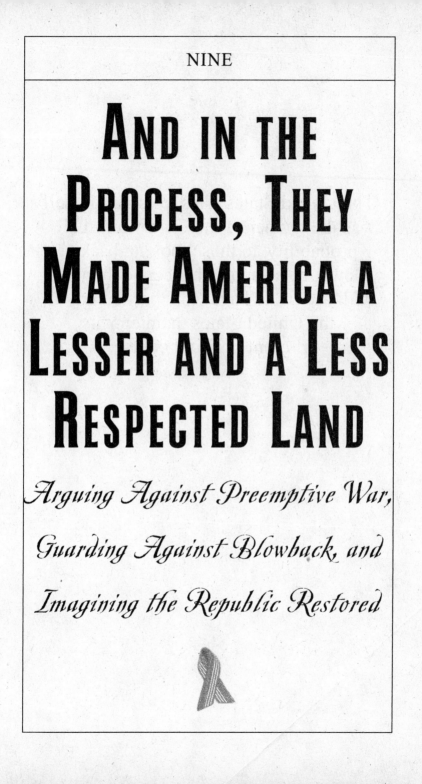

"The United States likes to think of itself as the winner of the Cold War. In all probability, to those looking back at blowback a century hence, neither side will appear to have won, particularly if the United States maintains its present imperial course.

—CHALMERS JOHNSON

America would end the twentieth century in much
the same manner as it was begun: with presidents intriguing to involve
the United States in distant wars for purposes that appeared more economic and expansionist than moral. The new targets of entanglement,
expansion, and empire were the Middle East countries that sat atop
the great oil riches that were coveted by the gas-guzzling nations of
the west. Replacing the old colonial powers that had drawn the
region's border lines, the United States became in the post-Cold War
era the dominant outside player in the region. And it played rough.

For dissenters against U.S. policy in the region, there were challenges. Critics of the U.S. allegiance to the government of Israel
sometimes found themselves charged with anti-Semitism, even as
they echoed the concerns expressed by Israeli progressives. And
those who argued that it was morally wrong and practically unwise
to send vast American armies to displace the leaders of oil-rich lands
were accused of favoring Fascism and fanaticism over freedom.

It was difficult even to frame the arguments, as the old language
of anti-imperialism had been cleansed from the lexicon of the era.
Even the critics of empire were cautious about raising valid arguments because they were, so frequently, dismissed as extremists or
fools. This unfortunate constraint, particularly during the first Gulf
War of 1991, prevented too many critics from stating the obvious:
that, once again, American troops were being sent to fight and die in
the service of corrupt monarchs and even more corrupt corporations.

When the first President Bush intrigued to send a massive U.S. force
to dislodge the Iraqi invaders of the oil kingdom of Kuwait in 1991, an
antiwar movement challenged him in the streets, carrying banners that
read, "No blood for oil." Members of Congress who had come of age
during the Vietnam era fought to prevent another undeclared war, with
the essential Ron Dellums and others suing the president to force him

to consult Congress. Though the suit was unsuccessful, the Bush administration went to Congress seeking a measure of approval—which it received by a reasonable margin in the House and a narrower one in the Senate. The consultation never resulted in a genuine declaration of war, though only a handful of members, in particular Texas Representative Henry B. Gonzalez, chose to note the illegality.

The war was quick, and seemingly easy. The Kuwaiti royals were back in power, and their oil fields were back in the service of the United States, within months. Yet, a few of its foes continued to warn that America would suffer terrible consequences. "I think that relying on the military and not giving economic sanctions and diplomacy a chance has scrambled the Middle East, will unleash forces there that are unknown and unknowable. Tremendous anger will be directed at the United States, Beirut writ large," said Senator Paul Wellstone. A brilliant scholar, Chalmers Johnson, would give scope and character to Wellstone's concerns, coining the phrase "blowback" to describe the anger and violence that was directed toward Americans in response to U.S. meddling in the affairs of distant lands.

A decade later, after several smaller assaults by groups that traced their anger to the 1991 decision of an American president to dispatch U.S. troops to politically shuffle the deck of the Muslim world, thousands of Americans would be killed as nineteen members of a Saudi Arabian millionaire's terrorist sect flew jet planes into the World Trade Center buildings and the Pentagon. Those who suggested that America's entanglement in the affairs in the Middle East might have provoked the tragedy would be condemned for speaking their heresy. Yet, what developed was precisely as Wellstone had predicted.

The response to the September 11 attacks gave the imperialists of a new age a fresh excuse for the old career of empire. There was no question that those who had plotted the attacks needed to be brought to justice. But there should have been some debate about how best to achieve that purpose. Instead, the Congress issued a second President Bush a blank check for a "war on terrorism" that would bloat Pentagon budgets to historic levels and enable the expansionists of the twenty-first century to implement schemes that would have made Teddy Roosevelt wince. Only one member of the Congress challenged the rush toward unregulated and endless war. "In 1964, Congress gave President

Lyndon Johnson the power to 'take all necessary measures' to repel attacks and prevent further aggression. In so doing, this House abandoned its own constitutional responsibilities and launched our country into years of undeclared war in Vietnam," recalled the lone dissenter, California Representative Barbara Lee. "At that time, Senator Wayne Morse, one of two lonely votes against the Tonkin Gulf Resolution, declared, 'I believe that history will record that we have made a grave mistake in subverting and circumventing the Constitution of the United States. . . . I believe that within the next century, future generations will look with dismay and great disappointment upon a Congress which is now about to make such a historic mistake.' Senator Morse was correct, and I fear we make the same mistake today."

Lee's critics said her vote would ruin her politically. Instead, she was reelected by an overwhelming margin. Between, September of 2001 and November of 2002, when the election was held, however, Lee's worst fears would be confirmed. Without evidence of a connection to the terrorist attacks of 2001, and without legitimate intelligence to suggest that a threat was posed, the Bush administration was preparing to launch a preemptive war to remove the disfavored sovereign of Iraq. A tepid and uninspired Congressional debate had handed the president a second blank check to launch a war that Bush's own Secretary of State warned would leave America "owning" Iraq. "This is the Tonkin Gulf Resolution all over again. Let us stop, look, and listen. Let us not give this president or any president unchecked power. Remember the Constitution," warned Senator Robert Byrd, who seemed at times during the prewar debate to channel the arguments of La Follette, Borah, Norris, and Blaine. Byrd would condemn his contemporary colleagues for their pliant behavior. "We cower in the shadows while false statements proliferate," he charged. "We accept soft answers and shaky explanations because to demand the truth is hard, or unpopular, or may be politically costly."

Outside the halls of Congress, millions rallied against the war that, again, they charged would be fought for oil. As it had been at the start of a previous century, the charge of "war profiteering" was sounded— and, this time, it was directed toward the office of the vice president, who was, conveniently, the former CEO of a company that had collected the most lucrative contracts for reconstructing Iraq.

As the invasion turned to occupation, Robert Byrd repeated comparisons of contemporary America to ancient Rome. And a few of his colleagues came to recognize the crisis that was at hand. At Byrd's side stood Senator Edward Kennedy, whose brother had attempted in 1968 to open a national debate about morality and foreign policy. In January of 2004, Kennedy condemned the Bush administration in language that shocked a pliant and dysfunctional media. "It has broken faith with the American people, aided and abetted by a congressional majority willing to pursue ideology at any price, even the price of distorting the truth," Kennedy said of the White House. "On issue after issue, they have moved brazenly to impose their agenda on America and on the world. They have pursued their goals at the expense of urgent national and human needs and at the expense of the truth. America deserves better."

Yes, said Byrd, America deserves better. And, he reminded the Senate, America was better. "This Republic was founded in part because of the arrogance of a king who expected his subjects to do as they were told, without question, without hesitation," the senator said. "Our forefathers overthrew that tyrant and adopted a system of government where dissent is not only important, but it is also mandatory. Questioning flawed leadership is a requirement of this government. Failing to question, failing to speak out, is failing the legacy of the Founding Fathers."

It is not likely that Robert Byrd has ever listened to the music of Patti Smith. It is doubtful that he would recognize the name of the poet and punk rocker. But they were speaking the same language in the first months of 2004. A few days after Byrd recalled the founders, Smith had this to say, "To me, a patriot is someone who constantly asks questions of his government and demands answers. Thomas Jefferson counseled us to be vigilant in watching our government and to overturn it if it wasn't representing us properly." Smith would energize antiwar rallies by singing a song about the consent of the governed titled, "People Have the Power."

And so it would be again. A new century. A new war. A new call for America to rise, once more, against the beast.

President Bush appears to be on the verge of making a terrible mistake that will have tragic consequences for the whole world.

—U.S. SENATOR PAUL WELLSTONE, *from his first speech as a senator, January 10, 1991. Wellstone was speaking in opposition to President George Herbert Walker Bush's proposal to launch a war against Iraq, which the previous August had invaded Kuwait. Wellstone warned that waging a war on Arab soil "could lead to [an] unpredictable and uncontrollable escalation in the form of terrorist attacks around the world." He worried that military action by the United States could lead to the destabilization of regimes that were friendly to the U.S., "unleash forces of fanaticism in the Middle East," and encourage the development of "radical anti-American forces."*

As a member of the Vietnam generation, when I was privileged to be sworn in as a member of Congress, I promised myself at that time I would never be part of any undeclared war.

—U.S. REPRESENTATIVE MARCY KAPTUR, *statement explaining her decision to join U.S. Representatives Ron Dellums, Don Edwards, fifty other members of the House and U.S. Senator Tom Harkin of Iowa in filing a lawsuit that would have forced President George H. W. Bush to ask Congress to pass a declaration of war before undertaking military action in the Persian Gulf, November 1990. Judge Harold H. Greene of the U.S. District Court for the District of Columbia refused, on procedural grounds, to grant an injunction that would have blocked President Bush from "waging war against Iraq without a congressional declaration of war." But the judge agreed that Congress had the sole power to declare war. Within days of his decision, President Bush asked Congress for permission to launch the Gulf War. Michael Ratner, of the Center for Constitutional Rights, explained, "It was clear that Judge Greene's decision had a fairly heavy impact on the president's decision to get congressional consent." The House voted 250–183 for the use of military force, while the Senate approved it by a narrow 52–47 margin.*

I haven't changed my mind at all. I've had a sense of foreboding ever since November 8, with the massive troop build up. I'm more worried than ever about the direction we're heading . . . all the questions I had weeks ago before the outbreak of war, against the policy of war, I continue to have. And I continue to express my misgivings.

—U.S. SENATOR PAUL WELLSTONE, *interview with* The Progressive, *January 1991. The interview was conducted after the war began. While many war critics backed off their criticism of the war after polls showed President Bush's approval ratings soaring to 91 percent, Wellstone continued to speak out. Referencing Bush's talk of creating a "New World Order" in the aftermath of the Cold War, Wellstone said, "I've tried to think and speak about the postwar world, and I don't believe I see a New World Order, but rather a new world disorder, a primitive world order linked to violence. An opportunity to build some permanent structure to deal with problems in nonviolent ways is lost; we were unable to do that. I fear what the military solution will mean. I think that relying on the military and not giving economic sanctions and diplomacy a chance has scrambled the Middle East, will unleash forces there that are unknown and unknowable. Tremendous anger will be directed at the United States, Beirut writ large. Finally, in a domestic part of the picture, we will have an administration unwilling to fight any other war—the war against AIDS, the war against poverty, against illiteracy, against drugs. And, I believe if we don't fight those wars, we will see only further decline in our country, our economy, our society."*

∽

U.S. Middle East Policy: Oil

Since WWI, when the world began to move onto an oil-based economy, the Middle East has become central in world affairs, for the very obvious reason that it has, by far the largest and the most accessible petroleum resources—primarily in Saudi Arabia, secondarily in Iraq, and thirdly in the Gulf Emirates, and elsewhere. It is, as the State Department described it during the Second World War, when the U.S. was taking over, "It's a stupendous source of strategic power and the greatest material prize in world history. . . ."

Well, the U.S. took over from Britain in the Middle East and, in fact, much of the world, after the Second World War. In fact, actually, replaced Britain and France. France was summarily expelled—they weren't given the time of day. Britain however, was given a role. It was given the role of "junior partner," as the British foreign office rather ruefully described it, accurately. Britain was going to be our lieutenant—the fashionable word is "partner"—as they were described by a senior adviser in the Kennedy administration. That's reasonably accurate—you're seeing an example of it right now. The lieutenant is doing its job—the attack dog, maybe.

The United States took over from—inherited from Britain—the modalities of control over the region as well. These modalities had changed during and after WWI, when Britain no longer had the force to rule the empire directly by occupation, and therefore had to turn to airpower and high technology—advanced technology. So, it was explained pretty frankly. The distinguished statesman Lloyd George was commenting on Britain's success in undermining a disarmament conference—which would have barred the use of airpower against civilians. He pointed out that it was a success because, as he put it, "We have to reserve the right to bomb the niggers." Which kind of sums up world affairs rather nicely. . . .

On the political side, Britain—(we know from the British Foreign Office records—Colonial Office records, which have been declassified)—they developed a system, which in fact the U.S. has taken over. The idea was, the oil-producing states would be administered by what the British called—secretly, of course—an "Arab facade"— constitutional fictions behind which Britain would continue to rule. Now the facade has to be weak, because it has to be dependable. It has to do what you tell it. But then, there's a problem: If the facade is weak, it may not be able to control its own population, and its own population is "uncivilized and ignorant." They "do not understand." They "can be easily infected" by what is called "a virus of radical nationalism." Which was defined by the State Department back in the 1940s as "the belief that the first beneficiaries of a country's resources ought to be the people of that country."

That, of course, is intolerable because "any sane and civilized person" can understand that the "first beneficiaries of a country's resources" have to be wealthy investors in the United States, and so on. "These people just don't understand that," and, "They're always causing trouble," "They're uncivilized tribesmen," and so on. . . . So, you have to have some way of keeping the "Arab facade" in power. And to do that, the U.S. developed the system; there are two kinds of violence required. Actually, this is all over the world. Much of the history of the last half-century is the playing out of this issue; in Southeast Asia and Latin America, and all over the world. It's not put that way, but that's the way it is. In the Middle East, the way it was worked out, is that there are to be what the Nixon administration called "local cops on the beat," that is, local gendarmes who sort of keep order in the neighborhood. And it's best to have them be non-Arab 'cause they're better at killing "recalcitrant Arabs." So, there's a periphery of—in fact, what David Ben Gurion, Israeli prime minister, called the "periphery policy" non-Arab states, Iran (under the Shah), Turkey, Israel, Pakistan. They are there to be the "local cops on the beat," but the understanding, of course, is that "police headquarters" remains in Washington. And if things really get out of hand—the "local cops on the beat" can't handle it—there's British and U.S. muscle in reserve to be used when needed. That's essentially the modality of control.

—NOAM CHOMSKY, *talk at Columbia University in New York City, April 4, 1999. During the 1980s and 1990s, when many on the left shied away from the use of words such as "imperialism" and "empire," Chomsky kept the discourse alive with talks on university campuses. Talks by the internationally acclaimed academic drew huge crowds but little coverage in the so-called "elite media." Only after the September 11, 2001, terrorist attacks on the World Trade Center and the Pentagon did Chomsky begin to get a measure of attention from newspapers such as the* Washington Post *and the* New York Times. *Even then, however, he was not seen on broadcast television.*

The Consequences of Our Actions Abroad:
Americans Feeling the Effects of "Blowback"

Perhaps the term "blowback" can help us to re-link certain violent acts against Americans to the policies from which they secretly—as far as most Americans are concerned—sprang. From refugee flows across our southern borders from countries where U.S.-supported repression has created hopeless conditions, to U.S.-supported economic policies that have led to unimaginable misery, blowback reintroduces us to a world of cause and effect.

We also might consider widening the word's application to take in the unintended consequences U.S. policies may have for others. For example, even if the policies that our government fostered and that produced the economic collapse of Indonesia in 1997 never blow back to the U.S., the unintended consequences for Indonesians have been staggering. They include poverty, serious ethnic violence, and, perhaps, political disintegration. Similarly, our "dirty hands" in overthrowing President Salvador Allende in Chile and installing General Augusto Pinochet, who subsequently killed thousands of his own citizens, are just now coming fully into the open. Even when blowback from our policies mainly strikes other peoples, it has a corrosive effect on us, debasing political discourse and making us feel duped when the news finally emerges.

The United States likes to think of itself as the winner of the Cold War. In all probability, to those looking back at blowback a century hence, neither side will appear to have won, particularly if the United States maintains its present imperial course.

—CHALMERS JOHNSON, *"The Consequences of our Actions Abroad: Americans Feeling the Effects of Blowback,"* Los Angeles Times, *May 4, 2000. Johnson is the president of the Japan Policy Research Institute and authored* Blowback: The Costs and Consequences of American Empire *(Metropolitan Books, 2000).*

℘

Mr. Speaker, I rise today with a heavy heart, one that is filled with sorrow for the families and loved ones who were killed and injured in New York, Virginia, and Pennsylvania. Only the most foolish or the most callous would not understand the grief that has gripped the American people and millions across the world.

This unspeakable attack on the United States has forced me to rely on my moral compass, my conscience, and my God for direction. September 11 changed the world. Our deepest fears now haunt us. Yet, I am convinced that military action will not prevent further acts of international terrorism against the United States.

I know that this use-of-force resolution will pass although we all know that the president can wage a war even without this resolution. However difficult this vote may be, some of us must urge the use of restraint. There must be some of us who say, let's step back for a moment and think through the implications of our actions today—let us more fully understand its consequences.

We are not dealing with a conventional war. We cannot respond in a conventional manner. I do not want to see this spiral out of control. This crisis involves issues of national security, foreign policy, public safety, intelligence gathering, economics, and murder. Our response must be equally multifaceted.

We must not rush to judgment. Far too many innocent people have already died. Our country is in mourning. If we rush to launch a counterattack, we run too great a risk that women, children, and other noncombatants will be caught in the crossfire.

Nor can we let our justified anger over these outrageous acts by vicious murderers inflame prejudice against all Arab Americans, Muslims, Southeast Asians, or any other people because of their race, religion, or ethnicity.

Finally, we must be careful not to embark on an open-ended war with neither an exit strategy nor a focused target. We cannot repeat past mistakes.

In 1964, Congress gave President Lyndon Johnson the power to "take all necessary measures" to repel attacks and prevent further aggression. In so doing, this House abandoned its own constitutional responsibilities and launched our country into years of undeclared war in Vietnam.

At that time, Senator Wayne Morse, one of two lonely votes against the Tonkin Gulf Resolution, declared, "I believe that history will record that we have made a grave mistake in subverting and circumventing the Constitution of the United States . . . I believe that within the next century, future generations will look with dismay and great disappointment upon a Congress which is now about to make such a historic mistake."

Senator Morse was correct, and I fear we make the same mistake today.

And I fear the consequences.

I have agonized over this vote. But I came to grips with it in the very painful yet beautiful memorial service today at the National Cathedral. As a member of the clergy so eloquently said, "As we act, let us not become the evil that we deplore."

—U.S. REPRESENTATIVE BARBARA LEE,
speech on the floor of the House, September 15, 2001.
Lee cast the sole vote in the House or Senate in opposition to a
resolution granting President George W. Bush authority to use
"all necessary and appropriate force" to the attacks.

∽

BARBARA LEE SPEAKS FOR ME!

—POSTER, *displayed in U.S. Representative Barbara Lee's*
congressional district initially and then by antiwar activists
nationwide, 2001. While it was suggested that Lee had destroyed her
political career by opposing the use-of-force resolution, she was
easily reelected in 2002 by an overwhelming margin.

∽

A WIDOW'S PLEA FOR NON-VIOLENCE

My husband, Craig Scott Amundson, of the U.S. Army lost his life in the line of duty at the Pentagon on September 11 as the world looked on in horror and disbelief.

Losing my twenty-eight-year-old husband and father of our two young children is a terrible and painful experience.

His death is also part of an immense national loss and I am comforted by knowing so many share my grief.

But because I have lost Craig as part of this historic tragedy, my anguish is compounded exponentially by fear that his death will be used to justify new violence against other innocent victims.

I have heard angry rhetoric by some Americans, including many of our nation's leaders, who advise a heavy dose of revenge and punishment. To those leaders, I would like to make clear that my family and I take no comfort in your words of rage. If you choose to respond to this incomprehensible brutality by perpetuating violence against other innocent human beings, you may not do so in the name of justice for my husband. Your words and imminent acts of revenge only amplify our family's suffering, deny us the dignity of remembering our loved one in a way that would have made him proud, and mock his vision of America as a peacemaker in the world community.

Craig enlisted in the army and was proud to serve his country. He was a patriotic American and a citizen of the world. Craig believed that by working from within the military system he could help to maintain the military focus on peacekeeping and strategic planning—to prevent violence and war. For the last two years, Craig drove to his job at the Pentagon with a "Visualize World Peace" bumper sticker on his car. This was not empty rhetoric or contradictory to him, but part of his dream. He believed his role in the army could further the cause of peace throughout the world.

Craig would not have wanted a violent response to avenge his death. And I cannot see how good can come out of it. We cannot solve violence with violence. Mohandas Gandhi said, "An eye for an eye only makes the whole world blind." We will no longer be able to see that we hold the light of liberty if we are blinded by vengeance, anger, and fear. I ask our nation's leaders not to take the path that leads to more widespread hatreds—that make my husband's death just one more in an unending spiral of killing.

I call on our national leaders to find the courage to respond to this incomprehensible tragedy by breaking the cycle of violence. I call on them to marshal this great nation's skills and resources to lead a worldwide dialogue on freedom from terror and hate.

I do not know how to begin making a better world: I do believe it must be done, and I believe it is our leaders' responsibility to find a way. I urge them to take up this challenge and respond to our nation's and my personal tragedy with a new beginning that gives us hope for a peaceful global community.

—AMBER AMUNDSON, *"A Widow's Plea for Non-Violence,"*
Chicago Tribune, *September 25, 2001. Amundsen was the wife of the late Craig Scott Amundson, an enlisted specialist in the army.*

∽

A JUST CAUSE, NOT A JUST WAR

Voices across the political spectrum, including many on the left, have described this as a "just war." One longtime advocate of peace, Richard Falk, wrote in *The Nation* that this is "the first truly just war since World War II." Robert Kuttner, another consistent supporter of social justice, declared in *The American Prospect* that only people on the extreme left could believe this is not a just war.

I have puzzled over this. How can a war be truly just when it involves the daily killing of civilians, when it causes hundreds of thousands of men, women, and children to leave their homes to escape the bombs, when it may not find those who planned the September 11 attacks, and when it will multiply the ranks of people who are angry enough at this country to become terrorists themselves?

This war amounts to a gross violation of human rights, and it will produce the exact opposite of what is wanted: It will not end terrorism; it will proliferate terrorism. I believe that the progressive supporters of the war have confused a "just cause" with a "just war." There are unjust causes, such as the attempt of the United States to establish its power in Vietnam, or to dominate Panama or Grenada, or to subvert the government of Nicaragua. And a cause may be just—getting North Korea to withdraw from South Korea, getting Saddam Hussein to withdraw from Kuwait, or ending terrorism—but it does not follow that going to war on behalf of that cause, with the inevitable mayhem that follows, is just. . . .

We might examine the idea of pacifism in the light of what is going on right now. I have never used the word "pacifist" to describe myself, because it suggests something absolute, and I am suspicious of absolutes. I want to leave openings for unpredictable possibilities. There might be situations (and even such strong pacifists as Gandhi and Martin Luther King believed this) when a small, focused act of violence against a monstrous, immediate evil would be justified.

In war, however, the proportion of means to ends is very, very different. War, by its nature, is unfocused, indiscriminate, and especially in our time when the technology is so murderous, inevitably involves the deaths of large numbers of people and the suffering of even more. Even in the "small wars" (Iran vs. Iraq, the Nigerian war, the Afghan war), a million people die. Even in a "tiny" war like the one we waged in Panama, a thousand or more die.

Scott Simon of NPR wrote a commentary in the *Wall Street Journal* on October 11 entitled, "Even Pacifists Must Support This War." He tried to use the pacifist acceptance of self-defense, which approves a focused resistance to an immediate attacker, to justify this war, which he claims is "self-defense." But the term "self-defense" does not apply when you drop bombs all over a country and kill lots of people other than your attacker. And it doesn't apply when there is no likelihood that it will achieve its desired end.

Pacifism, which I define as a rejection of war, rests on a very powerful logic. In war, the means—indiscriminate killing—are immediate and certain; the ends, however desirable, are distant and uncertain.

Pacifism does not mean "appeasement." That word is often hurled at those who condemn the present war on Afghanistan, and it is accompanied by references to Churchill, Chamberlain, Munich. World War II analogies are conveniently summoned forth when there is a need to justify a war, however irrelevant to a particular situation. At the suggestion that we withdraw from Vietnam, or not make war on Iraq, the word "appeasement" was bandied about. The glow of the "good war" has repeatedly been used to obscure the nature of all the bad wars we have fought since 1945.

Let's examine that analogy. Czechoslovakia was handed to the voracious Hitler to "appease" him. Germany was an aggressive nation expanding its power, and to help it in its expansion was not wise. But today we do not face an expansionist power that demands to be appeased. We ourselves are the expansionist power—troops in Saudi Arabia, bombings of Iraq, military bases all over the world, naval vessels on every sea—and that, along with Israel's expansion into the West Bank and Gaza Strip, has aroused anger.

It was wrong to give up Czechoslovakia to appease Hitler. It is not wrong to withdraw our military from the Middle East, or for Israel to withdraw from the occupied territories, because there is no right to be there. That is not appeasement. That is justice.

—HOWARD ZINN, *excerpt from "A Just Cause, Not a Just War,"*
The Progressive, *December 2001.*

༽

Since the time of Thomas Paine and John Adams, our founders implored that we were not to be the new Rome. We are not to conquer and suppress other nations to submit to our will. We were to inspire them.

The idea of America using its power solely for its own ends is not consistent with the idealistic moral force the world has known for over two centuries.

We must rejoin the world community. America is far stronger as the moral and military leader of the world than we will ever be by relying solely on military power. We destroyed repressive communist regimes without firing a shot, not simply by having a strong military, but because we had a better ideal to show the world.

Every American president must and will take up arms in the defense of our nation. It is a solemn oath that cannot—and will not—be compromised.

But there is a fundamental difference between the defense of our nation and the doctrine of preemptive war espoused by this administration. The president's group of narrow-minded ideological advisors are undermining our nation's greatness in the world. They have embraced a form of unilateralism that is even more dangerous than isolationism.

This administration has shown disdain for allies, treaties, and international organizations alike.

In doing so, they would throw aside our nation's role as the inspirational leader of the world the beacon of hope and justice in the interests of humankind. And, instead, they would present our face to the world as a dominant power prepared to push aside any nation with which we do not agree.

Our foreign and military policies must be about America leading the world, not America against the world.

—FORMER VERMONT GOVERNOR HOWARD DEAN,
*speech in Burlington, Vermont, announcing his
candidacy for president, June 23, 2003.*

∽

Neither I, nor any of the religious leaders represented here, pretend to be politicians. The job of the prophets was often to say "No" to the king, and sometimes that is our job as we continue in a prophetic tradition. Tonight we say "No" to the king, no to first strike! We are not that kind of people! Our "Yes!" is that peace is a result of justice, and non-violence is a means. As a prophetic people, consecrated through Baptism to share with Jesus in His prophetic role, we are called to be a voice of conscience in our land. It is right and good that there be debate about our foreign policy. However, the voice of military intelligence should not be the most decisive. Part of our task as a people linked to a faith-tradition is to try to apply moral principles to specific problems in the debate of foreign policy.

1. We cannot really be peacemakers around the world unless we seek to protect the lives and dignity of the vulnerable in our midst.
2. We cannot turn to military force to solve the world's problems or to right every wrong. We need creative U.S. leadership in

foreign affairs that can resist dangers of both isolationism and unwise intervention.

3. We must reshape our programs of foreign aid to become a priority of development aid for the world's poor and the common good.

4. Through the UN and regional organizations, our nation must be positively engaged in devising new tools for preserving the peace. The kind of non-violence we advocate is not simply a non-resisting pacifism, but a stand to resist stark public evil with means other than force, e.g., dialogue, negotiation, protest, (strikes, boycotts, civil disobedience), etc. As a country, we do not yet know how to do this very well, but maybe we can learn how to do that and relate non-violently with countries we consider enemies. It may be difficult to learn to apply conflict resolution internationally, but we pray that the Lord will teach us the way, and that we be willing to learn . . .

Our heavenly King calls us to peace, not war! Say, "Yes!" Tonight, we rededicate ourselves to justice through nonviolence, and prayerfully pray to the Lord for the church, for civil authority, for the poor and oppressed, and for all victims of violence whether in this country or anyplace in the world.

Lord, please hear our prayer!

—REVEREND JUAN ROMERO, *using the commemoration of the thirty-second anniversary of the Chicano Moratorium demonstrations against the Vietnam War in Los Angeles to express his opposition to an attack on Iraq, August 29, 2002.*

∽

CONGRESS CAN CONTROL A WAR WITH IRAQ BY CONTROLLING THE PURSE STRINGS

I don't doubt that a technical legal argument can be made that George W. Bush does have authority for the current war, under the Operation Dessert Storm Resolution that his father obtained from Congress.

But that argument would be technical indeed. After all, that earlier Congress certainly did not believe it was authorizing the present war the younger Bush is planning. It is a different time, a different president, and very different circumstances—with the war on terrorism, the volatile Mid-East situation, and the increased weapons of mass destruction threat, which cuts both ways.

It is also clear that under the War Powers Resolution, Bush II can engage in hostilities with Saddam without violating either the letter or spirit of the law for at least sixty days. Or, like Clinton, he can simply ignore the law, and proceed. But in the end, the power resides with Congress, not the president, for one power the president cannot take away is the power to approve and withhold funds; it is Congress's alone.

If (hypothetically) no one in Congress, once hearings are held, is persuaded that war with Iraq is necessary or appropriate; if Republicans remain divided and our allies remain horrified; if only the chest-pounding hawks surrounding the president want war; and, if, nevertheless, the president says he is going to go forward with the war, Congress will still be in control.

Congress can always pull the purse strings. Wars demand a great deal of money, and the president can't reach into the U.S. Treasury without an authorization and appropriation. To spend money, he needs Congress's approval.

An excellent monograph, entitled "Pulling the Commander In Chief's Purse Strings," explains such use of purse power. The authors, William C. Banks and Peter Raven-Hansen, note that this was how the Vietnam War ended. It wasn't pretty:

> Eventually, Congress adopted Senator Thomas Eagleton's amendment . . . which provided that "none of the funds herein appropriated under this act or heretofore appropriated under any other act may be expended to support directly or indirectly combat

activities in, over or from off the shores of Cambodia or in or over Laos by United States forces." Although this first end-the-war effort was successfully vetoed by the president [Nixon] on June 27, on June 29, Congress approved and the embattled President signed the Second Supplemental Appropriations Act, which required an end to all U.S. "combat activities" in Southeast Asia by August 15. The June 29 measure was a compromise: The restriction was broadened to include all of Southeast Asia, but was put off to give the president forty-five more bombing days. . . .

Upon the withdrawal of U.S. forces from Southeast Asia, the U.S.-supported governments in the region rapidly collapsed. Operating under the strict limits of the end-the-war amendments, President Ford authorized limited use of U.S. military force in the final evacuations of Cambodia and South Vietnam in 1975.

In short, there is only one sure way Congress can stop President Bush from going to war with Saddam: cut off his funds. Without money there can be no war.

But this would be doing indirectly what Congress should do directly—either declare war, or not. And if Congress does not, and the president proceeds anyway, the president should be taken to task for ignoring the Constitution.

—JOHN W. DEAN, *excerpt from* Pursuant to the Constitution, and Despite Claims to the Contrary, President Bush Needs Congressional Approval Before Declaring War on Iraq, *FindLaw, August 30, 2002.*
Dean was the legal counsel to President Richard Nixon.

∽

I believe that this country is faced with probably the biggest vote that any of us in Congress have ever made or perhaps will make because we're changing the rules in the civilized world. We are saying that the United States can decide to wipe out another country's leader whenever we don't like them.

We are not saying there has to be a vote of the Security Council. The president, when he has this resolution in his hand, will have a blank check that whenever he feels, he, one person, can make the decision that diplomatic means will not work, he can move.

Now, from my point of view, that is way too much power.

> —U.S. REPRESENTATIVE JAMES MCDERMOTT, *declaring his*
> *opposition to a proposal to grant the Bush White House the authority*
> *to use force against Iraq, October 2, 2002. The Use-of-Force*
> *Resolution was debated by the House and Senate in October of 2002.*
> *A Vietnam-era veteran who represents the Seattle area in the House,*
> *McDermott said, "If we pass this resolution, we are setting precedents*
> *that we will regret: that America can start preemptive wars and that*
> *Congress can turn over authority to start a war to a president."*

∽

He's trying to establish a new doctrine of international law which changes the definition of self-defense. The implications of that for the future stability of the world are huge.

> —U.S. SENATOR CARL LEVIN, *explaining his opposition to*
> *President Bush's request for authority to use force against Iraq,*
> *October 9, 2002. Though Bush promised to use force only after*
> *exhausting diplomatic initiatives, Levin, the chair of the*
> *Senate Armed Services Committee, objected to the*
> *president's doctrine of preemptive war.*

∽

This is the Tonkin Gulf resolution all over again. Let us stop, look, and listen. Let us not give this president or any president unchecked power. Remember the Constitution.

> —U.S. SENATOR ROBERT BYRD, *speaking in opposition*
> *to the Senate Use-of-Force resolution on Iraq, October 8, 2002.*
> *Byrd, the senior member of the Senate observed, "Suffice it to say*
> *that this is a blank check . . . given over to the chief executive,*
> *not just this one but chief executives who will succeed him."*
> *The senator complained, "This resolution authorizes the president to*
> *determine, and authorizes the president to use, military forces*
> *as he will, when he will, how he will, and wherever he will*
> *as long as the threat is tied to Iraq. That is the way it is written.*

Lock, stock, and barrel. Congress might as well just close the doors,
put a sign over the doors, and say 'going fishing.'" Despite
Byrd's warning, the Use-of-Force Resolution passed the Senate
by a vote of 77–23. It passed the House by a 296–133 margin.

∽

Lewis Lapham, writing in the March 2002 *Harper's*, quoted the diplomat, George Kennan, a major architect of the Cold War between America and the Soviet Union, as saying this in 1948:

"We have about 50 percent of the world's wealth, but only 6.3 percent of its population. . . . In this situation, we cannot fail to be the object of envy and resentment. Our real task in the coming period is to devise a pattern of relationships which will permit us to maintain this position of disparity without positive detriment to our national security. To do so, we will have to dispense with all sentimentality and daydreaming."

Kennan added that we should steer away from "unreal objectives such as human rights, the raising of living standards, and democratization."

Propelled by the fanaticism of Manifest Destiny, the second half of the nineteenth century saw our imperial conquests in the Mexican-American War of 1848; in a militarily imposed Open Door trading policy on Japan in 1850; in the demolition of Native American tribes through military suppression and treaty abrogation between 1860–1880; and in Caribbean and Philippine conquests of 1898's Spanish-American War.

Implementing the Monroe Doctrine in our hemisphere led us to invade, occupy and then dictate the governments of Haiti under the repressive Duvaliers, Cuba under the dictator Batista, Dominican Republic under Trujillo, Nicaragua under the vicious Somoza dynasty. Panama has been a virtual U.S. satrapy. The U.S. came out of WWII as a highly-aggressive superpower eager to expand its control. There has rarely been a moment when United States soldiers were not involved somewhere, "protecting U.S. interests." Greece, in the late 1940s, quashing a socialist revolution; Korea, in 1950 (we still maintain a troop presence of thirty-seven thousand there);

Lebanon, in 1958. We funded a coup in Guatemala, in 1954, to over-throw the elected progressive Arbenz government, replacing it with a series of dictatorships that the World Council of Bishops once declared were committing genocide against their own people in a country dominated by U.S. interests. We were major players in over-throwing the progressive Mossadegh in Iran, in 1953, and replacing him with the tyrannical Shah: Iranians have hated us ever since. We backed the creation of Israel in 1948, which dislocated over a million Palestinians from their homeland, and we have never effectively lob-bied for a just solution to that situation.

The CIA was involved in the assassination of the Congo's first prime minister after independence, the leftist Patrice Lumumba in 1961, the last compassionate leader in that sad country, and a national hero today.

We trained and funded the right-wing militarists led by General Suharto who overthrew Sukarno in Indonesia in 1965 and then slaughtered two hundred thousand so-called "Communists." The his-tory of our involvement in Vietnam, from support of the French throughout the 1950s, to our thirteen years of subversion, manipulation, assassination, and outright warfare is a grim history that left four million Vietnamese dead, 60 percent of their arable land destroyed, generations crippled. In 1965, Lyndon Johnson sent twenty-five thousand marines into the Dominican Republic to defeat Juan Bosch, a liberal leftist, and install an autocratic right wing military coup. Our support for reactionary governments in Brazil and Uruguay, and our involvement in the 1973 right wing Pinochet military coup in Chile, are a dismal part of the record.

For decades, our country shored up Zaire's sorry dictator, Mobutu Sese Seko, and we long supported Portugal's harsh colonial regime in neighboring Angola. When Angola achieved independence in 1975, the United States and South Africa armed Zairan mercenaries to invade Angola, and we promoted the reactionary leader of right wing UNITA forces, Jonas Savimbi, who was finally killed on February 22 this year after causing the deaths of an estimated one million Angolans during a twenty-seven year civil war he could not have waged without our support. The ruin of Angola today owes much to American policies and aid over the last three decades.

And the 1991 Gulf war in Kuwait and Iraq, where we killed an estimated two hundred thousand Iraqis in seventy-two hours (while incurring almost no U.S. casualties) to keep American oil prices cheap, endeared us to nobody, and managed to offend many Arab states and people of Islamic religion. Recent aerial warfare in Kosovo and Serbia, resulting in not a single American casualty, has been a brutally bizarre phenomenon to the rest of the world.

No other country on earth has even remotely invaded so many foreign nations to promote its self-interest.

We may speak of democracy and human rights at home, but abroad, in support of U.S. commerce, we trample on human rights and environment. We maintain actual, or stand-in military presences far and wide. Our domination is sustained by the largest and best equipped army of anyone. Here are some facts taken out of a recent *World Almanac,* facts that don't even mention U.S. training, supply and support of military regimes where our soldiers aren't directly involved. But as of four years ago we had: a million soldiers in the continental U.S., 16,000 in Alaska; 36,000 in Hawaii; 5,000 in Guam; 35,000 roaming U.S. possessions; and 127,000 on ships supplying these soldiers. We also had 1,500 in Belgium; 15,000 in Bosnia/ Herzegovina; 4,000 in Croatia; 49,000 in Germany; 6,500 in Hungary; 1,900 in Iceland; 12,500 in Italy; 500 in Macedonia; 750 in the Netherlands; 1,000 in Portugal; 2,700 in Spain; 2,900 in Turkey; 11,500 in the United Kingdom; and 4,000 on ships in those areas. Then we had 43,000 in Japan; 37,000 in Korea; 15,000 on ships in that area. Also, 500 in Bahrain; 900 in Diego Garcia; 1,000 in Egypt; 5,500 in Kuwait; 1,500 in Saudi Arabia; 4,000 on ships in the area. And finally 1,800 in Cuba/Guantanamo; 300 in Haiti; 900 in Honduras; 6,500 in Panama; and 1,500 afloat. Dozens of countries entertain a U.S. military of under five hundred soldiers and commanders and advisors. Even a force of twenty-five U.S. military and its material demands constitute a significant political and economic American presence.

These figures above from four years ago do not include the U.S. in Afghanistan and Pakistan, nor do they suggest the amount of U.S. training and material for Israel, which is our largest recipient of foreign aid, for a country smaller than New Jersey with approximately six million inhabitants. The figures above do not include our training and manipulation of undemocratic governments and their military or counter-terrorist apparatuses, for example in Columbia, or now in the Philippines. The figures also do not include current U.S. bases for three thousand personnel under construction in Krgystan, another three thousand Americans in Uzbekistan, more in Tajikistan, a new base in Oman, and the three hundred U.S. military who recently entered the former Soviet republic of Georgia to help them "combat terrorism," i.e., meddle in their civil war.

"The imperial perimeter is expanding into Central Asia," said Thomas Donnelley, the deputy executive director of the Project for the New American Century.

Our country and our economic system is far and away the dominant occupying force on earth. We are seen as such by everyone. We are the largest arms dealers on earth, selling weapons or giving them as aid to reactionary regimes, outfitting many of the wars in Africa, Asia, Latin America, Europe, the South Pacific. Our cultural imperialism sets universal tastes and buying habits and values through films, music, products, and advertising around Coca-Cola, Marlboros, Microsoft. The world is governed, i.e., intimidated, by Bush/Rumsfeld, Fallwell/ Robertson, Disney/Time Warner. Our might and our wealth effectively seduces, co-opts, or terrorizes everyone. Our rhetoric speaks about human rights, democracy, liberation of women in Afghanistan, but we care little or nothing for these issues in Rwanda, Burundi, Iraq, Congo, Egypt, Chechnya, Azerbaijan, Guatemala, Salvador, Honduras, Bolivia, East Timor, Haiti, Jamaica, Angola, Liberia, Nigeria, Zimbabwe, Mozambique, Russia, and so forth. As the diplomat George Kennan advised in 1948, "we have maintained a position of disparity without positive detriment (so far) to our national security," and have not kowtowed to "unreal objectives, such as human rights, the raising of living standards, and democratization." A war in Iraq simply promotes this cynicism once again.

—JOHN NICHOLS, *speech at a Taos, New Mexico, antiwar rally,*
October 26, 2002

Peace is Patriotic

—UNITED FOR PEACE AND JU*
protesting against the Bush administratio
February 15, 2003. Demonstrations took p
of cities across the United States. Ba
President Bush ordered th

∽

Today's wars are about oil. But alternate energies exist now—solar, wind—for every important energy-using activity in our lives. The only human work that cannot be done without oil is war.

So, men lead us to war for enough oil to continue to go to war for oil.

—GRACE PALEY, *"Why Peace Is (More Than Ever) A Feminist Issue," Ms., Spring 2003. Recalling a lifetime of activism against U.S. military adventurism, the poet told the* New York Times *in February 2003, "Some of us were in the street about the Vietnam War in 1961, but there were no big demonstrations for four years. This is moving much faster, but so is Bush."*

∽

Millions are watching and waiting in mute frustration and hope—hoping for someone to defend the spirit and letter of our Constitution, and to defy the intimidation that is visited upon us daily in the name of national security and warped notions of patriotism.

—TIM ROBBINS, *speech by the actor at the National Press Club, April 15, 2003.*

∽

CROWN JEWEL OF THE AMERICAN EMPIRE

ake up the white man's burden," Britain's poet of empire, Rudyard Kipling, admonished Teddy Roosevelt's America in 1899. The United States had just triumphed in the Spanish-American War to liberate Cuba and, as war booty, had annexed the Philippine Islands.

We must "Christianize" them, President McKinley explained.

Defeating Spain had been as easy as crushing Iraq. But holding the Philippines would require three years of Vietnam-style fighting against the guerrillas of Aquinaldo, which cost tens of thousands of Filipino lives. And many more Americans died fighting the Filipinos to keep the islands than had died fighting Spain to take them.

Soon after we began that first American imperial war, the American press had a change of heart.

Wrote the *New York World*:

We've taken up the white man's burden
Of ebony and brown;
Now will you kindly tell us, Rudyard,
How we may put it down?

But in 1903, Aquinaldo surrendered, the insurrection ended, and the United States converted the islands into what we thought was a Pacific fortress. Yet, as Teddy Roosevelt had ruefully come to admit, the islands were actually our "Achilles heel." They were lost to Japan in the first six months of World War II and only retaken—to be set free in 1946—at an immense cost in blood and treasure.

Our new imperialists view Iraq much as McKinley's generation of imperialists saw the Philippines, as an outpost of empire and a strategic base camp for the projection of American power.

Senator Richard Lugar, chairman of the Foreign Relations Committee, says "we ought to be thinking of a period of five years," at least, before an Iraqi government takes control in Baghdad. The *New York Times* reports that the Pentagon has already selected four sites as permanent U.S. air bases—inside Iraq.

But has anyone consulted the Iraqis on whether they wish to play their assigned role in the Pentagon's script? Or will we have to first put down Iraqi resistance, as we did Filipino resistance, to pacify the country and convert it into a U.S. Middle-Eastern bastion? For the vision of the neoconservatives—that Iraqis would embrace Americans as liberators and democracy would spread like brushfire across the Arab world—has yet to be realized. Consider:

- Last Friday, after prayers, fifty-thousand Shias and Sunnis took to the streets of Baghdad chanting, "No to Bush, no to Saddam, yes to Islam," and, "Leave our country, we want peace."
- In Kut, militant Shia cleric Syed Abbas walked into the town hall and took it over, accompanied by hundreds of Islamic backers who had crossed from Iran. Thousands attend his meetings, which feature calls for an Islamic republic and an end to U.S. occupation.
- In Najaz, a religious moderate was knifed to death in that holy city's ancient mosque. Grand Ayatollah Sayyed Alo al-Sistani refuses to leave home—some say, for fear of his life.
- Up to two million Shi'ites are expected to converge Thursday on Karbala. While the mass pilgrimage to the site of the martyrdom of Imam Ali Hussein, a grandson of the prophet, has been peaceful, there have been signs also of deep hostility to the U.S. presence.
- On Friday, a *London Observer* reporter ventured into Saddam City, a poor Shia area of Baghdad where U.S. troops do not patrol. There, he found the armed militia of the Sadr Movement, named for a Shia cleric martyred with his sons by Saddam Hussein. Goal of the Sadr Movement: an Islamic state under sharia law.

The Pentagon has bet America's chips on Ahmed Chalabi of the Iraqi National Congress to lead Iraq. But before last week, Chalabi was last seen in Baghdad when John Foster Dulles was secretary of state. And reaction to Chalabi appears to range from indifference to violent hatred.

Many Iraqis see him as a Pentagon puppet.

Writes the *London Telegraph*: "On Friday . . . a car carrying the flag of the Iraqi National Congress and a large photograph of Mr. Chalabi was sprayed with automatic gunfire. After Friday prayers at the Salati Jimad mosque, when thousands of militant supporters of the late Ayatollah Mohammed al Sadr spilled into the streets, Mr. Chalabi's name was openly derided." ·

Bush's dilemma? If America is to make good on his promise to build a free, stable, democratic Iraq, it simply cannot be done in months. It will require years. But with many Iraqi Shias already looking on us as imperial and infidel occupiers, we may not have that much time.

Having crushed Saddam's Republican Guard, are we willing to crush an Iraqi intifada to hold onto the country. It may come down to that.

Meanwhile, how do you like the empire?

> —PAT BUCHANAN, *April 23, 2003. From "Crown Jewel of the American Empire," an essay that appeared on Buchanan's Web site. The conservative commentator and former presidential candidate was the most prominent member of a group of traditional conservatives who objected to the Bush administration's career of empire. In Congress, a small circle of Republicans—six in the House and one in the Senate—opposed authorizing the president to launch a preemptive invasion of Iraq.*

∽

Throughout our history, the United States has been viewed by the world as a beacon of freedom and a pillar of democratic principle. . . . The United States was seen as a constructive force in the world. Right now we are seen by many as a destructive force in the world. That is not the vision for America that I have, and it is not the vision that Americans have.

> —U.S. REPRESENTATIVE TAMMY BALDWIN, *explaining why she would vote against authorizing supplemental appropriations to pay for the occupation of Iraq, October 16, 2003.*

∽

The citizens of our democracy have a fundamental right to debate and even doubt the wisdom of a president's policies. And the citizens of our democracy have a sacred obligation to sound the alarm and shed light on the policies of an administration that is leading this country to a perilous place.

I believe that this administration is indeed leading this country to a perilous place. It has broken faith with the American people, aided and abetted by a congressional majority willing to pursue ideology at any price, even the price of distorting the truth. On issue after issue, they have moved brazenly to impose their agenda on America and on the world. They have pursued their goals at the expense of urgent national and human needs and at the expense of the truth. America deserves better.

The administration and the majority in Congress have put the state of our union at risk, and they do not deserve another term in the White House or in control of Congress.

I do not make these statements lightly. I make them as an American deeply concerned about the future of the Republic if the extremist policies of this administration continue.

By far, the most extreme and most dire example of this administration's reckless pursuit of its single-minded ideology is in foreign policy. In its arrogant disrespect for the United Nations and for other peoples in other lands, this administration and this Congress have squandered the immense goodwill that other nations extended to our country after the terrorist attacks of September 11. And in the process, they made America a lesser and a less respected land.

—U.S. SENATOR EDWARD KENNEDY, *"America, Iraq, and Presidential Leadership," speech to the Center for American Progress gathering at the Mayflower Hotel, Washington, D.C., January 14, 2004. Reviewing the rising death toll and the declining sense of security in Iraq, as well as the collapse in respect for the United States, Kennedy warned, "We are reaping the poison fruit of our misguided and arrogant foreign policy. The administration capitalized on the fear created by 9-11 and put a spin on the intelligence and a spin on the truth to justify a war that could well become one of the worst blunders in more than two centuries of American foreign policy."*

Very few wars are necessary. Very few wars are good wars. And this one [the invasion of Iraq] does not qualify. Most wars are costly beyond measure, in life and limb and economic hardship. In this regard, this war does qualify: 566 deaths, ten thousand casualties, and hundreds of billions of dollars for a victory requiring self-deception.

Rather than bragging about victory, we should recognize that the war raging on between the Muslim East and the Christian West has intensified and spread, leaving our allies and our own people less safe. Denying we have an interest in oil, and denying that occupying an Islamic country is an affront to the sensitivities of most Arabs and Muslims, is foolhardy.

Reasserting U.N. Security Council resolutions as a justification for the war further emphasizes our sacrifice of sovereignty, and only underscores how Congress has reneged its constitutional responsibility over war.

This resolution dramatizes how we have forgotten that for too long we were staunch military and economic allies of Saddam Hussein, confirming the folly of our policy of foreign meddling over many decades. From the days of installing the Shah of Iran to the current worldwide spread of hostilities and hatred, our unnecessary involvement shows so clearly how unintended consequences come back to haunt generation after generation.

Someday our leaders ought to ask why Switzerland, Sweden, Canada, Mexico, and many others are not potential targets of an Islamic attack. Falsely believing that al Qaeda was aligned with Saddam Hussein has resulted in al Qaeda now having a strong presence and influence in Iraq. Falsely believing that Iraq had a supply of weapons of mass destruction has resulted in a dramatic loss of U.S. credibility, as anti-Americanism spreads around the world. Al Qaeda recruitment, sadly, has been dramatically increased.

We all praise our troops and support them. Challenging one's patriotism for not supporting this resolution and/or policy in the Persian Gulf is not legitimate. We should all be cautious about endorsing and financing a policy that unfortunately expands the war rather than ends it.

—U.S. REPRESENTATIVE RON PAUL, *March 17, 2004, from a speech to the U.S. House of Representatives. A conservative*

Republican from Texas, Paul voted against authorizing the president to use force in Iraq and remained a consistent critic of the war. He made this statement during a House debate over a resolution (H. Res. 557) that sought a House endorsement of the doctrine of preemptive war.

⁓

I have watched with heavy heart and mounting dread as the ever-precarious battle to bring security to post-war Iraq has taken a desperate turn for the worse in recent days and hours. Along with so many Americans, I have been shaken by the hellish carnage in Fallujah and the violent uprisings in Baghdad and elsewhere. The pictures have been the stuff of nightmares, with bodies charred beyond recognition and dragged through the streets of cheering citizens. And in the face of such daunting images and ominous developments, I have wondered anew at the president's stubborn refusal to admit mistakes or express any misgivings over America's unwarranted intervention in Iraq.

During the past weekend, the death toll among America's military personnel in Iraq topped six hundred—including as many as twenty American soldiers killed in one three-day period of fierce fighting. Many of the dead, most perhaps, were mere youngsters, just starting out on the great adventure of life. But before they could realize their dreams, they were called into battle by their commander in chief, a battle that we now know was predicated on faulty intelligence and wildly exaggerated claims of looming danger. . . .

It is time we faced up to the fact that this president and his administration blundered . . .when they took the nation into war with Iraq without compelling reason, without broad international or even regional support, and without a plan for dealing with the enormous post-war security and reconstruction challenges posed by Iraq. And it is our soldiers, our own six hundred and more, who are paying the price for that blunder. . . .

The harsh reality is this: one year after the fall of Baghdad, the United States should not be casting about for a formula to bring additional U.S. troops to Iraq. We should instead be working toward an exit strategy. The fact that the president has alienated friend and foe alike by his arrogance in "going it alone" in Iraq and has made the task of internationalizing post-war Iraq an enormously difficult burden should not deter our resolve.

Pouring more U.S. troops into Iraq is not the path to extricate ourselves from that country. We need the support and the endorsement of both the United Nations and Iraq's neighbors to truly internationalize the Iraq occupation and take U.S. soldiers out of the crosshairs of angry Iraqis.

And from the flood of disturbing dispatches from Iraq, it is clear that many Iraqis, both Sunni and Shi'ite, are seething under the yoke of the American occupation. The recent violent uprising by followers of a radical Shi'ite cleric is by far the most troubling development in Iraq in months and could signal America's worst nightmare—a civil war in Iraq that pits moderate Shi'ites against radical Shi'ites. Layered over the persistent insurgency being waged by disgruntled Iraqi Sunnis and radical Islamic operatives, a Shi'ite civil war could be the event that topples Iraq from instability into utter chaos. . . .

Where should we look for leadership? To this Congress? To this Senate? This Senate, the foundation of the Republic, has been unwilling to take a hard look at the chaos in Iraq. Senators have once again been cowed into silence and support, not because the policy is right, but because the blood of our soldiers and thousands of innocents is on our hands. Questions that ought to be stated loudly in this chamber are instead whispered in the halls. Those few Senators with the courage to stand up and speak out are challenged as unpatriotic and charged with sowing seeds of terrorism. It has been suggested that any who dare to question the president are no better than the terrorists themselves. Such are the suggestions of those who would rather not face the truth.

This Republic was founded in part because of the arrogance of a king who expected his subjects to do as they were told, without question, without hesitation. Our forefathers overthrew that tyrant and adopted a system of government where dissent is not only important, but it is also mandatory. Questioning flawed leadership is a requirement of this government. Failing to question, failing to speak out, is failing the legacy of the Founding Fathers.

—U.S. SENATOR ROBERT BYRD,
speech to the Senate, April 7, 2004.

The present administration has confused the American people by linking nationalism to patriotism. To me, a patriot is someone who constantly asks questions of his government and demands answers. Thomas Jefferson counseled us to be vigilant in watching our government and to overturn it if it wasn't representing us properly.

—PATTI SMITH, *interview with* USA Today, *April 22, 2004.*

AFTERWORD
Standing Against the Beast

On a crisp fall day, just a few weeks before our country would choose a president, my daughter Whitman and I are driving west from our home in Madison to the Wisconsin village where her great-great-grandfather is buried. We are on our way to lay flowers at his grave. When we get to Blue River, I am happy for Whitman because she can see the town almost as her ancestors knew it. There is still a La Follette Street, named for the great progressive senator who fought to prevent the United States from invading Mexico and from joining in the mad warmaking of a British king and a German kaiser. There is still the front porch where John Blaine, home from fighting in Washington to end the U.S. occupations of Haiti and Nicaragua, would watch the Fourth of July parades, knowing that he was practicing the patriotism that the founders intended.

We have come to Blue River a few weeks before a vote that we are being told is the most important in our history. Yet, neither the Democrats nor the Republicans have nominated a La Follette or a Blaine. The debate, such as it is, revolves around how best to manage our country's growing list of occupations and entanglements. Save for a few honest voices, our politicians speak the language of empire. Yet, they are embarrassed by their excess. The Secretary of Defense has gone so far as to announce that the military occupation of Iraq is not "imperialism." It is strangely reassuring to hear the old lies dusted off and used once more. The men who rule our land do not quite trust the American people to share the lust for expansion that has gripped the governing class. And they are right to worry. America is growing weary, once more, of the vain impulses of economic royalists and military adventurers—an anti-imperialist is born.

Whitman will come to know that weariness. She is barely old enough to walk, yet she had already marched against war and rallied in opposition to our occupations. She has sat in the lap of her ninety-two-year-old Aunt Carolyn Fry, who remembers playing on that porch where John Blaine and my great-grandfather watched the parades of the 1920s. Whitman is too young to understand when Aunt Carolyn speaks of the madness of the "King George" who has occupied our White House. But she will know soon enough. The American story is one of frequent struggle between those who take the side of George Washington and Abraham Lincoln and Frederick Douglass and Helen Keller and Barbara Lee and Robert Byrd versus the dark forces that would set America on a career of empire. We are in such a struggle now. In these first days of the twenty-first century, what is left of the good name of America has again been assaulted by those who would make this good land the handmaiden of their crude self-service. Our treasury is being emptied into the folly of a distant war, our freedoms have been curtailed, our official discourse has been emptied of meaning. So we are called, once more, to take a side. On this afternoon in October, as the sun sparkles through the trees of the old graveyard, Whitman and I kneel to touch the monument of an ancestor who knew which side he was on. And in that instant we are connected to a patriotism that is stronger than fear. We rise, Americans, to stand against the beast.

$\mathcal{A}cknowledgments$:

Conversations with Gore Vidal at his grand home in Ravello gave birth to the idea for this book. I am deeply indebted to Gore for his career and his courage. But, most of all, I am indebted to him for confirming my faith that anti-imperialism is the truest patriotism. This project is informed from start to finish by his good spirit, as it is by insights gained from many hours spent reading the articles, essays, and books of the great University of Wisconsin historians, in particular William Appleman Williams and Fred Harvey Harrington, who contributed so much to this field. I am appreciative, as well, of Robert L. Beisner, whose *Twelve Against Empire: The Anti-Imperialists 1898-1900* is essential reading, along with anything written by Jim Zwick, a contemporary scholar whose research and writing on America's great anti-imperialist moment is remarkable for its scope, its intellect, and its humanity. I am indebted, as well, to Howard Zinn and Noam Chomsky for their example, and for their encouragement along the way.

The editor of Nation Books, Carl Bromley, embraced the idea of this book with the enthusiasm that every writer longs to know in his or her editor. Carl's colleague, Ruth Baldwin, had the patience and the grace to see it from the idea that Carl handed her to the reality that you now hold. I am deeply indebted to Carl and especially to Ruth, and to the editors at Avalon Publishing Group who were willing to give this book the time it needed to take shape.

My dearest comrade, Robert McChesney, championed this project from the start, even when it drew me away from our shared work on behalf of media reform. My editors at *The Nation,* Katrina vanden Heuvel and Karen Rothmyer, understood the importance of the project and supported me at every turn, as did Dave Zweifel, my editor at

The Capital Times in Madison, Wisconsin. I am indebted to them, as I am to *Nation* and *Capital Times* colleagues such as Phil Haslanger, Judy Ettenhofer, Linda Brazill, Roane Carey, Marc Cooper, Mike Webb, and Peter Rothberg. *The Nation* and *The Capital Times* have long stood together in opposition to entanglement, expansion, and empire, and I am proud beyond words to be associated with both of these publications. I am proud, as well, of my long association with *The Progressive* magazine, where the editor, Matt Rothschild, recognized the point of this project from the start.

Nothing I do would be possible without the support of my parents, Harrison and Mary Nichols, and the understanding Whitman Genevieve Nichols Bottari. The music of Phil Ochs, Patti Smith, Ani DiFranco, Kate Jacobs, Steve Earle, Jimmy Cliff, Bob Marley, and Johnny Cash put everything in perspective. Conversations with my Aunt Carolyn Fry, Tony Benn, Pat Buchanan, Bob Kimbrough, Phyllis Rose, Barbara Lawton, Midge Miller, Steve Cobble, Lorrie Moore, David Austin, Ed Garvey, Jen Rubin, Adam Benedetto, Ben Manski Anita Bottari, Sue Carter, Mike Ferner, Meredith Clark, Cindy Clark, Marc Rosenthal, and many other friends and fellow travelers helped advance the project, as did the enthusiasm of audiences I spoke with about it. That is especially true of peace activists such as Sue and Tom Holmes, Tricia Denker, and Tom Arbogast in the small towns and cities of Wisconsin, for whom such conversations are acts of homecoming. This book is dedicated to Mary Elizabeth Bottari, whose rage for justice—at home and abroad—knows no equal.

INDEX OF FIRST LINES

SUBJECT INDEX